Beyond
the Stars
III

Beyond the Stars III:

The Material World
in American Popular Film

Edited by

Paul Loukides
and
Linda K. Fuller

Bowling Green State University Popular Press
Bowling Green, OH 43403

Library of Congress Catalogue Card No.: 89-82334

ISBN: 0-87972-622-9 Clothbound
0-87972-623-7 Paperback

Cover design by Laura Darnell Dumm

Dedication

This one too is for Nora, Jason, and Cindy with love and gratitude.

Paul Loukides

To FWF IV, KKF, and ASF—SWMs who are adept, bright, creative, dauntless, enterprising, fun, genteel, handy, imaginative, joyful, kindhearted, loving, manly, nimble, open-minded, perceptive, quick-witted, real, sportsmanlike, talented, unique, versatile, witty, (un)xenophobic, yogurt- and Yorkshire Pudding-eaters, and zany.

Linda K. Fuller

Contents

Introduction
Conventions of the Material World in Popular Film

Paul Loukides
and
Linda K. Fuller

The material universe exists only in the mind.
Jonathan Edwards, *On Mind* 1720

In our continuing search for clues to the connection between American popular film and American social reality, perhaps nothing simplifies our task more than looking at "things" in motion pictures—the material world.

Take, for example, artifacts as common as cars. Automobiles are among the artifacts that are commonly used to establish a film's time period; they are also used to give viewers information about the owner/driver's social status and life style. Cars are so important in both American life and film that some have evolved into movie icons unto themselves, like Herbie the "Love Bug," Stephen King's demonic Christine, the Blues Brothers' "Bluesmobile," or the classic James Bond cars. While individual artifacts like cars are interesting in themselves, the conventions of material objects in motion pictures challenge us to make sense of them contextually within individual films and in the broader context of American popular culture.

To use another transportation example, consider trains in film. One of the first motion pictures, after all, was the Lumiere brothers' short, "Arrival of a Train at a Station." New York's Museum of Modern Art recently launched a major exhibit dedicated to trains, titled "Junction and Journey: Trains and Film." Laurence Kardish, MOMA's curator, chose this theme because, "Trains figure in the whole history of cinema and in all film cultures...they function as potent metaphors for a host of basically abstract ideas—sometimes contradictory ones. Trains represent progress and the past, and the future, and death. They always signify change. They're protean as a metaphor, and yet they're profoundly romantic objects in and of themselves" (Sterritt 13).

Trains have been part of film fare since its inception—culminating, perhaps, in a rash of them during the 1970s (Howard Hawks' *Rio Lobo*, 1970; Martin Scorsese's *Boxcar Bertha*, 1972; Joseph Sargent's *The Taking of Pelham One Two Three*, 1974; Sidney Lumet's *Murder on the Orient Express*, 1974; Arthur Hiller's *Silver Streak*, 1976). We might wonder why movies featuring

1

trains were so popular at that time; was there a particular societal sense of anomie, rootlessness, and/or desire for freedom then? Were train films precursors of 1980s films of nostalgia? When examining the material world of film the scholar needs to first ask if, then when, where, how, and why various objects are used, even abused; the next step is to make some educated judgments about these processes.

Materialism, the American Family Values study commission tells us, is on the decline in America. In a survey of 1,200 respondents around the country, "having nice things" declined ten points from the 1989 sample. Can we look to the movies to see if this really bears out? Filmgoers are inundated with stories of the fallen greedy, both real and fictional. Return-to-basics films like *Regarding Henry*, *The Doctor*, *Little Man Tate*, *Paradise*, *Prince of Tides*, even *The Addams Family* emphasize family/life style values more than merely collecting things. Is material wealth actually being de-emphasized in popular film?

Another question to be weighed is the target market for various films. Implicit in this approach is the notion that audience(s) readily interpret both overt and subtextual meanings from the physical trappings that make up the minutiae of physical detail within a film. We are familiar with "reel fashion," ranging from clothing and hairstyles (e.g., *Streetcar Named Desire*'s T-shirt, *Annie Hall*'s haberdashery, Bo Derek's *"10"* plaits, *Flashdance*'s off-the-shoulder sweatshirt). We hear that many moviegoers absorb ideas for interior decoration from the movies, or read that citizens groups are worried about teen movie fashions crossing over to the classroom. Must we continue to depend on anecdotal evidence to confirm our suspicions that the material world in film effects our social reality? "There has never been any 'school' of American film criticism," according to Grogg and Nachbar. "Nor is one needed now...What is needed, then, is not a revolution of perceiving what is on the screen. Rather, what is needed is the continuation of a growing trend about how the movies themselves are perceived" (1-9).

Our study of film as cultural artifact is not a new one; since the early years of film, social scientists have been interested in movies as mirrors of society, and sociocultural film studies have continued to grow ever since. Kathy Merlock Jackson finds ample reason for the proliferation of this form of film criticism: "It takes film out of a vacuum and places it in the realm of history, politics, economics, literature, art, music, and other far-reaching cultural factors. In essence, it looks squarely at the relationship between films and the social milieu of the people who produce and consume them."

As motion pictures enter their centennial decade, we recognize that they offer us a unique opportunity to study the visual record of our culture and reflect on the world caught on film. By focusing on the sheer physical "stuff" that makes up the universe of the movies, both its constants and its changes, we can begin to more fully understand the particular penchants and priorities of material life in America.

As Peter C. Rollins has commented, "American films often tell more about their times than their filmmakers consciously intended" (4). Perhaps the material texture of American film is not so much tied to the reality of twentieth-century material experience as to an idealized, even ritualized interpretation of that reality.

The essays in this volume, *Beyond the Stars III: The Material World in American Popular Film*, reflect the material world embedded in film. Its first section on conventions of "things" deals with food and other consumables, beginning with Parley Ann Boswell's study of food and eating scenes. It continues with Jay Boyer's analysis of food—or lack of it—as a comic motif in the silent comedies of Charlie Chaplin. Dick Stromgren reminds us of what a gourmet Alfred Hitchcock was, and how he used food as central metaphors for life (and death). And Denis Grady talks about another oral fixation in film: smoking marijuana.

Further interpretive clues to understanding American society can be found in our clothing choices. Movie journalists, Norma Fay Green points out, are usually bedecked in neutral beige outerwear, while nurses, doctors, scientists, and "all-around good guys" wear white. Philip Skerry and Brenda Berstler give yet another example: Western costumes as semiological indices.

In terms of art and media, Linda K. Fuller documents the year 1985 as a benchmark for studying the symbiosis between film and popular culture in terms of the specific case of self-advertising, when Susan Siedelman's treatment of the "personals" in *Desperately Seeking Susan* coincided with concern about the real-life growing AIDS epidemic. Eric S. Lunde and Doug Noverr examine Hitchcock's use of the fine arts in film, which they argue strengthened his cinematic vision, while Brooks Robards contributes a broader discussion of the visual arts as used in biopics, mystery/suspense films, and melodramas.

Further conventions of the material world are evidenced in tools and weapons. Ralph R. Donald discusses character relationships with air and space craft as metaphors for human affinities, arguing for the uniqueness of man/machine relationships, since no other interaction with objects in the material world permits humans to "slip the surly bonds of earth." Bats, balls, and gloves in contemporary baseball films, according to Howard Good, are more than playthings; rather, they are symbols glowing with meaning. So too are weapons, according to Gary Hoppenstand and John H. Lenihan. The former focuses on the urban vigilante film, seeing the gun as lethal weapon becoming a filmic icon, while the latter discusses superweapons in costume movies as projections of American fantasies and fears regarding atomic power. Steve Lipkin looks at objects in the Vietnam war film as a lens through which "a clearer moral perspective" might be gleaned. Finally, Martin F. Norden examines the presentation of wheelchairs and their users over the course of nearly a century of film.

The last category in this volume considers technologies, both old and new. Susanna Hornig writes about the role of intelligent computers in contemporary film—pieces of digital equipment that think, talk, interact and make decisions much like human beings. The morality of that technology is the subject of Donald G. Lloyd's essay, dealing with renegade robots and hard-wired heroes. In the final essay, by Greg Metcalf, the mobile home—or motor home, trailer, caravan, RV, whatever one may call it—is traced as a powerful American symbol for freedom, escape, modernity, and/or individuality.

The analysis of even a small sample of the objects ingested, worn, owned or used in film suggests that the conventions of film both reflect and distort the evolution of American social reality. As yet another means for providing insights into the images and illusions that reflect and define our society, consideration of the material world of film offers an illuminating perspective.

Works Cited

Grogg, Sam L., Jr., and Nachbar, John C. "Movies and Audiences: A Reasonable Approach for American Film Criticism," *Movies as Artifacts: Cultural Criticism of Popular Film* Ed. Michael Marsden. Chicago: Nelson-Hall, 1982.

Jackson, Kathy Merlock. *Images of Children in American Film.* Metuchen, NJ: Scarecrow, 1986.

Rollins, Peter C., ed. Introduction. *Hollywood as Historian: American Film in a Cultural Context* Lexington: UP of Kentucky, 1983.

Sterritt, David. "Thriller Trains Movies." *Christian Science Monitor* 15 July 1991.

Food and Other Consumables

Hungry in the Land of Plenty:
Food in Hollywood Films

Parley Ann Boswell

Could you tell me why it is that I'm still hungry?
>Beth Jarrett (Mary Tyler Moore)
>*Ordinary People*

When I watch you eat...I just want to smash your face in.
>Barbara Rose (Kathleen Turner)
>*The War of The Roses*

We always laugh at these sight gags when we see them in the movies: the slip on the banana peel, the pie in the face, the tablecloth pulled (often unsuccessfully) from beneath a set table. Why do we laugh? For many reasons—because we recognize the sight gag as it approaches, because we are delighted by our ability to predict the outcome, because we can make light of potential disaster by trivializing it. And, whether we realize this at the time, we also respond to these devices because they employ a property of film with which we are intimately, ultimately familiar: food.

Among film properties, food is a staple. Audiences respond to food, to eating, to dining scenes because we all understand something about food—we all eat. In the journeys we make when we watch movies, we can count on food as a marker to help guide us along. As films create their own closed worlds for us, food becomes a key to our entry into these worlds.

Mary Anne Schofield has aptly explored the value of food to literature. Food, she writes:

counts, because it articulates in concrete terms what is often vague, internal, abstract...Food cooked, eaten, and thought about provides a metaphoric matrix, a language that allows us a way to get at the uncertainty, the ineffable qualities of life. (1)

Like food in literature, food in film offers us a language and a sensual means by which to explore the complexities and unknowns presented to us. And, just as we may not understand the mysteries of how food enriches our bodies, we may not understand how scenes involving food contribute to our understanding of films.

8 Beyond the Stars III

Food scenes always look familiar to us. If we notice them at all, we may think that we are merely seeing food on a table and characters eating. We are really being exposed to much more. In movies, food is not just a basic need; it is most often the representation of a ritual act. A dining scene becomes a "tribal rite," one that suggests communion, epiphany, crisis, or conflict to us. Particular foods and how characters behave during dining scenes suggest a means by which we can begin to distinguish values in a film.

When we begin to consider food as a film property, we also begin to discover that food can be vital to our understanding of social class, ethnicity, or nationality in a film. We may also find that we use food and eating scenes to distinguish relationships between or among characters. There may be no scenes so valuable to our understanding of family dynamics or sexual relationships as dining scenes, which may explain why there are so few films—certainly few Hollywood productions—which do *not* include dining scenes.

Hollywood films rely on our understanding of dining traditions so often and so completely that individual scenes—and entire films which employ food and dining scenes often—deserve further consideration. When we examine the uses of food in American film, we may begin to understand not just how food is used as a device, but how Hollywood projects the nature of certain values presented to us in terms of food and eating scenes. As a reflection of an American culture which prides itself on being the "land of plenty," Hollywood offers us significant examples of how food figures into this American cliche.[1]

When characters come together to break bread in an American film, they sometimes truly *break* bread. Some of the most famous Hollywood food scenes—those which have become part of American "iconography"—are scenes in which food becomes a means to some end, often a violent or disturbing one. James Cagney, frustrated to the point of anger, smashes Mae Clarke in the face with a grapefruit in *Public Enemy* (1931). Jack Nicholson intends to humiliate a pedantic waitress when he orders wheat toast and then pushes his table to the floor in *Five Easy Pieces* (1970), and pies become projectile missiles for Jack Lemmon, Tony Curtis, Natalie Wood, and anyone else standing in the way in *The Great Race* (1965).

What each of these familiar food scenes shares with the hundreds of other less famous scenes is that in all of them, food becomes for the characters a tool, weapon, a means to some end which has little to do with the food itself. If we can learn anything about the nature of how food is used in American movies, it is that we are never just watching people who are eating food. We are almost always exposed to problems or complications during dining scenes, often complications which allow us to distinguish conflict in terms of plot or characters.

Certainly some Hollywood movies provide us with celebrations of food and dining. We watch characters fall in love while they eat: Katharine Hepburn and Spencer Tracy in *Pat and Mike* (1952), Faye Dunaway and Warren Beatty in *Bonnie and Clyde* (1967), Al Pacino and Diane Keaton in *The Godfather* (1972), and Amanda Plummer and Robin Williams in *The Fisher King* (1991). We also see scenes of dining which serve as happy resolutions in several films, including *A Tree Grows in Brooklyn* (1945), *The Big Chill* (1983), and *Moonstruck* (1987). And we experience entire meals where characters come together in a communion of friendship and love in *My Dinner with Andre* (1982) and *The Dead* (1987).

However, these scenes which suggest happiness, comfort, or fulfillment are exceptional among Hollywood productions. In American movies, food and dining are most often associated with crisis, frustration, conflict, or emptiness. No matter what the food, or what the meal being presented to us, Hollywood shows us not how Americans celebrate an abundance of food, but how this very abundance of food exposes other yearnings and other needs of American culture. By reviewing breakfast, lunch, and dinner scenes from several Hollywood movies, perhaps we can begin to distinguish and define Hollywood's vision of the "land of plenty."[2]

We know that Ted Kramer's (Dustin Hoffman's) wife has left home, but we are not aware of how difficult life will be for Ted until we watch him attempt to make breakfast for his eight-year-old son Billy (Justin Henry). Ted Kramer is at a loss. We begin to realize, from his inability to negotiate his way around his own kitchen, that Ted has never prepared breakfast for Billy, who seems more capable than Ted. Billy can at least point to where cooking utensils are located, and he can remember how his mother prepares French toast.

Ted's handling of breakfast with his son in this early scene is vital to our understanding of much of the conflict in *Kramer vs. Kramer* (1979). Because of this "burned French toast" scene, we recognize not only that Ted is out of touch with the day-to-day life of his family, but that he resists advice and attempts to do things "his way." When we watch him burn his son's breakfast, we realize how profoundly lost he is. Ted Kramer doesn't know where he is going, and he is taking us with him.

The food which Ted and Billy eat, and their behavior at mealtimes become our best ways to gauge the quality of their changing relationship during *Kramer vs. Kramer*. From the first breakfast scene to a later dinner scene, where Billy rejects his frozen dinner and defies his father by eating ice cream out of the carton, we watch the two of them struggle to define their positions in their new woman-less home. By the time Joanna Kramer (Meryl Streep) returns to claim Billy, we are aware that Ted and Billy have created a new life together, and most of what we know about these two males has been because we have watched them eat together. In one final, symmetrically-positioned eating scene, Ted and Billy work together to prepare their breakfast on the morning of the custody trial of Kramer v. Kramer. With little effort, they prepare French toast perfectly. This food scene becomes our evidence that Ted and Billy have become a family.

In *To Kill a Mockingbird* (1962), we watch another motherless family who are eating lunch. This scene, only one of two dining scenes in the film, is also one of the most crucial to our understanding of Atticus Finch (Gregory Peck) and his children Jem (Philip Alford) and Scout (Mary Badham). It is because of this dining scene that we begin to recognize not only the nature of the relationship between Atticus and his children, but the moral code by which the Finch family tries to live.

This has been Scout's first day of school, and she is not happy about wearing a dress, or about being told by her teacher that her father has taught her to read "all wrong." By lunchtime, a frustrated Scout has gotten into a fistfight with one of her classmates, Walter Cunningham, and, to smooth things over, her older brother Jem has invited Walter to the Finch home for lunch. We see Atticus and the children sitting around a dining room table while the Finch housekeeper, Calpurnia, moves back and forth from kitchen to dining room. Atticus serves each child a plate, beginning with Walter, who comments to Atticus that he has been eating "mostly squirrel and rabbit lately."

We, like the Finch family, already understand that Walter is not of their economic class; he is rural and poor, and his tastes are quite different from those of Jem and Scout. When Walter asks for the molasses, Atticus and then Calpurnia comply. When Walter pours the syrup over his entire plate of food, neither Atticus nor Jem says anything (although the camera shows us their surprised faces). Scout, however, does not stay silent: "Walter, what in the sam hill are you doing?" she asks, mortified. Walter lowers his head and begins to cry, and Scout is summoned to the kitchen by an angry Calpurnia.

We understand that Scout lacks the maturity and social graces of both her older brother and her father, and that the scene we are watching is a "lesson to be learned" for her. But she won't hear the lesson from her father. Calpurnia's becomes the voice that delivers the message: "That boy's your company, and if he wants to eat up the table cloth you let him, you hear?" The scene ends with Calpurnia's smacking Scout on the backside and sending her out onto the front porch.

There are several ways in which this scene becomes crucial for us. It establishes Atticus as the generous, reasonable father figure who maintains civility at his lunch table. Also, Atticus suggests certain values during the lunch conversation which will become significant for Scout, Jem, and the audience later in the film; it is during this scene that Atticus delivers his "mockingbird" speech to his children, a speech which Scout will recount to her father near the end of the film. Atticus's "mockingbird" speech is important to the plot of *To Kill a Mockingbird* because it suggests that Atticus's (and his children's) view of the world includes compassion and respect for life. Certainly, that Atticus's lunch table is open to guests of his children, that guests in the Finch home are to be made comfortable without question, and that Atticus shares with all three children his story about what it means to kill a mockingbird, are all significant aspects of this "food scene." Finally that Calpurnia, a black housekeeper, is the character who relates to Scout the "rules of the home" is also significant.

As the film continues, we will watch as the Finch children come of age during several summers when their lives are defined by community gossip and racial prejudice. For a black female housekeeper to teach a six-year-old white girl a lesson in gentility will become a meaningful and powerful gesture. This food scene in *To Kill A Mockingbird* suggests much to us about the challenges and the conflicts which the characters—and the audience—will struggle to understand during the course of the film.

This scene represents another characteristic of many Hollywood food scenes: it is an *interrupted* dining scene. Scout's behavior disrupts the dining experience of everyone in the Finch home, and, of course, we recognize that other disruptions are to follow. This pattern—a disrupted dining scene used to prepare us to for further conflict—occurs in innumerable Hollywood productions.[3] One of the most pointed examples of disrupted meals is *Saturday Night Fever* (1977), where not one, but three dinner scenes include major disruptions.

Tony Manero (John Travolta) arrives home from his job at the paint store in time to primp before his mirror and have dinner with his family before he joins his friends for a night of dancing. Before he begins to eat, he dons a bib so that he won't drip spaghetti on his good shirt. We notice this gesture, but his family seems otherwise occupied; they are busy fighting with each other as they fill their plates with food. Tony's father is angry with everyone because he has lost his job, and Tony's mother has bought food too expensive for their budget. When Tony serves himself two pork chops, his father slaps him across the face. Before this first meal is over, several members of Tony's family will have left the table in anger, and ultimately, several will either have slapped someone or will have been slapped.

This, and two later dining scenes, look to us to be "choreographed" dances which allow the audience to identify Tony's position within his family, and to compare this position, this "dancing" with the family, to his dancing in the club. The dining scenes serve as a foil for the scenes in which Tony dances gracefully—and without disruption—around a dance floor. We see Tony dining with his family before we watch him dance, and the contrast is stunning. While his family dinners are violent and unpredictable, his dancing is ordered and pristine. While the only attention Tony gets during family dinners is to be yelled at or slapped, on the dance floor Tony is admired by both men and women. By the time we have been to three dinners at home with Tony—all of which have been disrupted for some reason—we understand his desire to move away from his family. An unemployed and bitter father, a confused brother who has left the priesthood, a mother in tears: these are the problems we watch Tony face every time he sits down to eat a meal at home. Tony Manero is ready to leave this ritual dance of anger in Brooklyn to find what he hopes will be a better experience across the river in Manhattan. From the dining scenes especially, we have become aware of Tony's need to distinguish himself from his family.

Saturday Night Fever includes these powerful dining scenes which share another characteristic with many other Hollywood productions: food becomes one of our gauges to ethnicity in the film. Tony Manero's family is Italian/Catholic; we know this because every meal we watch them eat includes first, genuflection and second, spaghetti. We see ethnic food scenes in many other films as well. We realize that Michael Corleone (Al Pacino) will assume his father's position in the Corleone empire because of a scene in which he is taught to make spaghetti sauce by his father's Sicilian "associates" in *The Godfather*. Many of the scenes which help us to understand the relationships among the characters in *Once Upon A Time in America* (1984) take place in a New York city delicatessen. And, in one of the most pointed of all Hollywood food scenes, Woody Allen's Alvy in *Annie Hall* (1977) projects the differences between his Brooklyn Jewish family and Annie's Wisconsin waspish family by providing us with a split screen dining experience. While Annie's family sits politely in a large, sunny dining room, eating ham and drinking wine, Alvy's family sits in a crowded kitchen, all talking at the same time. Alvy comments to us about Annie's family: "I can't believe this family...they really look American, you know, very healthy.... Nothing like my family."

Alvy Singer has not just compared his family dining experience to Annie's in this scene. He has also identified a type of family dining scene that we see in countless other films. Most often, Hollywood gives us versions of this "American family" dining experience: white, middle class, healthy-looking families who are sitting around well-appointed tables, eating wholesome food. And, just as Alvy comes to realize that Annie's family has its problems (her grandmother is a "classic Jew-hater"; her brother has a morbid fascination with death), we also can begin to notice that these happy, healthy dining scenes in other films usually are deceptive. For almost every civilized, well-prepared meal set before us, we also find a "dysfunctional" American family who is trying to eat it.

The War of the Roses (1988) represents one such film in which a series of dining scenes show us a "healthy American family" that is anything but healthy. The dinners of Oliver and Barbara Rose (Michael Douglas and Kathleen Turner) are never happy meals. In one of the first dinner party scenes, when

Barbara cannot tell a story to Oliver's satisfaction, he interrupts her and tells the story himself. Barbara's response is to give Oliver the finger across the formal dining room table. In a later scene, we see the entire Rose family (Oliver, Barbara, their son and daughter), eating dinner in silence. Oliver breaks the uneasy silence: "We've always been a family that's communicated." We can't help but notice that the four of them could not be sitting further apart from each other, and are divided by gender into two groups of Roses: males on one side of the dining room, females on the other. And, in one of the most obvious examples of an unhealthy American dining experience ever presented by Hollywood, in a late scene we watch Oliver urinate on Barbara's gourmet dinner party.

The Roses are never happy, and we know this most pointedly by the way they use food to hurt each other. In this film, food becomes a weapon and a source of power for both Oliver and Barbara Rose; the kitchen and dining room of the Rose home become the battleground on which we most often watch them waging war. It is not unimportant that food actually becomes part of the plot development in *The War of the Roses*. As Barbara Rose becomes more successful in her career—a catering business—she begins to dislike her husband more and more. For Barbara, food represents success and a source of power and freedom. For us, then, *The War of the Roses* becomes not a movie where there are significant scenes involving food, but a "food movie," a film where food is vital to the plot.

There are many other American "food movies": the 1934 production of *Imitation of Life*, *Marty* (1955), *Crossing DeLancey* (1988), *Men Don't Leave* (1989), *Mystic Pizza* (1988), *Staying Together* (1989), *Baby Boom* (1987), and *Moonstruck* are just a few of the American films in which the production or preparation of food becomes significant to the plots. In these "food movies," the characters are most often struggling to be financially successful, to "find themselves," or to achieve some goal (getting the girl, gaining respect of a community), and food becomes the means by which they define themselves as successful or happy. In turn, we are also asked to equate their success, financial or otherwise, with the business of food.

Indeed, food and economic class are closely related in Hollywood films. We begin to understand economic status of entire families or contrasts between characters because we identify certain foods or certain table manners with lower, working, middle, or upper class characters. When we watch Rayette (Karen Black) trying to participate in the dining conversation with Bobby (Jack Nicholson) and his family in *Five Easy Pieces*, we are uncomfortably aware that Rayette does not understand the rarified environment of this upper class home (she inquires of another house guest, "Is your hair natural?" which silences everyone at the table). We recognize—painfully—that Rayette is more comfortable in a diner than she is in this dining room.

Five Easy Pieces is only one of many Hollywood productions which uses food to point out differences in class among characters. As in *To Kill A Mockingbird* we are asked to consider class differences because of characters' behavior and food choices. When the students in *The Breakfast Club* (1985) take out their lunch bags during their day of detention in the high school library, they unpack very different lunches which tell us much more about the characters than anything they say or do: one student has brought a peanut butter sandwich, one has brought homemade chicken soup, one has brought sushi and chopsticks, and one has brought no lunch at all. We immediately know who these teenagers are. Because of their lunches, we will probably be able to guess the incomes of their parents. We also realize that, as different as their lunches (and their parents' incomes) are, these students are all dissatisfied with themselves and their teenaged lives. In this film, as in so many other American films, we understand that abundance and quality of food do not guarantee happiness. That they have lunches does not make these students any happier. For us, that they have such interesting and varied lunches only serves to bring their problems out of relief. These are not fulfilled, healthy teenagers. They have needs that food will not satisfy.

Food and dining scenes, then, represent a most valuable film property which allows an audience to distinguish ethnicity, class and spiritual "famine." We have also seen that Hollywood often uses the film property of food to empower characters, as in the case of "food movies." In these films, where food becomes part of the plot development, we come to expect food to be a powerful means of our understanding. However, food and dining scenes show up in many American productions which might not be considered "food movies." There are many Hollywood productions which rely on our implicit understanding of food and dining behavior, and which use food and dining scenes throughout to help us understand other aspects of the films. Three major American films, *Bonnie and Clyde*, *Ordinary People* (1980), and *Driving Miss Daisy* (1989), can serve to illustrate the power of food to American film.

Throughout *Bonnie and Clyde*, we are exposed to various film properties which might suggest 1930s America to us: cars, clothing, newspapers and radio broadcasts among them. Perhaps the most surprising—and effective—cultural icon we see in this movie is food. Bonnie and Clyde do not just drive around robbing banks in this movie. They also *eat* their way through the American Dustbowl, and the food they eat tells us a great deal about them and about this Hollywood version of 1930s America.

Bonnie Parker (Faye Dunaway) spies Clyde Barrow (Warren Beatty) as he is about to steal her mother's car. When he boasts to her that he is carrying a gun, Bonnie challenges Clyde to prove that he is the gun-slinging adventurer that he says he is. He proves himself to her by taking her along while he robs a grocery store, and by then stealing a car for their getaway. We see them next sitting in a diner. While Bonnie eats a hamburger and Clyde drinks a Coke, he talks her into staying on the run with him. Clyde has guessed (correctly) that Bonnie is a bored waitress, and to convince her that he can offer her a more exciting life, Clyde points to the bored-looking middle-aged waitress who is serving them. By the end of this scene, the two of them have everything they need for their adventures: a gun, a car, and the food they have stolen. Because of this opening sequence, Bonnie and Clyde have become "Bonnie and Clyde."

As the Barrow gang grows and prospers, we watch them steal and eat food many times. Especially from the time that Buck and Blanche Barrow (Gene Hackman and Estelle Parsons) join Bonnie, Clyde, and C.W. Moss (Michael J. Pollard), we see a great deal of food in the film. Not surprisingly, the Barrow gang eats traditional American fare—hamburgers, french fries, Cokes, ice cream—which helps us establish the American landscape of the movie. What might be more surprising is how food functions as a property in *Bonnie and Clyde*. What we discover when we watch closely is that the scenes in which the characters talk about food, steal food, or eat, are almost always followed by scenes of violence or trouble for the Barrow gang. For the audience, food becomes a direct warning that "something bad is about to happen." In *Bonnie and Clyde*, food always means trouble.

After Buck orders groceries by phone, the delivery man overhears Blanche talking about Bonnie and Clyde, precipitating a shoot-out scene between the Barrow gang and the police which leaves two policemen dead, and the Barrows speeding away in their cars. Soon after, the Barrows steal a car from the home of a young woman who, with her boyfriend, chase the Barrows out into the country. The two lovers are eventually forced to take a ride with the Barrow gang, and they all eat hamburgers and french fries as they ride. When Eugene (Gene Wilder) tells Bonnie that he is an undertaker, he and his girlfriend are promptly ejected from the car, and are left standing by the roadside with their hamburgers still in their hands while the Barrow gang speeds off with their car. For Eugene and Velma, dining with Bonnie and Clyde has been a very expensive—and very dangerous—outing.

We watch the Barrow gang share meals with others as well. They picnic with Bonnie's family, after which Bonnie's mother warns them that they will probably die. In a scene shortly after this picnic, Blanche and C.W. buy food in a diner, and C.W.'s gun is spotted by another customer. In the following series of shoot-out scenes, we watch the Barrow gang begin to disintegrate: Buck dies, Blanche is blinded, and Bonnie and Clyde are both shot. By this point, we realize that buying groceries is a deadly necessity for the Barrow gang.

As C.W. drives the wounded Bonnie and Clyde through the country he stops to ask for water from a group of displaced families who have established a tent city in a field. Ironically, this is the only time we experience a "home-cooked" hot meal with the Barrow gang, and even this meal is only implied, when one of the women gives a bucket of hot food to C.W. to take with him in the car. Finally, when C.W. takes Bonnie and Clyde to his father's house to recover, his father takes him into the kitchen alone and becomes so angry that he hurls food at his son from a spoon.

During the final scenes of *Bonnie and Clyde*, the property of food continues to serve the way to violence and death. When C.W.'s father talks to the sheriff about his "houseguests," they are talking in an ice cream parlor. When his father warns C.W. about not riding with Bonnie and Clyde in their car, he is serving ice cream to his son. And finally, during the penultimate scene of the film, Bonnie and Clyde are shopping for, of course, groceries. As they speed out of town toward their deaths, Bonnie feeds Clyde a pear. For us, she might as well be feeding him an apple—they are the doomed Adam and Eve, moving toward their final damnation. We know this because we know how food functions in *Bonnie and Clyde*. The Barrow gang needs food to survive, but food always betrays them. We understand what they do not, that food, whether in a grocery bag, a wax paper wrapper, a picnic basket, or a tin bucket, means death.

At the time of its release in 1967, *Bonnie and Clyde* also represented a kind of Hollywood film that celebrated the dignity of "marginalized" Americans.[4] The most noble people in the film are the homeless, demoralized victims of the Depression whom the Barrow gang encounters on the road. Their willingness to share their hot food with C.W. is in sharp contrast to the lawmen and the people in the grocery stores and diners. This food scene helps us to understand the affinity between the Barrows and the other Americans they meet who live outside of the law. We watch them share food, but we know they share much more.

The Barrow gang always eats on the run, which helps us to recognize them as outlawed, disenfranchised Americans. They share this characteristic with many other film characters, whose meals and dining habits also suggest that they are somehow "marginalized" Americans. In recent American movies, the kind of greasy, processed fast food that Bonnie and Clyde ate has come to suggest a kind of deterioration of values and an unravelling of the family structure. Often we see fragmented families eating fast food—Ted and Billy in *Kramer vs. Kramer*, Elliot, his siblings and his divorced mother in *E.T.* (1982), the parent-less Joel in *Risky Business* (1983). Pizza, hamburgers, milkshakes, Chinese take-out food and TV dinners have become staple props in many Hollywood productions, among them *Nashville* (1975), *Smile* (1975), *Valley Girl* (1983), *Home Alone* (1990), and *Fast Times at Ridgemont High* (1982), a movie where much of the action takes place in a mall "food court" where several of the characters work.

In American films, if fast food helps us to understand that the characters are either on the run from the law or living in broken homes, then home cooking should tell us that all is well in these American homes. However, this is rarely the case. When we see entire families sitting around a table eating a home-cooked meal, we are almost never made to feel comfortable (the Roses, after all, ate gourmet cooking at home). In Hollywood productions of the last 20 years, home-cooked food and family dining scenes have been used to highlight unhealthy aspects of the American family. We may see plates full of good food, but the characters eating this food are anything but happy.

One of the most powerful examples of this "dysfunctional family" dining experience is *Ordinary People*, a film which, like *Bonnie and Clyde*, includes scenes of food throughout. So many scenes take place in the dining room or the kitchen of the Jarrett home that we begin to see these rooms as the "heart" of the family organism in this film. And, by the end of the film, they will represent a broken heart.

We meet the Jarretts in the kitchen for breakfast. Beth (Mary Tyler Moore) is setting the table; she asks her husband Calvin (Donald Sutherland), "Where's Conrad? This will get cold." She is referring to the French toast she has cooked, but we also understand, from her behavior, that she, too, is "cold." When her son Conrad (Timothy Hutton) tells her that he is in too much of a hurry to eat, we see her take his plate and force the French toast down the disposer. We realize, from this family's awkward and meaningless breakfast conversation, that no one is comfortable, that they can't seem to find any topic of conversation that is not painful. Our final shot is of Calvin, who has tried to engage his son in conversation, sitting alone at the table, calling after Conrad, who has bounded out the door.

As the movie continues, we will learn of the series of tragedies which have made the Jarrett family unable to communicate with each other. They are all struggling to come to terms with the drowning of Conrad's older brother Buck, and with Conrad's subsequent suicide attempt and hospitalization. Throughout the film, we will watch many scenes in which this upper-middle class, suburban family tries to eat meals together in their beautiful formal dining room. With each dining scene, we will be more and more uncomfortably aware of the family's anguished attempts to remain a family. Their conversations at mealtime become increasingly strained. Beth insists on talking about neighborhood gossip and repairmen, Calvin insists on trying to encourage Conrad to talk about anything, and Conrad cannot share anything with his parents.

We see many scenes in which Conrad is in restaurants: once when he has an upsetting reunion with a girl he had met in the hospital, and a later scene in which he takes Janine (Elizabeth McGovern) to McDonald's after their date. (It is also important to note here that, at the end of the film, Janine will take

Conrad into her house for breakfast. Our last shot of Conrad and Janine is a promising picture: she is bringing Conrad into her "heart" by bringing him into her kitchen for breakfast.)

Most of Beth's scenes take place in the Jarrett home, which we know is her family's "heart" as well. Beth is an apt homemaker who buys her son's clothes, sets the table, arranges Halloween treats, and does the dishes. We realize early in the film that Beth resists all conversation about the family's losses or problems by channeling whatever pain she has into running her home smoothly and maintaining an appearance of normalcy. When she is confronted with Calvin's or Conrad's attempts to talk about Buck, she retreats, usually into the kitchen.

We learn most about Beth from her behavior in the kitchen. The Jarretts have a particularly strained Thanksgiving celebration in which Beth's father attempts to photograph the three Jarretts together, and Beth resists. When Conrad becomes angry and swears, Beth breaks the stillness by asking "Who's hungry?" For her, preparing food is a way to avoid conflict. She and her mother go into the kitchen, where Beth breaks a plate. While her mother tries to talk with Beth about Conrad (and, it is not unimportant that her mother asks, "is he getting enough to eat?"), Beth avoids her mother by commenting on how she thinks that the broken plate "can be saved."

For Beth, her broken family can also be saved, but only by solving "these problems in the privacy of our own home" (she tells Calvin as they dine in a public restaurant). Throughout the film, her response to the needs of her husband and son is to engage in "damage control" by continuing to run her home smoothly and silently from her kitchen. We begin to realize, especially from the scenes where Beth is preparing or eating food, that she, not her husband or son, needs this control and this disciplined silence to survive—that behind her mask of the competent homemaker and good cook is a raging, anguished woman whose life has been devastated by the loss of one son and the illness of another. Preparing food becomes Beth's only means of control, her only means of comfort.

There are very few scenes in *Ordinary People* where the characters are *not* uncomfortable, and few scenes which allow us to feel happy for them. By the time Calvin takes Beth on a trip to Texas, and we hear her ask her brother, "why is it that I still feel hungry?" we understand that Beth truly *is* hungry, but not for food. Like Calvin and Conrad, she is hungry for relief from anger and grief.

The many food scenes are our best gauge to the depth of their pain, because we understand in these scenes the sharp contrast between their well-balanced diet of good food, prepared and eaten in a pleasant, affluent home, and their totally unbalanced and dysfunctional behaviors. The dining scenes in *Ordinary People* are particularly difficult to watch because they are the scenes in which we see the family together but alone, looking good but feeling badly, eating but hungry.

Near the end of the film, Calvin finally acknowledges and articulates his fears and feelings to Beth. He does so while he is sitting alone at the dining room table, crying, in the middle of the night. When Beth sees him, she asks, "Why are you crying? Can I get you something?" She means, of course, "Can I bring you some food?" We learn, as she does, that she cannot get him anything, that what he needs is not in the kitchen. When Calvin tells Beth that he doesn't think he loves her anymore, the dining room seems empty and cold to us. The Jarrett "heart" is empty as well; dining together has not allowed this family to heal, but has only emphasized, both for Calvin and for us, how truly starving these ordinary people are.

In *Ordinary People*, we find that the kitchen and dining room, and the preparation and presentation of food, become significant to our understanding of the tensions among Beth, Calvin and Conrad. Other recent films use kitchen and dining room scenes to help us distinguish conflict, most notably *Driving Miss Daisy*, in which the kitchen is the realm of the black workers, Idella the cook (Esther Rolle) and Hoke the chauffeur (Morgan Freeman), and the dining room belongs to Daisy (Jessica Tandy). We see food used often to define racial lines of the film. Food is Daisy's property and distinguishes her from her black servants. When she accuses Hoke of stealing food from the pantry, when Idella dies while preparing food in the kitchen, when Daisy and Hoke eat separately and alone in their respective parts of the house, we understand the racial lines which divide them, as if there were a line painted between Daisy's kitchen and dining room.

Throughout the film, we can gauge much about the relationship of Daisy and Hoke by their relationship to the food in Daisy's house. We understand how much their relationship changes during the film by remembering that although Daisy had accused Hoke of stealing food early on, in a much later scene (representing several years later), she tells him to "eat anything you want to out of the icebox." We may see this scene as progress, until we realize that in the next scene, Daisy dines at a formal dinner where Martin Luther King is the guest speaker and Hoke sits outside in the car, listening to Dr. King on the radio. Daisy and Hoke may have met in the kitchen of her private home, but we see that in the public forum, the line between black and white, between kitchen and dining room, remains for them.

Like *Bonnie and Clyde*, *Driving Miss Daisy* also uses traditional "American" foods to help define an American environment. After Idella dies, Daisy tries to fry chicken (she rejects Hoke's efforts to help her), and the final scene of the film is of Hoke feeding pumpkin pie to Daisy as she sits in her wheelchair in a nursing home on Thanksgiving Day. It has been the food, as much as any other property of this film, which has helped us to understand the racial divisions of Miss Daisy's Atlanta, and the changes in Miss Daisy's behavior toward Hoke. When we watch Hoke feeding her, we notice that they are both sitting at the same table. This is, sadly, the first and last time we see them in these positions.

Almost every movie presented to us by Hollywood uses food as a film property. As we have seen, some films use food in subtle ways and in only a few scenes, and some films are structured so that the food becomes an important guide to plot or character development. What food seems to suggest in almost all Hollywood movies is that American culture does not value that which it has in abundance; we are, in fact, suspicious or ignorant of the value of food. Hollywood films tell us that although food is plentiful in these United States, Americans are rarely happy because of food. Food can make us financially wealthy or physically fit, but food always betrays us, confines us, divides us.

In Hollywood movies, having and eating food makes us aware of those qualities which we do *not* have: respect, love, power. There are many scenes where food and dining become nightmares: Celie (Whoopie Goldberg) attempts to stab her husband (Danny Glover) during a dinner scene in *The Color Purple* (1985); Edna (Sally Field) watches helplessly as her murdered husband's body is laid out on her dining room table in *Places in the Heart* (1984); Roy (Richard Dreyfuss), by attempting to create a version of Devil's Tower out of his mashed potatoes, frightens his wife and children to tears in *Close Encounters of the Third Kind* (1977).[5]

Food, then, shows us an America that is hungry in the land of plenty. Yet Hollywood has always provided us some relief from this grim vision of America by allowing us to laugh at ourselves, often with the help of food or dining scenes. Perhaps because of this distrust of food in American film, food can function as a film property that can trick us or make us smile. We find many American movies in which we are encouraged to laugh because of food and dining experiences. *Life With Father* (1947), *My Favorite Year* (1982), *Best Friends* (1982), *Beetlejuice* (1988), *Tootsie* (1982), and *Terms of Endearment* (1983) are only a few of the hundreds of American films in which we laugh during scenes involving food. What we are laughing at will vary, but most often these funny food scenes are parodies or scenes in which food is used as a sight gag.

And we always understand sight gags, especially those involving food. To our initial list of banana peels, pies in the face, and sliding tablecloths, and to our menu of famous Hollywood "food icons," we might add the following American tidbits: Reese's Pieces in *E.T.*, raw eggs in *Rocky* (1976) and the cafeteria scene in *Animal House* (1978). We have food in such abundance in American films that we have the luxury of playing with it.

If the food presented to us in Hollywood films helps us understand American culture, then what we understand is that although Americans might be unaware of or hostile to their abundance of food they are not American without this food. Whether we eat it, grow it, cook it, sell it, or throw it, the powerful ways food is used in American films are a reflection of a society in which food always means something, whether we understand exactly what that something is or not. Beth McColley (Jessica Lange) tells us this when she applies for a job in a gourmet shop in *Men Don't Leave,* and she hesitates before groping for words about food: "I am interested in food. I love food. I know food. I eat food."

As we have seen in so many American film characters, we recognize in Beth a peculiar relationship to food; she relies on it, but she has never before given much thought to how she feels about food. Hollywood films have always been able to identify this ambiguity. Like it or not, Hollywood's America is forever the land of plenty, and Americans are forever uncomfortably hungry amidst an abundance of food.

Notes

[1]Because there are literally hundreds of American films which use food as a film device, I consider this essay to be an overview only; I would suggest that this essay represents a strategy for "reading" American films in terms of food and dining. Also, I have limited my discussion exclusively to American productions. The subject of food in films produced elsewhere in the world represents a much more complex topic and deserves its own discussion elsewhere.

I thank the following: S. and C. Carey, L. Coleman, K. Hutson, P. Loukides, B. Searle and N. Workman.

[2]There are no scholarly discussions which deal exclusively with food as a film property in American movies. There are several general discussions of trends in film and of specific films which have been valuable to this project, among them Christensen, Kolker, Levy, Ray, Shadoian, and, most especially, Reed, *American Scenarios.*

[3]There is an amusing chart which outlines interrupted dining scenes in eight recent Hollywood films in the October, 1990 issue of *Premiere,* "Why Hollywood Is Not the Headquarters of the Clean-Plate Club: Food For Thought—Not For Eating," 34.

[4]The significance of *Bonnie and Clyde* to American film culture and history is discussed in the following works: Gabree, Kolker, Levy, Reed, and Shadoian. Particularly useful is *The Bonnie and Clyde Book,* Wake and Hayden, eds.

[5]There are many other "nightmare" dining scenes in American films, including scenes in *Whatever Happened to Baby Jane?* (1962), *The Postman Always Rings Twice* (1981), *Fatal Attraction* (1987), *The Witches of Eastwick* (1987), and, in perhaps the most grizzly minglings of power, sex, violence and food: *The Silence of the Lambs* (1991).

Works Cited

Christiansen, Terry. *Reel Politics: American Political Movies from* Birth of a Nation *to* Platoon. NY: Basil Blackwell Inc., 1987.

Gabree, John. *Gangsters: From* Little Caesar *to* The Godfather. NY: Galahad Books, 1973.

Kolker, Robert Philip. *A Cinema of Loneliness: Penn, Kubrick, Coppola, Scorsese, Altman.* NY: Oxford UP, 1980.

Levy, Emanuel. *Small-Town America in Film: The Decline and Fall of Community.* NY: The Continuum Publishing Company, 1990.

Ray, Robert B. *A Certain Tendency of the Hollywood Cinema, 1930-1980.* Princeton, NJ: Princeton UP, 1985.

Reed, Joseph W. *American Scenarios: The Uses of Film Genre.* Middleton, CT: Wesleyan UP, 1989.

Schofield, Mary Anne. *Cooking By The Book.* Bowling Green, Ohio: Bowling Green State University Popular Press, 1989.

Shadoian, Jack. *Dreams and Dead Ends: The American Gangster/Crime Film.* Cambridge, MA: The MIT P, 1977.

Wake, Sandra and Nicola Hayden, eds. *The Bonnie and Clyde Book.* NY: Simon & Schuster, 1972.

"Why Hollywood Is Not The Headquarters of the Clean-Plate Club: Food For Thought— Not For Eating." *Premiere* Oct. 1990: 34.

Filmography

Year	Film	Director
1931	*Public Enemy*	William A. Wellman
1934	*Imitation of Life*	John Stahl
1945	*A Tree Grows in Brooklyn*	Joel Hardy
1947	*Life With Father*	Michael Curtiz
1952	*Pat and Mike*	George Cukor
1955	*Marty*	Delbert Mann
1962	*To Kill a Mockingbird*	Robert Mulligan
1962	*Whatever Happened to Baby Jane?*	Robert Aldrich
1965	*The Great Race*	Blake Edwards
1967	*Bonnie and Clyde*	Arthur Penn
1970	*Five Easy Pieces*	Bob Rafelson
1972	*The Godfather*	Francis Coppola
1975	*Nashville*	Robert Altman
1975	*Smile*	Michael Ritchie
1976	*Rocky*	John G. Avildsen
1977	*Annie Hall*	Woody Allen

1977	*Close Encounters of the Third Kind*	Steven Spielberg
1977	*Saturday Night Fever*	John Badham
1978	*National Lampoon's Animal House*	John Landis
1979	*Kramer vs. Kramer*	Robert Benton
1980	*Ordinary People*	Robert Redford
1981	*The Postman Always Rings Twice*	Bob Rafelson
1982	*Best Friends*	Norman Jewison
1982	*E.T. The Extra-Terrestrial*	Steven Spielberg
1982	*Fast Times at Ridgemont High*	Amy Heckerling
1982	*My Dinner With Andre*	Louis Malle
1982	*My Favorite Year*	Richard Benjamin
1982	*Tootsie*	Sydney Pollack
1983	*The Big Chill*	Lawrence Kasdan
1983	*Risky Business*	Paul Brickman
1983	*Terms of Endearment*	James L. Brooks
1983	*Valley Girl*	Martha Coolidge
1984	*Once Upon A Time In American*	Sergio Leone
1984	*Places In The Heart*	Robert Benton
1985	*The Breakfast Club*	John Hughes
1985	*The Color Purple*	Steven Spielberg
1987	*Baby Boom*	Charles Shyer
1987	*The Dead*	John Huston
1987	*Fatal Attraction*	Adrian Lyne
1987	*Moonstruck*	Norman Jewison
1987	*The Witches of Eastwick*	George Miller
1988	*Beetlejuice*	Tim Burton
1988	*Crossing DeLancy*	Joan Micklin Silver
1988	*Mystic Pizza*	Donald Petrie
1988	*The War of the Roses*	Danny DeVito
1989	*Driving Miss Daisy*	Bruce Beresford
1989	*Men Don't Leave*	Paul Brickman
1989	*Staying Together*	Lee Grant
1990	*Home Alone*	John Hughes
1991	*The Fisher King*	Terry Gilliam
1991	*The Silence of the Lambs*	Jonathan Demme

Cry Food:
The Use of Food as a Comic Motif
in the Films of Charlie Chaplin

Jay Boyer

Perhaps there's no more famous scene in silent comedy than the scene in Charlie Chaplin's *The Gold Rush* in which the Chaplin tramp is starving to death in a cabin in the Yukon. Across from him sits the bear-like Big Jim McKay. It's Thanksgiving day. With no food in the cabin, and no hope of acquiring any thanks to a raging Yukon storm outside, the two prospectors face imminent death. Amused, we watch as Chaplin prepares his boot to serve as a meal; perhaps a bit horrified, we watch as he and Big Jim set about making a meal of the boot. And, finally, caught up in the comic spirit of the sequence by this point, we laugh out loud as Big Jim, driven to the point of madness by hunger, begins to see the tramp not as a human being but rather as a chicken, one he has every intention of turning into a meal.

If not the most famous slapstick comedy sequence, it is at least the single most well-known work of Charlie Chaplin to contemporary audiences; from the preparation of the boot through Big Jim's pursuit of the tramp-as-chicken, it's a clip that's been used time and again in countless compendiums of silent comedies. But it almost got left on the cutting room floor. By the third week of March, 1924, Chaplin had yet another idea. Rather than big Jim's demented vision resulting in a chase of Charlie around the cabin, one that would end only once it had taken the two men into the perilous snowstorm outside, Chaplin thought about making it into a dream sequence with the tramp as the dreamer. The object of the dream was to be not a bird this time but rather a strawberry shortcake, and the central gag was going to be little more sophisticated than a pie in the face.

At this point in production, the female lead was being played by Lita Grey rather than Georgia Hale, the heroine in the version released for distribution. The daily continuity report for Saturday, 22 March contains the following passage:

Scene 14: Close-up. Dissolve. C. asleep in kitchen on couch. Lita standing over him with cake—awakens him—he sits up—she sits down beside him—smiles—takes berry—gives it to him—he turns forward—eats it—smiles—she takes another berry—starts to give it to him. She says: Close your eyes and open your mouth. He does so and she throws whole cake in his face and laughs. C. takes cake off—face all smeared with cream—Fade out and fade into close-up of cabin with C. asleep in cot—blanket over body but not on head—snow on neck and face—snow drops down from roof five times—he wakes up then sits up—and looks around room—brushes snow off—gets up—comes forward left of camera. O.K.

It's fortunate if not particularly surprising that Chaplin decided to forego this version in favor of the one we all know, and it's largely out of keeping with the kind of comedy he was employing by the 1920s, particularly in regard to food. Over a period of about ten years, Chaplin's use of food had evolved from the Sennett-esque pie in the face to something decidedly more complicated. Food was no longer simply a weapon, as it had been in so many of the Keystone comedies and Chaplin's early work as well. Food had begun to take on thematic dimensions as Chaplin pushed slapstick comedy toward the realm of filmic art. He had begun to employ extended gag sequences in which food and eating were used to explore the nature of humanity in the modern world.

Chaplin's Use of Food at Keystone, Essanay and Mutual Studios

In *My Autobiography*, Charlie Chaplin raises almost as many questions about how he worked as he answers, and for a man who lived so public and sometimes scandalous a life, the same might be said in regard to what he tells about himself. In fact, for an autobiography so thick, a book about 500 pages long in hardcover, *My Autobiography* tells us far less than one might anticipate.

About some things though, it tells us far more. His meals, for example. Why, one wonders, does Chaplin recount particular meals in his life in such a elaborate detail, and why does he recount so many? When so much else is left out, what relevance could Chaplin have thought there'd be in what he ate, and when he ate it?

The answer to this may have to do with the poverty of is youth. The poverty he knew as a child is legendary, and it certainly seems reasonable that someone who grew up living—sometimes literally—hand to mouth would be conscious of such events. Still, some of the meals Chaplin recounts occurred more than 50 years before the writing on the book; some of them he recounts in truly remarkable detail; and a reader gradually begins to suspect that throughout his life, through lean times and fat, food and eating and hunger were directly associated in Chaplin's mind with his place in the world.

One of Chaplin's earliest memories, for instance, is of being orphaned by his mother, then of going with his brother Sydney to the workhouse where their mother was an occupant and of spending that morning together.

Mother, Sydney and I looked a crumpled sight as we ambled out through the workhouse gates...Sydney had ninepence tied up in a handkerchief, so we bought half a pound of black cherries and spent the morning in Kennington Park, sitting on a bench eating them...At noon we went to a coffee shop and spent the rest of our money on twopenny teacake, a penny bloater and two halfpenny cups of tea, which we shared between us.

Often, hunger seems to be equated in Chaplin's memory with feelings of abandonment and helplessness; he sometimes speaks about them in virtually the same breath, as if hunger and abandonment were one and the same. Chaplin recalls a period when he and his brother were living with their alcoholic father and their father's lover. One afternoon Chaplin returned to the poor flat and found no one at home:

The room looked grim and unyielding and its emptiness frightened me. I also began to get hungry, so I looked in the larder, but no food was there. I could stand the gaping emptiness no longer, so in desolation I went out, spending the afternoon visiting nearby marketplaces. I wandered through Lambeth Walk and the Cut, looking hungrily into cookshop windows at the tantalizing, steaming roast joints of beef and pork, and the golden-browned potatoes soaked in gravy. For hours I watched the quacks selling their wares. The distraction soothed me and for a while I forgot *my plight and my hunger* (italics mine).

The particularity of Chaplin's memory is telling. One notes that there was not simply meat in the cookshops, but rather beef and pork, that these were "roast joints," that these joints were steaming. Nor is this sense of detail peculiar to this lone episode in his life. Chaplin sometimes recounts even the poorest and slightest of meals as though preparing to offer us the recipe:

After washing and scraping the cheese rinds we would add water and a little salt and pepper. Sometimes the boss would throw in a piece of bacon fat and a sliced onion, which together with a can of hot tea made a very appetizing meal.

Chaplin employs food in recounting the highest points of his life as well as the lowest. He recalls, for instance, the morning he conceived of the film that was to turn out to be his most beloved feature film, and Chaplin's personal favorite, "The Gold Rush." He'd spent the weekend with the Fairbankses. It was Sunday morning. He'd just had a large breakfast. Douglas Fairbanks offered him the stereopticon and an assortment of slides. One was a view of the Chilikoot Pass. A long line of prospectors were photographed as they climbed the frozen mountain. On the back of the slide was a list of the hardships they endured. He associated the scene with food and hunger. And this brought to mind a book he'd read about a party of prospectors who'd been driven to cannibalism:

I read a book about the Donner party who, on the way to California, missed the route and were snowbound in the Sierra Nevada mountains. Out of the hundred and sixty pioneers only eighteen survived, most of them dying of hunger and cold. Some resorted to cannibalism, eating their dead, others roasted their moccasins to relieve their hunger. Out of this harrowing tragedy I conceived of one of our funniest scenes. In dire hunger I boil my shoe and eat it, picking the nails as though they were bones of a delicious capon, and eating the shoelaces as though they were spaghetti. In his delirium of hunger, my partner is convinced that I am a chicken and wants to eat me.

Even a cursory look at Chaplin's films demonstrates the importance of food to their comedy. Sequences set in cafes and gags involving food are to be found in Chaplin's work long before *The Gold Rush*. They're to be found even in Chaplin's earliest films, *The Rounders*, to name but one, but the interest there is in drinking and liquor more than in eating and food. The first Chaplin film to put food at its center was one he starred in during his last months at Keystone, a film he directed himself entitled *Dough and Dynamite*, one of only seven two-reel comedies he appeared in while working for Mack Sennett. Charlie and Chester Conklin are semi-competent waiters. When the bakers go out on strike, the pair are left to handle the ovens as well. Unbeknownst to either, the strikers have snuck into the kitchen and put dynamite into a loaf before it's been put into the oven to be baked.

The film ends not with the usual Sennett chase but rather with a huge—and expensive, at $1000 the film would go way over the allotted Keystone budget—explosion. At its core though is the standard Keystone fare. Conklin and Chaplin bash one another repeatedly with the food they're supposedly preparing and serving, pies, bread and other baked goods, and what's somewhat surprising about a film so filled with gags dealing with food is how few times the food in question is eaten. As Gerald Mast lists in *The Comic Mind*, Chaplin employs the dough in the film's title in almost every way except as a way of making something to eat. Writes Mast, "Before the film has finished, Chaplin has used dough as boxing gloves, bracelets, quicksand, a mallet, a slingshot, a discus, a chair and something to occupy his roaming hands while flirting with a pretty girl."

Chaplin's break with Sennett came when he went to work for Essanay Studios in 1915. Indeed, the film that is normally cited as the birth of the Chaplin tramp, the film that was to capture the hearts of the world is *The Tramp*, an Essanay film. Yet food here is something of an afterthought. It's not used as a weapon the way it might have been at Keystone, but then neither is it employed as it will be later. It's used in two rather limited ways. Food, or more precisely, the paucity thereof, underscores the poverty of the title character, as, for example, when the tramp makes a meal of a single sausage boiled in soup can, or staves off his hunger with a handful of grass. But the meals he takes also remind us of the tramp's civility. He's a human being, and he stubbornly refuses to allow his circumstances to make of him anything less. Early in the film the tramp is given a bit of food in a handkerchief as a handout. He sits down to eat it. Before he begins his meal, he notices that his fingernails are in need of a polish. While he polishes his nails, another tramp steals the food and puts in its place a brick. Chaplin's circumstances reduce him to dining on grass. But even then, they never lessen his dignity. At one point in the meal he uses a tomato can as a finger bowl.

One of Chaplin's last Essanay films, *Shanghaied* (1915), and one of his earlier two-reel Mutual films, *The Fireman* (1916), both put food at their comic center. In *Shanghaied*, Chaplin becomes part of a plot to shanghai a trio of sailors only to be shanghaied himself; the majority of the gags though deal with his discomfort at sea. Chaplin is sick at his stomach from virtually the moment he sets sail, and as Sobel and Francis have chronicled in their 1977 study, *Chaplin: Genesis Of A Clown*, many of these gags are premised on Chaplin's revulsion at the sight and smell of food, a motif he would later employ in films such as *Behind the Screen*, and to still better advantage in such films as *The Immigrants*. The plot of *The Fireman* is reminiscent of the love triangles Chaplin often found himself involved in in the films of Keystone, triangles that put him in opposition to "heavies" who were inevitably larger and more threatening than himself. Here the heavy is the bushy-browed Eric Campbell, who, like Charlie, pursues the hand of Chaplin's leading lady of the period, Edna Purviance. The girl's father, played by Leo White, prefers Charlie's rival. The father sets fire to his own house in order to receive insurance money, and the ending of the film has Chaplin rescuing the heroine from the flames.

Like the earlier *Dough and Dynamite*, there's a rather spectacular quality to the climax on the screen, and as was true of *Dough and Dynamite*, Chaplin went over budget to get the ending he wanted: here he had to burn down two condemned houses before he finally got the cinematic effect he desired. But the middle of the film, in which Charlie performs his duties around the fire station, are on a much more personal and limited scale. Much of what Chaplin does around the fire station has to do with food, with preparing food and serving it to the other firemen. He flips plates on the table with the same flick of the wrist one might use in dealing cards; he draws coffee and cream not from the spigots of a coffee urn but rather from the boilers of the fire engine, etc.

The extant outtakes and daily records of production from *The Count* (1916) suggest that Chaplin may have been planning many more gags employing food than finally made their way to the screen; and even in what exists today of this story of a tailor's assistant (Chaplin) pursuing a rich woman's cook, there's both an extended kitchen episode and a long dinner table sequence putting Chaplin, Eric Campbell, and Edna Purviance together again. But there's little in either of these episodes that hadn't been done by Chaplin earlier, and the finale of the film, relying upon, among other things, gags with flying cake, is so familiar in madcap pace and violent tone that one wonders if it was done with any thought or invention at all.

A prolonged sequence in the kitchen involves Limburger cheese and Chaplin gets a series of laughs from the problems it poses, laughs not unlike those he got in *Shanghaied*, since food here virtually becomes his enemy. Too, a few scenes from *Behind The Screen* (1916), another Mutual film, call to mind this earlier work, such as his revulsion at the smell of onions in a co-worker's lunch and the ingenious ways he deals with this situation.

Since his days at Keystone, food had been identified with conflict and contention, with weaponry, assault, effrontery. Often it seemed to have a will of its own (the malodorous food in his films, for instance) or to be of use in enforcing one's will on another. And this would continue to be true as Chaplin's time at Essanay came to an end and he went to work at Mutual. In *The Rink* (1916), for instance, food is used as a comic prop over which to wage comic battles. Too, the film treats what's edible and what's not as one and the same— soap and other cleaning supplies are mistakenly served to a customer, for instance, instead of the meal that he ordered. *The Rink* is best known today for Chaplin's ballet-like roller-skating sequences, sequences he would bring to an artistic peak in his 1936 "silent" comedy *Modern Times*. But the first part of the film has Charlie as a waiter, much as he was in the beginning of *Dough and Dynamite* and, logically enough, the gags in this part of the film often have to do with serving food—or, more precisely, how not to—as Charlie negotiates his way through a gauntlet of competitive waiters and impatient customers.

There's a slight difference between Chaplin's use of food in these last films at Mutual and his use of food in his earlier work at Essanay and Keystone, however. Often one gag with food in his Mutual films leads logically to another, and that gag to another still. In the dinner table sequence in *The Count*, for instance, Chaplin skewers a roast turkey with his cane as if he is running through a foe with his lance, then uses the turkey at the end of his cane like a cudgel to crown a nearby man on the head; later he'll go to work on a finely iced cake with that same cane, in much the same manner. This repetition in which gags are structured around variations on one central action is to be found once again in the sequences in *The Rink* which deal with waiting tables. Chaplin manages to get three separate but related gags out of trying to serve a slippery roast chicken to an impatient couple; a number of things beside food are served by mistake in the restaurant, cleaning supplies, live animals, and more.

Chaplin's Use of Food at First National and U.A.

Chaplin's last films at Mutual relied heavily on modifications of earlier work he'd done with food as the stuff of physical comedy. Charlie's feeding of impoverished children with corn flakes in *Easy Street* (1917) is reminiscent of the poverty to be found in *the Tramp*, for instance; the restaurant sequences in *The Immigrant* (1917) owe much to Chaplin's work in the first sections of *The Rink*, just as surely as his sequences about life in steerage and *mal de mer* aboard the ship in *The Immigrant* call to mind individual gags from *Shanghaied.*

When Chaplin left Mutual and went to work at First National, though, he brought to his films a new consciousness—a new seriousness, perhaps?—of the capacity of motion pictures to comment and reflect on modern society; and with this sensibility came a new interest in how to employ food, and the serving of food, and the eating of food in his films.

In his book *The Silent Clowns*, Walter Kerr points out that the poverty in the streets of Chaplin's initial First National film, *A Dog's Life* (1918), seems real. It's not as if we're looking at the backlot of motion picture studio, says Kerr, and the sense of hunger that runs through the film is portrayed realistically as well. Kerr's right. There's something different about *A Dog's Life*. It's as funny or funnier than Chaplin's earlier work, yet, paradoxically, it's more serious somehow.

The film offers us a look at a dog-eat-dog urban environment—alleyways, tenements, brutal and thoughtless police, hunger and deprivation that reduce people to animalistic levels of life. Specifically, the structure of the film aligns the life of a homeless, starving mongrel dog, Scraps, and that of our hero, the Chaplin tramp. Five of the six major comic sequences that comprise the film deal with hunger, stealing food, eating food, or the like. The first will serve as a example. In the first ten minutes of the film, we meet first Charlie, the tramp, sleeping against a fence in a vacant lot, and follow along as he attempts to evade a menacing policeman and then feed himself. The film then cuts away from Charlie and takes us to Scraps, the mutt, who wakes up in a wash tub, aroused apparently by a smell of cooking food. We follow Scraps as he has a run in with the same cop, then finds himself having to fight for a bite of food; we watch as he is pursued by a pack of dogs seeking to keep him out of their territory and the sequence comes to an end as he is saved by Charlie, who just happens to be passing by. Within the frame, dog and man are virtually one as they flee, for, as Chaplin and his cameraman Rollie Totheroh photograph the scene, Chaplin is carrying the dog and the movement of Scraps hindquarters are not dissimilar from those of our hero.

The sequence with Scraps seeking food counterpoints and emphasizes the scene we've just witnesses involving the tramp. Chaplin swipes a hot dog from a passing vendor. He's seen by a policeman who pursues him. In the process of avoiding and outwitting the policeman, the tramp loses the hot dog he so deftly acquired. He's no better off than when he started; he's still hungry. Only now he's in flight from the law as well.

The hunger here is more tangible than it has been in Chaplin's earlier films. To be sure, one can find in his earlier work isolated gags that broach levels of pathos, such as the tramp salting grass in *The Tramp* in order to give it some taste, or Charlie feeding corn flakes to the gamins in *Easy Street* as if they were chickens in a farm yard; neither of these gags is paced in a way which might undercut their comedy, however. That's not quite so true in the sequence above, nor will it be true in the sequences to come. Scraps and Charlie work together in an attempt to put food in their stomachs, and we're given reason to believe that their stomachs are empty.

Here, food in general, and the feeding of someone else in particular, whether it's Scraps or later the penniless immigrant girl played by Edna Purviance, are equated with love, succorance, with a bond between caring parties, with the largely selfless, human act, and Chaplin uses food in motifs that point us toward what distinguishes a civilized society from a jungle.

Early in *A Dog's Life* Chaplin finds an abandoned milk bottle containing an inch or so of milk. He sits on the curb and considers what to do with it. Seeing he has no bowl with which to feed Scraps, he takes the dog's tail, dips it into the bottle, then gives it to Scraps to lick. This completes the bond between man and animal, and from this point forward in the film they will work as a team. At one point, in fact, when the tramp enters a restaurant where dogs aren't allowed, he puts Scraps into his pants. We see the couple from behind. Scraps' wagging tail protrudes from a hole in the seat of Charlie's pants. It's a wonderful bit of comic business, and the irony is striking. The character the camera identifies with an animal is the least animalistic of any male character we meet.

A similar act of feeding seals the bond between man and abandoned child in Chaplin's first feature, *The Kid* (1921), and underscores the tramp's humanity once again. Consider the first sequence in which the tramp appears. Two thugs have have stolen an automobile, unaware that an infant is in the back seat. When they discover the child, the thugs pull into an alley and dispose of the child amidst garbage cans. To them, the child isn't of value, hence it's disposable. Its humanity is never a consideration; it's little more than refuse that has to be gotten rid of. This begins a series of gags all premised on what is garbage in the modern, urban world and what isn't. We cut to the tramp coming through the alleyway in the distance. He dodges trash that is being thrown out a second floor window. He looks up. He moves deftly ahead. Just when he begins to relax, he's struck by trash thrown out of yet another window. He moves nearer to us. He removes a tin of cigarette butts from his pocket. Charlie depends on the trash of others in order to survive, we're to understand; they've been disposed of on the street and he's picked them up. Before he lights one, he daintily removes his glove. He inspects it. His glove is so worn that it's trash. He disposes of the glove. He comes upon the abandoned child next to the row of garbage cans. He looks overhead, assuming, apparently, that the child has been thrown out of second story window along with someone's morning trash. He doesn't appear to be dismayed. He understands the streets, the logic of city life. He starts to put it back where he found it, then stops. Thus far in the sequence, the tramp is the first one to see that there's a difference between a child and garbage and now begins a series of gags in which Chaplin tries to pawn off the child on others, a woman with a child of her own, another man. Charlie's not successful. Somehow, the child keeps winding up in his arms. Finally, he sits down on a curb. He's cradling the child, contemplating what to do next. He opens a sewer grate and starts to dispose of the infant, then thinks better of it. He knows he has no business trying to care for a child; he can barely fend for himself. Still, a child is a child—not garbage. He's asked by a group of prostitutes what the child's name is. It's the first time such a question has occurred to him. He disappears from our view. When he returns, he tells them, "John." He's found a private place where he can determine the child's sex, apparently. Next, we go with Charlie to his dilapidated room. The child is hungry. He's ill-equipped to care for the infant, but not unwilling. Ingeniously, he rigs up a coffee pot with the finger of a rubber glove for a nipple. From this point on the child belongs to Charlie.

As late as *Modern Times* (1936), Chaplin was employing this food motif to emphasize the tramp's humanity, his capacity for love, his ability to care for and comfort another human being. An orphaned girl played by Paulette Godard is living on the streets. In an attempt to keep from starving, she steals a loaf of bread from a retailer. A policeman apprehends her. The tramp has recently been released from prison. The Depression has swept the country while he was incarcerated and he's eager to return to prison where at least he's assured of a place to sleep and three meals a day. He tries to explain to the policeman that it was he, not the girl, who stole the loaf. The policeman won't buy it. He takes the girl away and puts her in a paddy wagon. This gives Charlie an idea. Chaplin goes into a cafeteria and orders a huge meal, eats it, explains to the cashier that he can't pay for it, and invites her to call for the police. A policeman soon arrives. He puts Charlie into the same paddy wagon where the girl was put. On the way to the police station, the paddy wagon is involved in an accident. Charlie and the girl are thrown clear. He urges her to flee. She urges him to accompany her. We next see them sitting outside a California bungalow. Charlie offers up a vision of what life must be like inside the house. He creates a vision in which food grows on trees, in which a cow appears at one's back door when a person wants milk. The girls explains to him that she hasn't eaten, that so much talk about food has only increased her hunger. He vows to feed her. He takes a job as a nightwatchman in a department store. He sneaks her in just after the store has closed, sits her down at a lunch counter, and feeds her royally.

From this point forward in the film, the girl and the tramp are a couple. The scene becomes something of a fulcrum upon which the rest of the action rests and Chaplin counterpoints it a number of times—to name one, the sequence in which Charlie encounters "a feeding machine." Chaplin may well have been mocking an often repeated slogan of the Depression, namely that machines and factories, whatever discomforts they caused aside, put food in the stomachs of America, for that's what happens here—more or less. Charlie, an assembly line worker, is chosen to help demonstrate the Biddle's Feeding Machine. Its creators are trying to convince the factory president that the machine they have to offer can increase productivity. Why give his workers a lunch break? They can continue working at the same time they're being fed. Chaplin's swiftly locked into the housing of the feeding machine. Only Chaplin's head is free. His face is in the center of the frame. Thanks to the camerawork, the rest of him appears to be composed of metal parts. It takes us a moment to realize what's happened. The machine has tubular, robotic arms, flange-like hands, and cameraman Rollie Totheroh emphasizes this meld of human and non-human parts by raising the camera and shooting Chaplin in high angle, creating a wonderful visual metaphor. Chaplin has become the perfect factory employee: Charlie-the-worker has become Charlie-the-mechanical man. The machine's robotic limbs are now his, apparently, and, at least in the beginning, he seems to be dining with a certain fluidity and mechanical grace. There's soup, an entree; there's tableware; there's even an automatic facsimile of a napkin with which to wipe his lips. But something goes wrong. Suddenly the hot soup is dumped into his lap. The machine goes haywire. It begins to pummel the tramp. At once pain and fear register on his face. Then, just as suddenly, it ends. The gears of the machine appear to have shifted into neutral. Oblivious to what the tramp has just gone through, the people from the Biddle company attempt minor adjustments of the machine's working parts and repeat the process from scratch. The same thing happens, but worse. Again the tramp is pinned, pummeled, abused. Again, minor adjustments are made. The demonstration begins for a third time, then a fourth, etc. For all intents and purposes, the machine becomes a device of torture—but no one seems to care. It's rejected by the factory president not because of what it has done to the poor abused Charlie, but rather because the machine isn't "practical."

In *The Kid*, Chaplin uses food to establish the humanity, dignity and compassion of the tramp, traits that set the tramp apart from much of the modern world around him. He does this again is *Modern Times*, using sequences such as the one above to underscore this point and show us the disparity between a civilized, human experience of the world and an experience which is not. But perhaps no Chaplin film makes this distinction clearer through comparison than does *The Gold Rush* (1925). Consider the Thanksgiving day scene in the Yukon mentioned earlier. Perhaps the fullest account of the making of this sequence for *The Gold Rush* is to be found in David Robinson's definitive biography, *Chaplin*. According to Robinson, the eating sequence in the cabin was among the first footage shot. Chaplin took three full shooting days and 63 takes just to get the parts in which Chaplin cooks and eats his boot. Chaplin seems to have begun shooting with little more in hand than the cooking and eating of the boot, and then, true to the way he worked, he gradually added to this as ideas occurred to him. "On The Set With Charlie," a publicity brochure credited to Sid Grauman, purports to tell us how Chaplin began to work his partner, Big Jim played by Mack Swain, into the sequence. Unlike Charlie, Big Jim was to be driven to the brink of madness through his hunger, apparently, and this seems to have occurred to Chaplin not by envisioning a visual bit of action, but rather through assigning Swain a few lines of dialogue.

Only three scenes were taken in the entire afternoon, but the proof that Mr. Chaplin is without doubt the hardest working individual in Hollywood is that each scene is shot at least twenty times. Any one of the twenty would transport almost any director other than Charlie; he does them over and over again, seeking just the shade to blend with his mood. And his moods are even more numerous than his scenes.

"Just once more—we'll get it this time!" is his continual cry, ceaseless as the waves of the sea. And each additional "take" means just three times as much work for him as for anyone else.

Perhaps in the middle of a scene when everything seems to be superlative, he will stop the action with a gesture, "Cut"—he walks over to a little stool beside one of the cameras and leans his head upon the tripod. The cameramen stand silently beside their cranks; everyone virtually holds his breath until Charlie jumps up with an enthusiastic yell:

"I've got it, Mack; you should cry: 'Food! Food! I must have food!' You're starving and you are going to pieces. See—like this!"

The tramp character's ability to transcend the poverty of his circumstances is evident as he serves up the boot he's boiled. He sets the table, sharpens the cutlery, divides the boot into a tender upper that, thanks to Chaplin's manner, seems to be more a tender capon than the upper of a boot, then accepts for himself the sole. He approaches the sole as if it were a filet of some kind, we see; then we get the pun: surely it's a filet of sole. He remains dainty, mannerly. He appears to be dining in a formal or even semi-formal setting, even though everything we see before us—the poverty of the cabin, for instance—denies this.

While Big Jim looks at him with dismay and wonder, Charlie approaches the boiled shoelaces as if they were pasta. Coming upon a bent nail in the sole, he crooks his little finger about it and offers it to Big Jim as though it were a wishbone. Big Jim looks at the tramp as if Charlie might well be going mad, but that's not our impression at all. We can see what the tramp's about. He's making the best of an overwhelmingly bad situation.

The madness, as things turn out, is Big Jim's, not Charlie's. He gradually begins to look on his dinner partner with cannibalism in mind. Big Jim's eyes glaze over. In his dementia, Charlie begins to take on the characteristics of a fowl, ripe for the plucking. Initially, Big Jim was to see a turkey—supposedly this is Thanksgiving day, after all. In its most primitive form, the scene dissolved from a shot of Mack looking at Charlie to a shot of a roast turkey sitting on a platter on the table, occupying more or less the same part of the screen as Chaplin occupied in previous cross-cuts. Big Jim reached out for the turkey. As he did, the turkey dissolved into Charlie. This happened several times. Seeing that he was in some danger, Charlie offered Big Jim a book to keep his mind off his hunger.

Several days were spent shooting the sequence in this form, never to Chaplin's complete satisfaction. Finally, apparently by the end of production on Saturday, 15 March, Chaplin hit upon something better. He had his costume department work through the rest of the weekend to prepare a man-sized chicken costume, and it was in this chicken costume that Chaplin resumed production on the following Monday.

David Robinson recounts how this modified sequence evolved. Rather than simply envisioning the bird, Charlie would actually become that bird before the audience's eyes. We would have the opportunity to share Big Jim's dementia.

Chaplin would start the scene in his ordinary costume. At a given moment the camera would be faded out and stopped. The scene and camera position would be kept unchanged while Chaplin rapidly changed into his chicken costume. At the same time the camera was wound back to the start of the fade, the place where the transformation was to begin while the camera started up and faded in, Chaplin would precisely retrace the action he had just filmed. In this way the two images of Charlie and the chicken would be exactly superimposed so that the two figures would seem to divide into one another. Precisely the same technique was needed to turn to chicken back into Charlie. During the pause for the costume change Mack Swain, who was also in the scene, had to stay absolutely motionless. To help him, he was seated at a table with his head firmly supported on his elbows.

That seems like a great deal of trouble to go to, especially for only a shot or two. Why spend so much effort—not to mention money—on a dissolve? Perhaps the answer is that there was no better way to show how Charlie was little more than meat to big Jim at that instant, and perhaps that was a point that Chaplin didn't want lost on his audience. It ties the first half of the sequence to the second once and for all. In the first half, Chaplin, thanks to his human grace, is able to transcend his lot in life and behave as a civil being. In his hands, a boiled shoe becomes a Thanksgiving meal, the inedible becomes food that makes possible his survival. This is counterpointed by the second half of the sequence. Big Jim lacks the little tramp's grace. He is reduced by his circumstances not only to a lower evolutionary level of behavior, but to a lower state of being. Through his eyes, the little tramp is simply one more creature in a food chain; at that instant, Big Jim's world is one in which the big eat the little, a world of the powerful and the powerless.

In *My Autobiography*, Chaplin recounts one of the lowest points of his life, the death of his father, and, with his father's death, the realization that Chaplin, his brother, and his mother were virtually penniless, abandoned, left with little more than the slimmest hope for the future. Not surprisingly, food, eating, and a concern with the preparation of food play a significant place in his account of the experience.

When we returned [from the funeral] there was not a particle of food in the cupboard except a saucer of beef dripping, and Mother had not a penny, for she had given Sydney her last twopence for his lunch money. Since Father's illness she had done little work, and now, near the end of the week, Sydney's wages of seven shillings as a telegraph boy had already run out. After the funeral we were hungry. Luckily the rag-and-bone man was passing outside and we had an old oil stove, so reluctantly she sold it for a halfpenny and bought a halfpenny's worth of bread to go with the dripping.

At a glance, this seems to be a curious detail to include, a particularly maudlin detail, perhaps. But as Chaplin describes these early years of his life, this is not a maudlin moment at all, and one has only to read a bit farther to see what he must have had in mind, for, within a few paragraphs, a new, wiser, more self-aware and self-sufficient Charlie is appearing, one determined to survive on his wits and human mettle. That his mother should find a way to feed Chaplin in the face of such circumstances, that succorance and love can stand firm in the face of tragedy, seem to be the fulcrum upon which these two experiences are balanced, as Chaplin recollects things. And that makes sense. In some ways insignificant, by some measure not worthy of inclusion in his story, that single act of feeding surely seemed important to Chaplin because of what it suggests about human beings doing their best to overcome the poverty of their circumstances in ways distinctly human.

It's much this same sensibility that's to be found in his later films; and like so much that's to be found there, it sets Chaplin aside from the standard slapstick fare of his day, from the pies in the face of Mack Sennett and Hal Roach and their brethren. There, food often becomes weaponry. In the hands of Roach's characters and Sennett's as well, food often becomes associated with the depths to which we can sink as we turn on one another; while, for Chaplin, as his career progressed, food became something more. It gradually became associated with the poverty of the circumstances in which we find ourselves, and, in the face of those circumstances, the capacity of the human spirit to triumph, if only we'll remain human.

Filmography

Food and eating of some sort can be found in the vast majority of the films Chaplin directed. Listed below are Chaplin silent comedies in which extended comic sequences employing food can be found. Each title is followed by the studio at which the film was make, its length at initial release, and its initial date of release.

The Rounders	Keystone, One Reel, September 7, 1914
Dough and Dynamite	Keystone, Two Reels, October 26, 1914
A Night Out	Essanay, Two Reels, February 15, 1915
The Champion	Essanay, Two Reels, March 11, 1915
In The Park	Essanay, One Reel, March 18, 1915
A Jitney Elopement	Essanay, One Reel, April 1, 1915
The Tramp	Essanay, Two Reels, April 11, 1915
Shanghaied	Essanay, Two Reels, October 4, 1915
The Fireman	Mutual, Two Reels, June 12, 1916
The Count	Mutual, Two Reels, September 4, 1916
Behind The Screen	Mutual, Two Reels, November 13, 1916
The Rink	Mutual, Two Reels, December 4, 1916
Easy Street	Mutual, Two Reels, January 22, 1917
The Immigrant	Mutual, Two Reels, June 17, 1917
A Dog's Life	First National, Three Reels, April 14, 1918
Shoulder Arms	First National, Three Reels, October 20, 1918
Sunnyside	First National, Two Reels, June 15, 1919
The Kid	First National, Six Reels, February 6, 1921
The Gold Rush	United Artists, Nine Reels, August 16, 1925
The Circus	United Artists, Seven Reels, January 7, 1928
City Lights	United Artists, Nine Reels, February 6, 1931
Modern Times	United Artists, Nine Reels, February 5, 1936

"Now to the Banquet We Press:"[1]
Hitchcock's Gourmet and Gourmand Offerings
Dick Stromgren

The book-length interview that Francois Truffaut conducted with Alfred
Hitchcock concluded with Hitchcock outlining his idea for a future film which
centers on 24 hours in the life of a city. It was an idea perhaps inspired by the
early German expressive documentaries known as "City Symphonies." The
film, Hitchcock suggests, might have as a central motif

an anthology on food, showing its arrival in the city, its distribution, the selling, buying
by people, the cooking, the various ways in which it's consumed. What happens to it in
various hotels; how it's fixed up and absorbed. And, gradually, the end of the film would
show the sewers, and the garbage being dumped out into the ocean. So there's a cycle,
beginning with the gleaming fresh vegetables and ending with the mess that's poured
into the sewers. (Truffaut 241)

Hitchcock finally got to make the film in which food serves as a central
metaphor for life (and death) in a city. The film, *Frenzy*, completed a long line
of works in which the director used the settings and actions associated with both
food and drink to enhance plot, develop characterization and manipulate
audiences. It was Hitchcock's next to last film, near the end of his own life in
which food and drink had become something more than means of sustenance
and aesthetic and social pleasantries.

The imagery and plot intrigues involving food and drink, and the settings
and trappings of social convention in which they are prepared and consumed
became a central and absorbing feature of the Hitchcock oeuvre. From the wine
bottles filled with uranium in *Notorious* to the potato sack filled with
Hitchcock's final murder victim in *Frenzy*, one finds a veritable feast of
delicacies (some not so delicate) that sustained characters and both delighted
and confounded audiences through the mischievous context in which they
appeared. Hitchcock's films are replete with ironies of all sorts, but one of the
recurring and prominent forms in which such ironies are cast is through the
unusual, frequently perverse context in which he placed the subject of food,
drink and dining.

Hitchcock had, in the words of one biographer, "a fierce indulgence in
food and drink" and "his life was a relentless pursuit of the best food and wine"

(Spoto 8-9). What prompted this obsessive preoccupation with food and drink remains a matter of speculation, but the modest if not spartan table to which he attended as a child and the admitted sense of insecurity that gnawed at him throughout his life probably provide part of the answer. In his biography Donald Spoto speaks of the Hitchcock family's dependence on "the bumper crop of potatoes for a cheap, filling, and nutritious (if somewhat monotonous) diet. Boiled, baked, double-baked, and mashed potatoes accompanied every dinner, even when there were guests" (Spoto 166). It should be mentioned that in spite of the lavish dinner parties for which he became noted, Hitchcock's own tastes were rather conservative, with steak, dover sole, roast chicken, or a boiled ham being served with a vegetable and, of course, potatoes, accompanied by a salad with ice cream for dessert.

By his own words and actions, it is clear that food and drink provided Hitchcock with the security and defense against the unexpected and uninvited, against isolation as well as confrontation, and against a depravation that soon became more social and aesthetic than physical. In addition to his entertaining at elaborate dinner parties, he scrupulously sought out the finest restaurants wherever he traveled—Simpson's in London, 21 Club in New York, Chasen's in Beverly Hills. The kitchen and wine cellar in the Hitchcock Bel Aire home became a testament to gracious living rivaling many gourmet restaurants. Meals were frequently flown in from Paris, London and New York, and produce dispatched from all over the globe in preparation for lavish dinners.

The indulgence in food was second only to Hitchcock's indulgence in wine and other spirits, which he constantly referred to as "medicine." As a connoisseur of fine wines, he would have these brought in from around the world to complement gourmet menus. But social drinking gave way to excessive consumption and ultimately to alcoholic dependence which left him virtually dysfunctional in the latter years.

This central roles that food and drink played in Hitchcock's own life, inevitably were to become a fixture in virtually all of his films. They were to provide not only much of the plot intrigue and motivation for characters, but also became a significant device whereby Hitchcock could manipulate his audience as well.

The films made in England between 1925 and 1939 were already providing ample evidence of the significance of food and drink to the Hitchcock oeuvre and to the innumerable ways in which the director could incorporate the elements in narrative design and in style of presentation. These pioneer works, the first nine silent, were embellished in mood, supported in character delineation, and provided with lessons on human frailty and moral ambiguity through the ways in which food and drink were procured, prepared and consumed.

Examples of the symbolic function served by wine and comestibles in these early films abound. The opening shot of *Champagne* (1928) is of a cabaret dancer taken through the bottom of a tilted champagne glass to suggest a life of abandon and vice. In his 1927 *The Ring*, the boxer husband of an unfaithful wife is left alone with a glass of champagne that has gone flat, as has the marriage. A marital relationship is again given a symbolic reference in *Manxman* (1929) when, during a wedding party, the bride cuts her finger while cutting the wedding cake—a symbol of an adulterous affair. Later in the same film, her husband arrives home to an empty house where the table is set for one, with a note and a wedding ring.

Further subtleties in human relationships are explored by way of some repast in several other early works, including *The Farmer's Wife* (1928), *The 39 Steps* (1935) and *Sabotage* (1936). In a comic vein, Hitchcock stages a scene in the *Farmer's Wife* with the hostess of a tea party holding a plate of jelly which quivers in her hand as the film's protagonist, Sweetland, offers a blustering proposal of marriage. He has previously said to his housekeeper, "There be a female or two floating around my mind like the smell of a Sunday dinner" and when his proposal of marriage is rejected by the town's fussily attired postmistress, he angrily responds with, "You're too fond of dressing your mutton lamb fashion."

On a more somber note, much of the action of *Sabotage* involves the preparation and consumption of food at the Verloc table, reaching a climax with Verloc's wife stabbing him with a carving knife during dinner. The scene provides one of the most intriguing ambiguities in all of Hitchcock's work as it is never clear whether the fatal wound is directed or self-inflicted.

The ultimate in dinner table intrigue, however, is the splendidly low-key scene involving the fleeing Hannay in *The 39 Steps*. With a mutual attraction developing between a crofter's young wife and the fugitive, the three sit down to dinner where the crofter proceeds to say grace. With heads supposedly bowed in prayer, the wife glances at a newspaper and realizes their dinner guest is a murder suspect. Hannay makes a nonverbal plea for her silence, while the crofter glances suspiciously from one to the other, sensing the visual communication going on between the two.

Overindulgence in drink was also to become a fixture in a preponderance of Hitchcock's American-made films. It had its comic antecedence in *Rich and Strange*, where the inebriated protagonist tries to set his watch by the dial of an elevator, by the drunk in *Champagne* who walks effortlessly on board a tossing ship but staggers on firm ground, and by the comic lush in *Number 17* who boards the runaway train and lands in a shipment of wine.

By the time Hitchcock joined the Selznick studio to begin the American phase of his career, he had set down an extensive "menu" of actions, themes and allusions evoking the imagery of food and drink. These ranged from the simple choice of location and routine actions of characters to the subtle and at times complex imagery that informed a scene, while at the same time confounding the expectations of viewers.

On the more basic level, and in keeping with his tour of famous sites—the Royal Albert Hall, Westminster Cathedral, Lincoln Memorial, Mt. Rushmore, Golden Gate Bridge, Radio City Music Hall and the Statue of Liberty, to mention just a few—Hitchcock would occasionally set the action of his intrigues in a famous or at least recognizable eating or drinking establishment. Simpson's restaurant in the Strand is featured in his British-made *Sabotage*, and the Plaza Bar and Mt. Rushmore Restaurant provide settings in *North By Northwest*. But it is the unidentified pubs, bars, restaurants and particularly the family dinner table that figure so prominently in virtually all the Hitchcock films.

The centrality of food and drink and the settings with which they are associated is hardly a uniquely Hitchcock trademark. But the director never missed an opportunity to use this most familiar and basic form of human activity to set the scene, define characters, and carry significant social, psychological and moral values as well. Food and drink as a prominent narrative fixture, even serving as the key propellant (or "MacGuffin") of plot progression, distinguish such films as *Notorious* with its uranium-enriched wine and poisoned tea, the suspect glass of milk in *Suspicion*, and a spy's camera hidden in a sandwich in *Topaz*.

Notorious provides some of the most intriguing examples of the way in which wining and dining become central to the narrative development and carries the responsibility for what Hitchcock is most famous: suspense. A particularly chilling domestic dining scene occurs at the Sebastian mansion which houses a covert Nazi spy organization. Emil, a member of the group, causes a scene over the particular bottle of wine being served, and is later put out of the way as a security risk. One of the film's most suspenseful moments, for both the protagonists and the audience, comes when the dwindling supply of wine at an elegant reception sends the Nazi host Alex (Claude Rains) off to the wine cellar where his wife, Alicia (Ingrid Bergman), and the C.I.A. agent Devlin (Cary Grant) are about to make a startling discovery. The complexity of their relationship at this point in the film is given a particularly ironic twist when they "feign" a romantic tryst rather than be discovered as counter-spies.

Still more in evidence is the way in which scenes of eating and drinking help to delineate character, providing the viewer with a ready profile of class standing, state of mind and motivation. Hitchcock was a careful observer of speech and behavior patterns that revealed levels of refinement and social standing. He began to incorporate table manners as a means to this end as early as the British silent features. In *The Farmer's Wife* the handyman drops good manners when guests go into the garden, throws a spoon at the maid, drinks coffee from a saucer, and devours several small cakes; in *Juno and the Paycock*

(1930) Boyle's attack on a sausage, along with his drinking habits, reinforces his lack of refinement; and Old Will, the china mender in *Young and Innocent* (1937) is painfully out of his element at a tea dance. He asks the waiter for two cups of tea and when the waiter asks, "India or China," he responds, "Naw, tea!"

These, however, were warm-up exercises for putting characters in their place or revealing their vulnerability. In the American-made films, food and drink take on a heavier role in character delineation. In the first film for Selznick, *Rebecca* (1940), the nameless heroine is immediately put in her place by Max de Winter (Laurence Olivier) when he utters, "I should have asked you to have lunch with me even if you hadn't upset the vase so clumsily." The line immediately establishes the nature of the relationship. There follows a number of scenes with Max and his new bride at opposite ends of a long banquet table, a vivid reminder of the estrangement caused by the haunting presence of the first wife. Vulnerability of a character is very much central to the scene in the remake of *The Man Who Knew To Much* (1956) where Ben (James Stewart), seated awkwardly at a low table in a Arab restaurant, has difficulty breaking bread and violates local custom by eating a small roast bird with both hands instead of the prescribed first and second finger and thumb of the right hand. Hitchcock could, with the simplest of actions, establish a character's nature. Even the C.I.A. agent Prescott in *Notorious* is given the extra edge of crassness and lack of sensitivity as he lies on a bed, artfully applying spread to crackers while discussing the fate of the American spy married to a Nazi agent.

As a connoisseur of fine wine, Hitchcock never misses an opportunity to ply his characters with spirits. Characters taking or offering a "stiff drink" under stressful circumstances abound and are too numerous to detail but occur, according to Spoto, in 51 of Hitchcock's 53 films (119), even in *Lifeboat* when poor Gus is offered a shot before his leg is amputated. And the social niceties and manners of the elegant cocktail party often give way to chronic drunkenness, and even murder, or an attempt thereof by poisoned drink. As Alicia Huberman (*Notorious*) and Lady Henrietta (*Under Capricorn*), Ingrid Bergman falls prey to alcohol. Other characters prone to overindulgence include the guests at a cocktail ball in *To Catch a Thief*, Jo and Ben's guests in The *Man Who Knew Too Much*, Scottie in *Vertigo*, the composer in *Rear Window*, Roger Thornhill in *North By Northwest*, and a patron of the Tides Cafe in *The Birds*. By way of comic relief Hitchcock offers the town drunk, including the Robert Benchley character in *Foreign Correspondent* (1940), and the drunk in the same film who, during a chase sequence, tries stepping off the curb as several cars round the corner, gives up, and returns to the tavern.

Aside from the rather innocent spoofing of table manners and drinking habits previously mentioned, there are numerous instances when wining and dining provide an opportunity to comment, either explicitly or by way of allusion, on a character's psychological profile, his/her motivation and/or relationship with other characters within the narrative. Meals eaten in silence in *Rebecca* and *Dial M for Murder* (1953) and the uneaten one in *Notorious* all comment upon the estrangement of a couple. In the latter, between sensuous kisses, Alicia offers the "chicken in the icebox" for a private candlelight dinner. Devlin has offered to return with the wine but his preoccupation over a C.I.A. plan to marry Alicia off to the Nazi spy, Alex, results in his forgetting the wine. His conflict in feelings for Alicia finally results in the dinner going cold, along with the romance. Romance for "Miss Lonely Heart" in *Rear Window* (1954) is long in coming and she resorts to preparing a candlelight dinner for an imaginary suitor. At the conclusion of the film, "Miss Torso's" army sweetheart arrives, embraces her, then pulls away with, "Hey, the Army pays me monthly, what do you have in the icebox to eat."

The preparation, handling, and consumption of food is frequently used by Hitchcock to reveal the darker side of character and to prefigure sinister deeds to come. In *The Paradine Case* (1947), Judge Horfield at dinner compares the human brain to a walnut, which he then proceeds to pick from its shell. After his wife makes a desperate plea for compassion for the accused, he cruelly orders her to bed, saying Mrs. Paradine will hang, then sits and picks his teeth. The association of food and villainous intent takes on a darker and more urgent tone in *Rebecca* just after the inquest into Rebecca's death when Jack Favell attempts blackmail. A lunch basket has been sent down from Manderley and the second Mrs. de Winter has just sipped the wine (which she finds distasteful) when Jack bounds into the car with, "Lunch, I say, what a jolly idea, rather like a picnic isn't it." He munches on a chicken leg, then in a maliciously taunting way says, "By the way, what do you do with old bones" (of family skeletons we presume), as he tosses the bone out the window and proceeds to talk blackmail.

It should be noted that chicken, or some form of roast bird, is a favorite repast for Hitchcock characters (birds of course are generally a harbinger of danger or a sign of foreboding in many of his films). Childhood experiences related to his father's trade as a poulterer were perhaps responsible for the prominence of this imagery, as well as that of the often misused egg for which Hitchcock seems to have had an aversion. In *The Ring*, a black circus performer is suspended over a tank of water and is periodically hit with rotten eggs as a crowd gleefully looks on. Young Stevie in *Sabotage* announces that he hates eggs and says that Ted also does, while in an earlier scene the cashier of the Verloc movie theatre speaks of having to eat eggs in the dark when power fails and having "half of it in my ear." In *To Catch a Thief*, an egg is thrown at a window of a restaurant kitchen by one of Robbie's former resistance pals while Mr. Stevens (Jessie Royce Landis) in another scene stubs out a cigarette in an egg yolk.

Much is made by the several biographers and by Hitchcock himself of an almost desperate need for security that the filmmaker experienced throughout his life. This preoccupation resonates in several of his films, where characters are frequently deprived of their security. In the words of Maurice Yacowar, "His art is always the art of false appearances, especially where smug security is upset by the revelation of deeper disorder" (12). It is in pursuit of the more suspenseful setting that Hitchcock frequently used the sense of security, serenity and civility one associates with dining to put his characters (and audience) off guard by the intrusion of distasteful, threatening or otherwise unexpected occurrence.

Spoto refers to dinner as "a favorite ironic setting for the disunity among relatives in Hitchcock's films" (119). In *Suspicion* (1941), tension between Lena and her father mounts at the dinner table over her seeing Johnny, whom he reveals to be a scoundrel, while in the same breath, complaining to his wife that he "can't stand things out of bottles." No family in Hitchcock films is more typical of wholesome, all-American values than the one in *Shadow of a Doubt*. The intrusion by Uncle Charlie sets up the ironic linking of this image with the dark and sinister mood and detail associated with the psychotic "Merry Widow" murderer. The association is frequently made at the family dinner table, first on Uncle Charlie's arrival when he tips over a glass on hearing his niece identify the waltz she keeps whistling as "The Merry Widow Waltz." Later, at a festive dinner in which Uncle Charlie offers sparkling Burgundy, he delivers his diatribe on "silly wives, useless women…faded fat, greedy women." The mood is further dampened when the neighbor Herb (Hume Cronyn) arrives with mushrooms (a possible method of poisoning), and he and young Charlie's father, Joe, begin to discuss the means to the perfect murder.

Other seemingly civil and secure dining scenes that mask evil plotting include the discussion of dual murders during a dining car luncheon in *Strangers on a Train* (1951), and in *North By Northwest* (1959), where the preparations for receiving dinner guests at a Glen Cove mansion provide the cover for another deadly game of espionage. In *Lifeboat* Hitchcock uses the deprivation of food to the point of near starvation as an opportunity for an ironic comment on a character's anticipation of finally being fed. As a Nazi rescue crew approaches in a launch, Constance (Tallulah Bankhead) speaks contemptuously of the prospect of being served German food, "Wienerschnitzel, and pig's knuckles and sauerkraut and apple strudel."

The ironic linking of food with "unsavory" details of setting and action were to become a distinctive Hitchcock trademark in his latter American works. Such ironic treatment was already blossoming in earlier works like *Champagne*. Here Hitchcock introduces an ironic comment on epicureanism in a sequence in which food is being prepared most unattractively with dirty hands and then served on expensive china. In the restaurant kitchen, a roast bird is being pulled apart, food dropped on the floor, picked up, brushed off, and arranged on a serving platter. A cut then follows to the elegantly laid table with the same food being served.

The most violent of intrusions on a seemingly benign or secure scene would have to include the attack of birds in the friendly atmosphere of the Tides Cafe, and during the quiet dinner and boisterous children's birthday party in *The Birds* (1963). These pale, however, beside Bob Rusk's intrusion on his ex-wife's office lunch in *Frenzy*, or the scene which follows Norman's return to the office of the Bates Motel with milk and sandwiches for himself and the only guest in *Psycho*.

The dark humor of such scenes would not seem to offer the best examples of Hitchcock's meeting his stated role of entertainer and his desire to satisfy audience expectations. They do, however, represent the central and pervasive function that satire and irony play in virtually all of his work. His satirical agenda is splendidly varied, often complex, and frequently profound in its perspective on the human condition. In his dedication to controlling audience mood and expectations, Hitchcock takes great care in the construction of a screenplay to create the required twists and turns in plot design and scenic detail. This is his way of keeping viewers off balance through the unexpected joining of disjunctive elements. Yacowar states it most succinctly: "For Hitchcock irony is both a matter of technique and style of life...Hitchcock continually tricks his audience with...a persistent subversion of the viewer's expectations" (13).

It is in the juxtaposition of sex and death with food that Hitchcock becomes his most mischievous and his most ironic. The irony is in the fact that while audiences are being entertained by being willingly manipulated, they are being made to feel, in Robin Wood's words, "a growing discomfort as we are made aware of our own involvement in desires and emotions that are the reverse of admirable" (40).

It is in some of the major Hollywood films that Hitchcock introduces the food and drink imagery to play with his character's and audience's sense of discretion by linking it with the "delicate" subjects of sex and murder. When asked if he were going to be murdered, how he would choose to have it done, he replied, "Well, there are many nice ways: eating is a good one" (Spoto 344). And so the combining of food and eating with death (if not necessarily murder) became a fixture in many of the more celebrated American-made works—*Rope*, *Rear Window*, *The Trouble With Harry*, and *Frenzy* to name a few.

In his lengthy interview with Truffaut, Hitchcock speaks of "fetish love" in connection with several of his films—*Vertigo* and *Marnie* in particular (227). Such perversion of love interest might well be applied to Hitchcock's own food fetish in relation to sexual fantasies and encounters that find their way into many of his works. Mention has already been made of the erotic kissing scene in *Notorious*, where Cary Grant and Ingrid Bergman feast on one another's lips while making plans for dinner. A similar scene occurs in *To Catch a Thief*, where Grant and Grace Kelly kiss rapturously over a picnic lunch (cold chicken this time). With her head in the lunch basket Kelly asks, in her most seductive voice, "Do you want a leg or a breast?" To which he replies, "You make the choice."

Several allusions to food and drink, once again in a lighter vein embellish *The Trouble With Harry*, the fanciful comedy that Hitchcock concocted in collaboration with John Michael Hayes. Here we find Jennifer (Shirley MacLaine) and Sam (John Forsythe) commenting on their preference as to the sweetness of lemonade which she is serving on the occasion of their first meeting. While she recounts her ill-fated wedding night, a mutual attraction begins to blossom. Similarly, in expressing his attraction to Miss Gravely (Mildred Natwick), Captain Wiles (Edmund Gwenn) suggests to Sam that Miss Gravely is "well preserved" and that "preserves eventually need to be opened."

In *Psycho*, the relationship between Marion Crane (Janet Leigh) and both Sam (John Gavin) and Norman (Anthony Perkins) are suggested through an association of food and drink with sexual appetite. At the conclusion of the lunch hour liaison with Sam in a seedy hotel room, Marion appeals for more respectable meetings, "in my house, with mother's picture on the mantle and my sister helping me broil a big steak for three." She leaves an uneaten sandwich in the room as she departs. In ironic contrast it is Norman's "mother" who later in the film upbraids her son with, "I won't have you bringing strange young girls in for supper. By candlelight, I suppose, in the cheap, erotic fashion of young men with cheap, erotic minds...tell her she'll not be appeasing her ugly appetite with my food, or my son!"

If, as Donald Spoto suggests, food and drink became a substitute for sex in Hitchcock's own life, they became complementary to sexual encounters in many of his films. In addition to the aforementioned, there are the crofter's wife's hunger for a loving relationship in the dinner scene from *The 39 Steps*; Scottie's first sight of Madeleine in the rapturous scene at Ernie's Restaurant in *Vertigo*; and Eve's sensuous proposition to Roger Thornhill in the dining car in *North by Northwest*.

Although it has a particularly perverse erotic quality at times, the linking of food and sex is not uniquely Hitchcockian. Luis Bunuel, Tony Richardson, Mel Brooks, Woody Allen, Peter Greenway, among others, have each given it their own twist (or parodied one another). What is more the Hitchcock signature and confounds the expectations of viewers, however, is the juxtaposition of food and drink with death, the dead and the act of murder. Putting murder "back in the home where it belongs" had been central to Hitchcock's idiosyncratic mission, and if it took place during mealtime, so much the better. In reference to the scissors murder in *Dial M For Murder* the director says, "But there wasn't enough gleam on the scissors, and a murder without gleaming scissors is like asparagus without the hollandaise sauce—tasteless." What characterized the Hitchcock style (and won him the reputation for tastelessness among some critics) was his literally joining the asparagus and hollandaise sauce with the murder and other macabre embellishments. Spoto reproduces the "Carte de mort" menu for the "Ghost-Haunted House Party" that Hitchcock hosted for Warner Brothers' executives and the press in 1956. Included among the delicacies were "suicide suzettes,...corpse croquettes, barbecued banshee,...mobster thermidor...and formaldehyde frappe" (Spoto 378).

The grisly details of murder frequently became the subject of dinner conversation and cocktail chatter. In *Suspicion*, Johnny (Cary Grant) and Lina (Joan Fontaine) are invited to a dinner party where the physician brother of the hostess expounds on murder by poison and the exhuming of bodies, while busily slicing the roast bird. In *Strangers on a Train*, Babs (Patricia Hitchcock) and an investigating policeman discuss an axe murder in which the victim was "left in the ice box with the left leg for six hours." It should be noted that one of Hitchcock's favorites among his *Alfred Hitchcock Presents* television series was "Lamb to the Slaughter" (1958), in which the murder weapon is a leg of lamb which the murderess cooks up and serves to the police conducting the investigation.

The presence of a body failed to inhibit some of Hitchcock's characters from casual or polite conversation about dining, anticipation of some repast, or actually engaging in mealtime activities. In *The Trouble With Harry*, Miss Gravely invites Captain Wiles to her house for blueberry muffins and elderberry wine as they stand on opposite sides of Harry's body. This innocent and bucolic scene stands in stark contrast to the central setting and situation in *Rope* (1948). Here the victim of a thrill murder committed by two homosexual classmates is placed in a chest that graces their apartment. With the father, aunt and fiancee of the victim in attendance, a buffet dinner is served from the chest which has been elaborately set with dinnerware, flowers and silver candlesticks.

The screenplays for such mordant creations were usually the work of others or the result of a collaboration with the director, and much of the dialogue must be credited to such screenwriters as Arthur Laurents, Ben Hecht, Charles Bennett, Alma Reville and John Michael Hayes, to mention just a few. Hitchcock acknowledges that Hayes was responsible for the droll exchange between Stella (Thelma Ritter) and Jeffries (James Stewart) in *Rear Window*. In one comic interlude, Stella munches on a celery stalk and contemplates on the Therwold murder while he eats breakfast: "Where do you suppose he cut her up? Of course, the bathtub! That's the only place he could've washed away the blood!" Jeffries at this point nearly chokes on his coffee. Hayes confirms that the lines were his. "The attempt was to unite the audience, to bring people together early in the film. Just as a dynamic speaker can unite an audience, so a comic person can weld a film audience."[2]

Other screenwriters were no doubt responsible for macabre bits of dialogue and situations in other films, but it was finally Hitchcock who gave ultimate approval and direction to the material and made it a part of his own penchant for the macabre. Though not anxious to credit others for such bursts of inspiration, Hitchcock must have been particularly pleased with the Hayes' lines for *Rear Window*.

Of course the final pièce de résistance in juxtaposition for Hitchcock was the "triple threat" linking of food—sex—and death, a gastronomic-erotic-necrophilic specialty of this mischievous filmmaker. It was his next to last film, *Frenzy*, that featured Hitchcock's last four murder victims.[3] The film also became a veritable cornucopia of food and drink imagery linked with the most aberrant of sexual reference. Here food becomes the central and pervasive motif in a setting—the last days of the Covent Garden vegetable, fruit and flower market in London's West End—which suggests a corrupted Garden of Eden.[4] The rape/murder of Blaney's wife Brenda takes place during her "frugal lunch" (an apple), to which Rusk, the murderer, helps himself as he makes sexual overtures and which he finishes after the strangulation.

A gruesome combination of murder with food-stuff follows Rusk's next murder. Having concealed Bab's corpse in a sack of potatoes, he realizes his stick pin is clasped in her hand, and in an attempt to retrieve the incriminating evidence, he becomes entangled in the limbs of the corpse and a cascade of potatoes as the produce truck speeds along the highway. This link between gastronomic and sexual appetite is reinforced later when the Scotland Yard inspector is enjoying a hearty English breakfast at his office while instructing an assistant on the nature of the psychotic rapist. "We've got to find him before his appetite is whetted again," he exclaims. The inspector's own appetite is ill-served by his wife's gourmet cooking, and in the comic highlight of this otherwise dark film she inflicts various culinary creations on him while the two discuss details of the latest murder.

Hitchcock makes his customary cameo appearance as part of the crowd observing the film's first victim floating in the river. He is within easy earshot of an exchange between a couple that makes an even more literal association between corpse and food. The wife says in reference to the killer, "He's a regular Jack the Ripper." To which her husband replies, "Not on your life, he used to carve them up. Sent a bird's kidney to Scotland Yard once, wrapped in a bit of violet writing paper...or was it a bit of liver."

What had become an obsessive fascination with this combining of sex, murder and food was not limited to the film itself. In a promotional short that he made for *Frenzy*, Hitchcock gets into the act and is seen floating on the Thames (as was the first victim of the feature); then in the bustling Covent Garden Market where he is found stuffing the film's third victim's foot back into a sack of potatoes—"I've heard of a leg of lamb but never a leg of potatoes"—and finally on the highway standing next to the corpse which has tumbled onto the roadway amid a shower of potatoes. Retrieving the necktie twisted around the victim's neck, he proceeds to tie it neatly around his own and in a burst of self-satisfaction says directly to the camera, "How do you like my tie."

With *Frenzy*, and its accompanying promotional short, Hitchcock had finally realized his ambition of the "City Symphony," replete with an array of produce and refuse seldom more inelegantly displayed.

Notes

[1]From the first and second act finales of the Gilbert and Sullivan operetta, *The Sorcerer*.

[2]From a conversation the author had with John Michael Hayes in June 1986.

[3]The adoptive parents of the villain in *Family Plot* have been murdered by him previous to the film's opening. The only "body" in the film is ironically that of Hitchcock—his familiar silhouette seen behind the frosted glass door of the "Registry of Births and Deaths."

[4]See Lesley Brill, *The Hitchcock Romance: Love and Irony in Hitchcock's Films* (Princeton: Princeton UP, 1988), for an extended analysis of the ironic nature of this film.

Works Cited

Spoto, Donald, *The Dark Side of Genius: The Life of Alfred Hitchcock*. Boston: Little, Brown and Company, 1983.

Truffaut, Francois. *Hitchcock*. New York: Simon and Schuster, 1976.

Wood, Robin. *Hitchcock's Films*. London: Tantivy P, 1977.

Yacowar, Maurice. Hitchcock's British Films. Hamden, CT: Archon Books, 1977.

Hitchcock Filmography

Silent Films

1925	*The Pleasure Garden*	Gainsborough
1926	*The Mountain Eagle*	Gainsborough
1926	*The Lodger*	Gainsborough
1927	*Downhill*	Gainsborough
1927	*Easy Virtue*	Gainsborough
1927	*The Ring*	British International
1928	*The Farmer's Wife*	British International
1928	*Champagne*	British International
1929	*The Manxman*	British International

British Sound Films

1929	*Blackmail*	British International
1929	*Juno and the Paycock*	British International
1929	*Murder*	British International
1931	*The Skin Game*	British International

1932	*Rich and Strange*	British International
1932	*Number Seventeen*	British International
1933	*Waltzes From Vienna*	Gaumont—British
1934	*The Man Who Knew Too Much*	Gaumont—British
1935	*The 39 Steps*	Gaumont—British
1936	*Secret Agent*	Gaumont—British
1936	*Sabotage*	Gaumont—British
1937	*Young and Innocent*	Gainsborough
1938	*The Lady Vanishes*	Gainsborough
1939	*Jamaica Inn*	Mayflower

American Sound Films

1940	*Rebecca*	Selznick International
1940	*Foreign Correspondent*	United Artists
1941	*Mr. and Mrs. Smith*	RKO
1941	*Suspicion*	RKO
1942	*Saboteur*	Universal
1943	*Shadow of a Doubt*	Universal
1943	*Lifeboat*	20th Century Fox
1945	*Spellbound*	Selznick International
1946	*Notorious*	RKO
1947	*The Paradine Case*	Selznick International
1948	*Rope*	Warner Brothers
1949	*Under Capricorn*	Warner Brothers
1950	*Stage Fright*	Warner Brothers
1951	*Strangers on a Train*	Warner Brothers
1952	*I Confess*	Warner Brothers
1954	*Dial M For Murder*	Warner Brothers
1954	*Rear Window*	Paramount
1955	*To Catch a Thief*	Paramount
1956	*The Trouble With Harry*	Paramount
1956	*The Man Who Knew Too Much*	Paramount
1957	*The Wrong Man*	Warner Brothers
1958	*Vertigo*	Paramount
1959	*North by Northwest*	MGM
1960	*Psycho*	Paramount
1963	*The Birds*	Universal
1964	*Marnie*	Universal
1966	*Torn Curtain*	Universal
1969	*Topaz*	Universal
1972	*Frenzy*	Universal
1976	*Family Plot*	Universal/MCA

There is no known extant print of *The Mountain Eagle*. With the exception of *The Pleasure Garden, Downhill,* and *Waltzes from Vienna,* all of Hitchcock's feature films are now available on video cassette.

From *Reefer Madness* to *Freddy's Dead*:
The Portrayal of Marijuana Use in Motion Pictures
Dennis P. Grady

When high school student Jeff Spiccoli walks into his history class on the first day of school in the comedy film *Fast Times at Ridgemont High* (1982), one student whispers to another, "This guy has been stoned since the third grade." At the end of the film we are told that Jeff saves model Brooke Shields from drowning and uses his reward money to hire the rock group Van Halen to play at his birthday party. Several years after the release of *Fast Times*, audiences attending a screening of the movie *No Way Out* were exposed to the difficulties faced by a young man whose drug use forces him into prostitution and eventually leads to his death. Although these examples oversimplify the changes that are occurring in the American film industry, it does illustrate a shift in the way drugs are presented in motion pictures.

This essay is an attempt to examine these changes by looking at the way marijuana usage is portrayed in films. In the last decade marijuana was used by four times as many people than any other illicit drug in the country (Mann 32). As writer Adam Weisman stated in *The New Republic*, marijuana use is "entrenched socially and economically" in our culture (16). This essay begins with a brief history of marijuana use as it is portrayed in American cinema. It then offers a detailed analysis of several motion pictures made in the 1980s which feature one or more characters smoking marijuana. After identifying common themes in these various films, the essay concludes by looking at how the role of drugs has changed in films of the 1990s.

The depiction of marijuana use in motion pictures is almost as old as the film industry itself. As the use of marijuana spread from Mexico into the United States during the 1920s, it began to appear in movies made or set in the West, such as *The Cloud Rider* (1925) and *High on the Range* (1929) (Starks 31). In 1932 hysteria about the dangers of marijuana spread across the country, spurred on by the newly created Federal Bureau of Narcotics. In the next few years the only films to deal with marijuana use were vehement anti-drug movies, such as *Assassin of Youth* (1935), *Reefer Madness* (1936) and *Marijuana: Weed with Roots in Hell* (1937) (Starks 102). The morality code against marijuana and other drugs in films was broken in 1956 by the critical and public success of a film on heroin addiction, *The Man with the Golden Arm* (Morganthau 20). Less than a decade later drugs (especially marijuana) became extremely common in films seeking to appeal to younger audiences. Drugs were freely and seriously discussed in such 1960s films as *The Trip, The Wild Angels*, and of course *Easy Rider* (Starks 58). This trend peaked in 1972 when the movie *Dealing* had to delete some pro-marijuana dialogue to avoid an X rating (Starks 111).

In contrast to the strong anti-drug films of the thirties, some films of the 1980s filled the big screen with humorous scenes of marijuana use. The most overt examples of this trend are found in the movies of the perpetually stoned Cheech and Chong, but other notable examples include *Fast Times at Ridgemont High* (1982) and *Desperately Seeking Susan* (1985). These films echo previous movies (such as *Arthur*) in which humor was derived from the wit and comical behavior of characters who were drunk or even alcoholic, by merely substituting the effects of marijuana for alcohol. Unlike the other films discussed in this essay, the use of marijuana in these movies is included primarily as a way of generating audience laughter, without fulfilling any deeper narrative or rhetorical functions. It is not surprising, then, that the films falling into this category are basically comedies. In these films, getting high does not prompt characters into intimate self-disclosure, nor does it lead them to form lasting friendships; instead we are offered more humorous and light-hearted views: Jeff Spiccoli stumbling and rolling out of a smoke-filled van in the school parking lot in *Fast Times at Ridgemont High*, or Gary giggling and answering the phone by identifying himself as "the spa king of New Jersey" in *Desperately Seeking Susan*. Scenes of smoking marijuana in these films are played strictly for laughs. Although other films portray the effects of marijuana in a humorous vein, their scenes of marijuana use serve more than simple comedic purposes. One such example is the 1985 film *The Breakfast Club*, in which writer/director John Hughes chronicles a day in the life of five high school students serving an eight-hour detention. The five students serving the detention are stereotypes of the kinds of students you typically find in high school films. They include Andrew (the jock), Brian (the brain), Claire (the Prom Queen), Bender (the rebel) and Allison (the recluse).

Initially the students try to ignore, bother, or make fun of each other during the detention. This gradually changes as the day wears on. A transformation takes place soon after the teens start smoking the marijuana that Bender supplies for them. They begin talking *to* instead of *at* each other. As film critic Denis Wood noted, "instead of prom queen to brain, she talks to him; instead of jock to weirdo, he talks to her" (63). By the time they are allowed to leave they become friends and begin to see the people that exist beneath the stereotypes.

The antics of the students as they begin to get high are humorous, and this scene usually evoked laughs when it was shown in the theater. However, marijuana has other purposes in *The Breakfast Club* than simply providing a few laughs. It also serves the function of advancing the narrative. The heart of *The Breakfast Club* is the serious conversation the students have in the latter part of the film. This discussion could not have taken place if they continued the constant bickering that characterized the first few hours of the detention. Screenwriter John Hughes needed a method of turning five initially hostile students into a cohesive group. Marijuana was the answer. One reviewer could not understand why the marijuana sequence was included in the film, and describe it as "completely gratuitous" (Walters 87). It does serve a purpose, though. It brings the students together. The drug acts as a catalyst by providing them with a way to overcome their negative resistance to each other.

Eventually the students settle down and begin talking to each other. This leads them to the realization that they are more alike than they originally believed (for example, none of them are happy with their parents or home life). In reviews of the film this scene is usually described in terms of group therapy or as an encounter session. As a result "new friendships will be formed, class barriers breached, old suspicions and hostilities swept away" (Denby, "Snap" 95). Before smoking marijuana their conversation consists of insults and put downs. Then they share a few joints and things start to change. They slowly but surely begin to share more personal things with each other. Smoking marijuana leads them to reveal their innermost feelings. Brian admits to having thoughts of suicide, Bender tells how his father abuses him, and Claire says that her parents give her things but not love. Self-disclosing this information is a positive experience for two reasons. First, the group gets to share some of the things they have been keeping inside of them. It increases their awareness of other people as well as of themselves. Second, they become friends as a result. When the detention is finally over they leave as either platonic friends or romantic partners.

Pauline Kael summed it up best in her review of the film when she wrote

In the course of the day, under the prodding of the rebel and the mellowing effect of the marijuana he provides, they peel off the layers of self-protection, confess their problems with their parents, and, after much shedding of tears, are stripped down to their true selves. When the doors are open, they walk out transformed. (Stanton 306)

The characters in the movie *Nine to Five* undergo a similar liberating experience. Comedienne Lily Tomlin is joined by actress Jane Fonda and country singer Dolly Parton as three employees of Consolidated Companies, Inc. They work under the supervision of company vice-president Franklin Hart, Jr. (Dabney Coleman). Tomlin portrays Violet Newstead, a senior office manager who wants to move into upper management. Parton is Doralee Rhodes, Hart's personal secretary; while Fonda is Judy Bernly, the newest addition to the company's large typing pool. An early scene in the film shows Violet at home installing a garage door opener and complaining to her teenaged son about Hart, who took credit for a report she wrote. Her son offers her a joint to help her relax. Violet is initially opposed to taking it, but she acquiesces as soon as he reminds her of the amount of time she has been waiting for a promotion. The scene ends with Violet's son slipping the joint into her purse.

Once Violet has the joint, it is inevitable that she will use it (or else it would be pointless to include that scene in the film). A few days later Mr. Hart calls Violet into his office to inform her that she has been passed over for promotion in favor of a less experienced male employee, because he feels that clients world rather deal with a man than with a woman. Violet furiously storms out of the building and heads to the corner bar for a drink. She is joined by Doralee, who discovered that Hart has been spreading rumors that she has been sleeping with him; and Judy, who is angry because a fellow employee was fired for revealing her salary.

The three women sit at the bar and complain about the miserable way Hart treats his employees. When Violet volunteers to pay for another round of drinks, she reaches into her purse and discovers the joint her son had given her. She twirls it in the air and suggests they have an "old fashioned ladies pot party." Judy replies that she smoked "mary-wana" (her pronunciation) at a party once, but could never figure out what the big deal was.

The next scene reveals exactly what the "big deal" is. The women have moved from the bar to Doralee's house. We see them laughing and passing the joint to each other, as Judy shares her fantasies for murdering their boss. A large feast, which appears to consist of everything that was in the refrigerator, is spread on the kitchen table in front of them. They are obviously experiencing the "munchies." Judy, eating and inexplicably wearing a link of paper rings in her hair, says, "Everything tastes so wonderful. I can't get over it." The scene ends with Doralee and Violet disclosing their own fantasies for eliminating Hart.

The next day the three women arrive at the office together laughing and talking. It is surprising how quickly the co-workers have become good friends. Twenty-four hours earlier they barely talked to one another. Violet resented the fact that she was assigned to train Judy, and only gave her minimal instructions for performing her job. The entire office shunned Doralee, assuming she was sleeping with Mr. Hart. Marijuana serves the same purpose in *Nine to Five* that it does in *The Breakfast Club*. Acquaintances find themselves in an unpleasant situation (a Saturday detention/working for an unfair and chauvinistic boss), smoke marijuana together, and become friends as a result. The marijuana scene in *Nine to Five* was described by one critic as a "sisterhood pot party" (Kael 112). Marijuana helps the women to break down the barriers between them and really get to know one another.

Marijuana is also used to help them forget the work-related injustices they suffer. Violet was originally convinced to take the joint from her son when he reminded her of how long she had been waiting for a promotion. As they sat at the bar the co-workers confessed they didn't know what to do about their supervisor. The only "solution" they could come up with was to have another round of drinks. That was when Violet discovered the joint stashed in her purse. The marijuana helped them to cope with the indignities inflicted upon them. While they are stoned mentioning their boss evokes only comical images (hunting him like an animal), instead of the anger they usually associate with his name. In her review of the film, critic Carol Slingo makes this point when she writes

The immediate solution to "we've got to do something" is to get drunk or stoned—i.e. do something pleasant and friendly and fun—and to dream of revenge. They relate their fantasies for murdering Hart, and the warmth of the scene of women coming together to act out their anger leads viewers to accept the fantasies as positive answers. But the fantasies only provide a catharsis for the three secretaries; the following day they talk about how much fun they had, Delgado (the employee fired for revealing her salary) being forgotten with the barbecue and smoke. (678)

Just as smoking marijuana seems to make Judy's food taste better, it also "improves" her vision: Mr. Hart is viewed as a fool, and as someone to laugh at, rather than the tyrant he normally appears to be.

The "acquaintance to friend" motif found in *Nine to Five* is paralleled in the 1984 film *Romancing the Stone*. Romance novelist Joan Wilder (Kathleen Turner) travels to Colombia to search for her kidnapped sister. Once in Colombia she mistakenly boards the wrong bus, which eventually breaks down, and she is forced to walk through the jungle. Jack Colton (Michael Douglas), an American who captures and sells exotic birds for a living, stumbles across her. The two share several misadventures before discovering a cargo plane that has crashed in the jungle. To escape the heavy rain that has left them thoroughly drenched, they enter the plane only to find it full of bales of marijuana. Joan, failing to recognize the plane's cargo, innocently inquires about it. After Jack tells her it is marijuana, he asks, "You smoke it?"

Joan replies rather indirectly, "I went to college."

To help dry off, they use the marijuana to build a fire inside the plane's hull. Jack finds a case of whiskey, and before long they are both comfortable and dry. Up until this point in the film Jack and Joan behave antagonistically toward one another. Jack accuses her of being a jinx, while Joan claims he has no finesse or style and cares only about himself. However, the alcohol and the smoke from the marijuana fire help to create a more relaxed and intimate setting. Instead of berating Joan, Jack begins to talk about his love of the ocean and his dream of buying a boat and sailing around the world. They snuggle up to one another , and the scene ends with Joan falling asleep in Jack's arms.

Once again, two people, initially hostile, come together through the use of marijuana. *Romancing the Stone* varies this theme by introducing the prospect of romance in addition to friendship. Jack originally agrees to help Joan only if she pays him for his effort. After a night together in the plane, drinking and inhaling the smoke from the marijuana fire, a more intimate relationship begins to develop. Although they have their ups and downs throughout the film, they live happily ever after in the traditional Hollywood style. From a cinematic perspective, marijuana is again used as a way of advancing the narrative, as Jack and Joan then unite against the dangers of the jungle and the criminals who are chasing them.

Not surprisingly, films portray friends as well as acquaintances smoking marijuana. Perhaps the most notable example from the 1980s is *The Big Chill*. The plot of *The Big Chill* (1983) revolves around seven University of Michigan alumni as they gather for the funeral of Alex, an old college friend who has committed suicide. As they sort out their feelings, they wonder why Alex decided to end his life. Most of the two days they share together is spent talking about how they have changed since graduation. Once idealists bent on changing the world, they have now become part of the establishment they used to hate. The only exception is Nick, who supports himself by selling drugs.

In one respect *The Big Chill* differs from the other films previously discussed in this paper. Getting high does not change Nick's view of the world, not even temporarily. Unlike the office workers in *Nine to Five*, he is just as cynical stoned as he is sober. Nick eventually finds a way out through his friends, not through his drugs. At the end of the film Harold and Sarah, who are hosting the wake, allow Nick to remain behind with plans for him to repair an old cabin Alex was working on when he committed suicide. This offers Nick an alternative to selling drugs for a living.

The other characters in the film clearly disapprove of the way Nick supports himself. The primary reason Harold and Sarah set him up in the cabin is to provide him with a alternative to dealing drugs. All the main characters in *The Big Chill* seem to smoke marijuana at one point or another during the weekend, and it would be hypocritical of them to chastise Nick for getting high. The difference seems to be one of degree. The movie implies that it is okay to use drugs casually, as long as they do not physically or financially dominate your life.

It is Alex's death that reunites the group. As the funeral procession leaves the church, Nick offers to give a ride to his friend Meg. She tells him how terrible she feels, so he gives her some marijuana to smoke on the way to the cemetery. Nick shares his marijuana with Meg to help ease the depression she is feeling after Alex's death. It is his way of offering her support. As Hubert Cohen noted in his review of the film, Nick's "unflinching self analysis as well as his training have sensitized him to people, and that his own alienation has made him aware of how impossible it is for one person to help another except by offering him drugs" (80). As in *Nine to Five*, marijuana is used as a way of coping with an unpleasant situation. It is a way for one person to help another person feel better.

Meg is one of several characters in *The Big Chill* who smokes marijuana. After dinner the first night the group sits down to talk about old times. There is a joint that they pass back and forth between them. Meanwhile another friend, Michael, is rolling more joints at a second table. Very little attention or discussion is focused on their drug use in this scene—unlike *The Breakfast Club*, when Andy faces a personal crisis trying to decide if he should smoke marijuana. In *The Big Chill* it is something that is done casually.

A similar scene takes place the next night. As Michael rolls a joint, the discussion focuses on Alex, as they try to figure out what drove him to commit suicide; and on themselves, as they evaluate their lives and feel guilty about their success. These late night conversations have been describe as the "where-have-we-gone group therapy scenes" (Denby, *Chill* 92) and as "boozy, druggy confessions" (Canby C14). The group uses marijuana as a way of dealing with Alex's death, just as Meg used it before his funeral. It also helps them face the realization that they have not accomplished their original ambitions. One critic described it by saying, "Their lives are at a midpoint and they are feeling a sense of loss, of angst, of guilt. So what do they do? They get stoned." (Edelman 88).

Marijuana plays a large part in establishing the emotional climate for these discussions. Many of the feelings the characters are experiencing are disclosed while they smoke marijuana. It is similar to the scene in *The Breakfast Club* in which the students smoke joints and then reveal how unhappy their home life is. Not every emotion or belief that is revealed in *The Big Chill* is greeted with mutual support, but in the end they re-affirm their love for one another. When they leave the next morning their friendship is stronger. They once again feel that special bond between them that had been missing since college. Marijuana serves the purpose of helping to create an environment conducive to self-disclosure. By sharing their guilt and fear with each other, they purge themselves of these feelings.

In *The Big Chill* occasional drug us is okay, but dealing drugs for a living is not. Moderation is the key. There is a clear distinction between Meg, who gets high to cope with Alex's death, and Nick, who takes and sells a variety of drugs. Nick goes beyond the acceptable limit, which results in Harold and Sarah attempting to "reform" him by allowing him to stay in Alex's cabin.

The way marijuana and other drugs were depicted in motion pictures like *The Big Chill* lead people both inside and outside the film industry to attempt a "reformation" of their own. In the mid 1980s concern was raised over the positive portrayal of illicit drugs in American movies and the effect such as a portrayal may have on the nation's youth. For instance, former president Ronald

Reagan commented that "there have been some pictures in which there was a gratuitous scene in there for a laugh about drug use, that made it look kind of attractive and funny, not dangerous and sad" (18). As director of the Scott Newman Foundation, Susan Newman (actor Paul Newman's daughter) worked toward a more realistic and less glamorizing depiction of drugs in popular films, but she admitted that in the first half of the decade progress was "frustratingly slow" (Morganthau 20).

However, in the late 1980s the manner in which marijuana and drugs were shown in American motion pictures began to change. The first observable sign of this change occurred when a number of scripts had drugs in their first drafts but not in their second. For example, writer Jim Crumley was forced to remove the casual cocaine use by the protagonist in his *Dancing Bear* script. Robert Ward could not even find a studio that would read his adaptation of the novel *Budding Prospects*, which focuses on three friends who are tricked into tending a marijuana farm (Cooper 54). Stories that dealt with drugs (even those that lightly held an anti-drug position) were now taboo. Instead, audiences were offered films with strong and explicit anti-drug messages, such as *Jo Jo Dancer Your Life is Calling*, *No Way Out*, and *Drugstore Cowboy*. Two notable exceptions to this trend were the Oliver Stone producions *Platoon* (1988) and *The Doors* (1991). However, these films take place in the late 1960s and the early 1970s, and are a reflection of a previous period in American history and culture. As a result they are granted what may be called a "license to sin." They are permitted to show marijuana and drug use because their stories are framed in the past rather than in the present.

The current portrayal of marijuana in motion pictures is best epitomized by the release of *Freddy's Dead* (1991), the final installment in the *Nightmare on Elm Street* series. Although *Freddy's Dead* makes fun of an anti-drug commercial frequently shown on television ("this is your brain on drugs"), the film itself contains an anti-drug message. In the movie a teenager, Spencer, has some marijuana and offers to share it with two of his friends. They decline by telling him they don't do drugs (in other words, they "just say no"). This forces Spencer to smoke it alone, after which he falls asleep. While asleep he is potential prey for the villainous Freddy, who inhabits the dreams of teenagers and kills them, which is precisely what happens to Spencer. Spencer is thus "punished" for smoking marijuana. His friends, who can only save him by waking him up, are unable to do so. They blame their inability to rescue Spencer on the marijuana he smoked, which put him into a sleep so deep it was impossible to save him from Freddy's clutches. In stark contrast to previous films which showed the group bonding that occurred when people smoked marijuana, Spencer is noticeably alone after failing to find anyone who was willing to get high with him. The new depiction of marijuana use reveals it to be an isolated and lonely activity.

Another example of how times have changed is found by comparing the original release of *Fast Times at Ridgemont High* with the cable version currently being shown on television channels such as "superstation" WTBS. The original film contains a scene that shows Jeff and a friend talking on the phone, discussing the particular type of marijuana they just smoked and the various side effects associated with it. The "new" version of this phone call has Jeff and his friend discussing the possibility of taking a trip to Mexico, with all references to marijuana edited from the scene (this second conversation was not part of the film when it was initially released). It is interesting to note that in the scene cut from the original movie Jeff and his friend were merely talking about marijuana. They were not shown using it. However, even a conversation about marijuana use was judged to be inappropriate for a nighttime cable television audience.

There may be several reasons behind this cinematic shift in the portrayal of marijuana use. One studio official stated that the public is simply "bored" by the topic (Morganthau 20). Other Hollywood executives say the change is a reflection of the conservative shift in American society and politics. Tom Craig, vice-president at United Artists, said

Studio people don't want to glorify what has become a notional problem. Drugs aren't a laughing matter anymore, and people, therefore, aren't going to come to see a movie that makes light of the issue. (Cooper 55)

One major writer is certain, though, that Hollywood's new anti-drug attitude will fade.

This is not a new McCarthy period. Studios will ultimately be guided only by the market place. Eventually a drug script will come in with big revenue potential. All that will be necessary then is to provide the audience with the moral and aesthetic justification to come in and see the freaks. And they will, even if the freaks are druggies. And if that movie makes it, then it will be a whole new ball game. (Cooper 56)

Conclusion

Throughout the first half of the 1980s, scenes of marijuana use in American motion pictures shared several common themes, most of them involving positive consequences for the characters involved. In these films characters were often reluctant to smoke marijuana, but acquaintances or friends managed to overcome their initial resistance. Lasting interpersonal bonds were formed as a result of getting high together and, while high, characters were better able to cope with unpleasant or unhappy situations (ranging from a chauvinistic boss to the death of an old friend). Marijuana use was also conducive in creating a supportive environment for self-disclosure. At a more general level, marijuana was depicted as a humorous element in a variety of comedy films.

In the late 1980s and the early 1990s the use of marijuana and other illicit drugs was notably absent in most American films. When it did make its way into a motion picture, drug use was depicted as having negative, rather than positive, consequences. The only exception to this rule seems to be films which are granted a "license to sin" because they are set in a previous time period or purport to tell true stories (*Platoon, The Doors, La Bamba*). Now that drug dealers and smugglers are routinely replacing communists and terrorists as the "bad guys" of motion pictures (in films such as *Die Hard, Robocop* 2), it appears that this trend is going to continue.

Works Cited

Canby, Vincent. "The Big Chill." *The New York Times* 23 Sept. 1983: C14.

Cohen, Hubert. "The Big Chill." *Magill's Cinema Annual* Ed. Frank Magill. Englewood Cliffs: Salem P, 1984.

Cooper, Marc. "Up in Smoke." *American Film* March 1987.

Edelman, Rob. "The Big Chill." *Film Review Annual*. Ed. Jerome Ozer. Englewood Cliffs: Film Review Publications, 1984.

Kael, Pauline. "The Current Cinema." *New Yorker*. 9 March 1981.

Mann, Peggy. *Marijuana Alert*. NY: McGraw-Hill, 1985.

Morganthau, Tom. "Going After Hollywood." *Newsweek*. 11 Aug. 1986: 20.

Reagan, Ronald. Interview. *Newsweek* 11 Aug. 1986: 18.

Slingo, Carol. "Nine to Five." *Film Review Annual*. Ed. Jerome Ozer. Englewood Cliffs: Film Review Publications, 1982.

"Snap, Crackle, and Pop." *New York* 18 Feb. 1985.

Stanton, Louise. "The Breakfast Club." *Films in Review* 36 (1985).

Starks, Michael. *Cocaine Fiends and Reefer Madness*. East Brunswick: Cornwall Books, 1982.

Walters Gordon. "The Breakfast Club." *Magill's* Cinema Annual. Ed. Frank Magill. Pasadena: Salem P, 1986.

Weisman, Adam Paul. "I Was a Drug-Hype Junkie." *The New Republic* 6 Oct. 1986.

Wood, Denis. "Seeing and Being." *Film Quarterly* Spring 1986.

Filmography

Year	Film	Director
1925	*The Cloud Rider*	
1929	*High on the Range*	
1935	*Assassin of Youth*	
1936	*Reefer Madness*	
1937	*Marijuana: Weed with Roots in Hell*	
1956	*The Man with the Golden Arm*	Otto Preminger
1966	*The Wild Angels*	Roger Corman
1967	*The Trip*	Roger Corman
1969	*Easy Rider*	Dennis Hopper
1972	*Dealing*	
1980	*Nine to Five*	Colin Higgins
1980	*Caddyshack*	Harold Ramis
1982	*Fast Times at Ridgemont High*	Amy Heckerling
1983	*The Big Chill*	Lawrence Kasdan
1984	*Romancing the Stone*	Robert Zemeckis
1985	*The Breakfast Club*	John Hughes
1985	*Desperately Seeking Susan*	Susan Seidelman
1986	*Jo Jo Dancer Your Life is Calling*	Richard Pryor
1987	*La Bamba*	Luis Valdez
1987	*Less than Zero*	Maret Kanievska
1988	*Platoon*	Oliver Stone
1989	*Drugstore Cowboy*	Gus Van Sant
1991	*The Doors*	Oliver Stone
1991	*Freddy's Dead*	Rachel Talalay

Clothing

Press Dress:
The Beige Brigade of
Movie Journalists Outdoors
Norma Fay Green

Despite a Union general's suggestion that Civil War correspondents "should wear a white uniform to indicate the purity of their character," (Knightley 19) movie journalists have usually been confined to neutral beige outerwear with on-screen white costumes reserved for actors portraying nurses, doctors, scientists and all-around good guys. Through exposure to hundreds of films over nearly a century of film portrayals, moviegoers have come to quickly decipher the occupational shorthand symbolized in the ubiquitous trenchcoat and the bush, or safari, jacket as they relate to cinematic newsgatherers.

Though the British military-styled garb is by no means the exclusive property of journalistic film characters, viewers have come to understand that trenchcoats are literal coverups for spies, private investigators, police and roving reporters, with bush jackets designating explorers, hunters, traders and journalists in global hot spots. Clothing historian Anne Hollander observed that "messages could be exchanged through clothing, based on common cinematic experience" (344). She noted that stock character representation through apparel has been achieved through the cumulative effect of popular films:

Certain of the early-movie ways of suggesting characterization through dress have passed completely into the general public consciousness of clothing as if they were natural laws. A trench coat and sheath-like, glittering evening dress have continuing visual resonance; they carry suggestions that have less to do with their intrinsic looks than with their movie meaning. (341)

Surely the importance of costume design was not an alien concept to early Hollywood moguls, many of whom had come to film making from the garment industry. Few silent films about journalism were produced compared with the noisy newspaper movie genre popularized in the 1930s, but the bridge between early portrayals such as *The Old Reporter* of 1912 and *Big News*, an early talkie from 1929, was the similarity in the office attire among the ink-stained wretches of the newsroom. Though this study of journalism films deals mainly with the occupational cues suggested by the outdoor wear of journalists, it seems

65

important to briefly discuss the typical in-office clothing viewed in hundreds of American motion pictures.

Indoors, if journalists were depicted anywhere besides the newsroom milieu, it often was difficult for audiences to discern reporters from regular office workers. Since the days of Charlie Chaplin's screen debut as a would-be photo-journalist in the 1914 *A Busted Johnny* or *Making a Living*, cinematic reporters have been dressed in standard issue white collar office wear. Business suits—double or single-breasted jackets, depending on the fashion of the era and the body of the actor, usually with matching trousers for men and matching or contrasting skirts or trousers for women—have been the official uniform in the corporate world and celluloid culture of American urban journalism for most of the twentieth century. Editors, who stayed indoors most of the time, were routinely shown in shirtsleeves, with vests and visors as frequent accessories. Through the 1930s and 1940s, when the journalism film genre proliferated, eye-shades were as commonplace in newsroom settings as candlestick telephones.

The proportionately few women reporters depicted in journalism films early on adopted the tailored look of male prototype suits for most of their assignments. An interesting wardrobe versatility is demonstrated in the 1931 *Five Star Final* when a woman reporter (Kitty Carmody played by Ona Munson) arrived for a job interview at the *Gazette* in a low-cut hip-hugging outfit. The camera ogles her bosom as she smoothes her clothes in anticipation of meeting the editor (Randall, played by Edward G. Robinson) who is dressed in a boxy dark suit. It is obvious that she has dressed to call attention to her anatomical traits rather than her journalistic skills. After she is hired, she shows up for her first assignment in a demure dress with a high and prim collar which is either for the sake of the people she is going to interview (a cloak of innocence to gain their confidence) or her true self. In her final scene, she is dressed in a jazzy plaid suit. It appears that she had adapted the business uniform to her style in terms of cut and material, so that she still stands out in a conservatively-garbed office.

But women reporters, who only adopted some elements of male dress, were often impeded in their work when they gave into voguish style (Bisplinghoff 227-31). Likened to some sort of fashion hermaphrodite, the much-analyzed female version of Hildy Johnson in the 1940 *His Girl Friday* wears an efficient-looking suit jacket,[1] matched to an immobilizing straight skirt and high heels, not good for running up and down stairs or tackling sources—both of which are required to garner her exclusive stories. Women journalists who wanted to be taken seriously by their peers and sources dressed liked men. In the 1953 *Deadline U.S.A.* editor Ed Hutcheson (Humphrey Bogart) relies heavily on the only female crime reporter on staff, Mrs. Willebrandt (Audrey Christie) who wears vests and shirts with skirts throughout most of the film, unlike publisher (Ethel Barrymore) or staff researcher Barndollar (Florence Shirley) who wear dresses, with Barndollar often adding a bow tie, not unlike editor Bogart's.

By the early 1970s, newsroom apparel had loosened up considerably and younger male reporters were seen in shirt and tie with jeans while women sported pants suits. *Miami Herald* crime reporter Edna Buchanan noted that film crews who came to shoot on location in the newsroom were often unimpressed by actual journalistic attire. She quotes Linda Benedict, a wardrobe woman for the 1985 *Mean Season* as observing, "Reporters don't care how they look, do they?" (76). But that was not always the case. The corporate dress-for-success syndrome pervaded the *Herald's* newsroom in the 1981 *Absence of Malice* where female reporter Megan Carter (Sally Field) dutifully wears business suits and tailored pants and vests while her male city editor is seen in sweaters. Perhaps Carter, who is less experienced and more insecure, feels more respectable in a suit than her immediate boss, who no longer goes outside to cover stories and establish credibility with sources. In most scenes, Carter is shown in outfits with matching or color-coordinated accessories. She appears to be unified and in control of her look. After a source commits suicide because of her story, Carter begins to lose her sartorial discipline. She goes to visit the subject of her investigation and he rips her blouse. When she picks herself up off the floor, we notice that her shoes and handbag do not match; they are blue and brown respectively. Moreover, her shoes are open-toed and seem to represent the vulnerability of the reporter who stumbled into something she cannot escape. She ends up borrowing a sweater to cover up her torn clothes as if suddenly she is ashamed of being exposed. Her garments unravel with the concluding events of the film and perhaps the literal uncovering of Carter is meant as figurative retribution for all the subjects of stories she exposed and lives she ultimately tore asunder. Most of the time, however, reporters only strip down to shirtsleeves at work and robes at home when they sit down to write their stories. For the first half of this century, the key transitional wardrobe accessory was the reporter's hat—worn at almost all times, indoors and outdoors.

For any pre-1960 American film, the main material distinction between male reporters and other office characters was the ever-present headcovering. Most of the fedoras were snap-brimmed and worn up or down, depending on the characterization or the lack of continuity between takes. They were often worn tilted to one side or high back on the head with a band wide enough to hold a press pass prominently (though few were found in the films perused for this study). Wearing hats indoors has been interpreted as the height of male impudence—something not done in polite society—and irreverence for etiquette. Other interpretations indicate the hat was a sign of readiness to spring into action and rush outdoors to cover breaking news or a practical way to keep the head warm in drafty pressrooms. Women journalist's hats, while acceptable to wear indoors, reached absurd heights and widths in the 1940s (Gaines and

Herzog 242). Ethan Mordden blames Columbia studio's poor fashion sense for Hildy's headgear in *His Girl Friday*, "shaped like those children's birthday-party favors that explode when you pull the string" (*Hollywood Studios* 186). In the 1942 *Woman of the Year*, Katherine Hepburn as international columnist Tess Harding calls attention to herself and away from a baseball game when she wears a shoulder-width light-colored picture-brimmed hat (with trim to match her checked dress and gloves), which blocks the view of at least one guy sitting in the stands behind her who asks sports reporter Sam Craig (Spencer Tracy) to "tell her it ain't raining." She seems oblivious to the game or her intrusive accessory. But if she had been mindful of any storms, she might have donned a trenchcoat because the tan or khaki-colored water-repellent garment, originally designed for the British army around World War I, had been appropriated by civilian journalists covering the Great War and co-opted into service for future generations of news representatives.[2]

Clark Gable is often credited with starting the occupational fashion trend of trench-coated journalists in his role as newspaper reporter Peter Warne in the 1934 *It Happened One Night*. But his later off-screen wife Carole Lombard was filmed in one six years earlier as newspaper reporter Margaret Banks in the 1929 *Big News*. Regardless of which journalist wore the first trenchcoat on screen, the question remains of why it became a requisite part of every movie reporter's wardrobe. From a purely technical point of view, the color was right.

Whites photographed with a glare, so most whites were greyed or were actually pastels, which photographed white. Plaids, stripes and polka dots, used to connote certain character types, had to be worn judiciously as they looked "busy" and the potential clash with backgrounds had to be considered. Academy Award-winning costume designer Edith Head declared that the on-screen clothing should convey a strong enough message about characters so that the attire became a visual equivalent of the audio portion "if the sound went off in the theatre" (36). Also, there was an ongoing relationship between the military and media representatives. The idea of a war reporter adapting a design dating back to 19th century military coats, styled with epaulets and a double yoke at the shoulders (O'Hara 244), is not far-fetched if the correspondent is trying to stay as warm and dry as the troops and establish credibility—what better way than to look like one of them? Perhaps some of the real-life reporters who later turned to writing screenplays, along with costume researchers, were inspired by reporters such as William Howard Russell, who is described as having elaborate quasi-uniforms made up when he was assigned to cover various wars (Knightley 9). It is possible that various Americans saw photographs of this scribal dandy and decided to duplicate it, especially if they were journalists with romantic notions about war correspondents. The feedback process of fashion, with fictional film following authentic dress but also creating new consumer demand by exaggerating existing styles, was alive and well by the time of the Great War.[3] Clothing historian Anne Hollander observed that form of vestigial detail had become meaningless to the function of the outfit:

A great number of modern garments stemming originally from...military costumes have preserved some of the look but none of function of its characteristic trim: lapels, cuffs, snaps, pocket flaps, extra buttons, buckles, and sometimes rings have been traditional decorative elements in tailored informal clothing for both sexes during two centuries of stylistic modifications. Their military connotations were eventually lost, after the early atrophy of their function. (474)

While combat conditions dictated the design elements of many garments, civilian journalists most likely adopted them because they looked good and were versatile for socially and climatically-mobile reporters. The World War I vintage trenchcoats, manufactured by Burberrys and Aquascutum, were expensive investments characterized by detachable epaulets, buttoned down at shoulder; raglan sleeves; large button-over lapels; buckled wrist-strap with tab holding strap in place; belt with D-rings; buttoned welt pockets; throat latches and back yoke. But an American knockoff dubbed "King of the style Parade" was advertised in the 1931 Sears catalog for $2.98 postpaid and well within the reach of low-paid real-life reporters. The coat could do double duty as a raincoat and overcoat, with a button-in lining.

Stateside reporter Johnny Jones (Joel McCrea) probably became the most famous movie mannequin for the trenchcoat when he went to Europe under the byline of Huntley Havistock to be *The Foreign Correspondent*, a 1940 film directed by Alfred Hitchcock with costumes credited to I. Magnin & Co. McCrea's portrayal of the *New York Globe* reporter, more accustomed to covering urban crime than international politics, features one of the few instances where the movie journalist actually buttons the storm flap of his coat against the bad weather. His new coat also proves to be an occupational hazard when it gets caught in the gears of a windmill where he has discovered an espionage ring. Almost 40 years later, Christopher Reeve played the bumbling Clark Kent who gets his raincoat caught in the ladies room door as he tried to pursue a conversation with Lois Lane in *Superman I*.

Trenchcoats, properly tied rather than belt-buckled, were worn well by Jimmy Stewart playing newsman Christopher Tyler in *Next Time We Love* and John Wayne who, as newsreel cameraman Bob Adams in *I Cover the War*, kept a pet monkey in his generous trenchcoat pocket. Both Humphrey Bogart (playing Matrac, a fugitive French journalist) and John Lader as British journalist Manning sport trenchcoats in *Passage to Marseille*. While the trenchcoat figures prominently in *It Happened One Night* as both Gable's protection against the rain and Colbert's bathrobe and blanket, it had been reduced to a regular raincoat, stripped of its epaulets and D-rings (originally used for carrying hand grenades and water bottles), by the time of the 1956 remake *You Can't Run Away From It* starring Jack Lemmon. After World War II, it appeared that there was no use for military details. A scene in *Deadline U.S.A.* features newspaper editor Humphrey Bogart confronted by a journalism school graduate asking for a job. They both have on the same, simple raincoat and the clothing seems to bond the older journalist with the kid who aspires to be a foreign correspondent in Egypt. Bogart looks at his clothes double and remarks: "It may not be the oldest profession but it's the best." By 1979, when Jane Fonda appeared as TV reporter Kimberly Wells in *The China Syndrome*, all real-life and reel-life journalists had the requisite trenchcoat. Dutifully, Wells carries hers around but never covers up in it. If the audience reads her clothing as communication, it becomes apparent that she is unprotected and vulnerable as she gets involved in her investigation. In the 1984 *Killing Fields*, Sam Waterson plays the *New York Times* Cambodian correspondent Sydney Schamberg. On his home turf he is seen gazing at the Manhattan skyline, with his back to the camera, dressed in a trenchcoat. The reporter has returned with quite a story to tell. Interestingly, he is never pictured in Southeast Asia with what became another symbolic outfit for American journalists: the safari jacket.

Michael Herr, a Vietnam war correspondent and later screenwriter for *Full Metal Jacket*, was captivated with the romantic image of reporters covering "…wars in places where the climate was so cool that you could wear a trench coat and look good" (188). He and several hundred other journalists of the post-World War II baby boom never really got the chance to experience many chilly assignments as conflicts erupted closer to the equator over the last three decades. One of the early on-screen performances of journalists in bush jacket country involved Spencer Tracy playing a *New York Herald* reporter of 1871 in *Stanley and Livingstone*. The 1939 production, filmed on location in East Africa, featured Tracy in quasi-bush jacket that looked like a belted and booted version of the tropical-weight suit he wore on board the ship enroute to meet the famous doctor. His light-colored single-breasted jacket featured two patch pockets at the hip.

The traditional bush jacket, with four patch pockets with box pleats and button flaps and an all-around belt, is based on a British army tunic first worn in India and Africa in the mid-nineteenth century.[4] While *Esquire* magazine noted that the bush jacket, "which had been out of fashion for several years, staged a comeback in 1943," (Schoeffler and Gale 63), most World War II correspondents from the United States wore combat fatigues when covering war zones in films such as *Guadalcanal Diary* and *Objective Burma*. Yves Saint Laurent is credited with reviving the safari jacket in 1968 for non-tropical civilian use (O'Hara 218). By then, Americans had seen a few real-life television correspondents reporting from Vietnam in such attire and it was only a matter of time before the style was co-opted by pacifists and some armchair adventurers. Feature films about Vietnam were slow in coming, and few portrayed war correspondents. One of the earliest, *Green Berets*, included a jaded newspaper reporter, George Beckworth (David Janssen), who is first seen stateside in his dark suit and tie. Challenged to find out more about the war up-close, he soon arrives in Vietnam wearing a freshly-pressed safari jacket which remains so throughout the rest of the film. When he goes out with the troops, he dons camouflage wear, but is seen more often in his immaculate bush clothes. Perhaps he was the fashion inspiration for what real-life Vietnam correspondent Michael Herr described as the tell-tale look of newly-arrived reporters "dressed in one of those jungle-hell leisure suits that the tailors on Tu Do were getting rich cranking out, with enough flaps and slots and cargo pockets to carry supply for a squad" (37). American broadcasters also became role models during the Vietnam era with British journalist Phillip Knightley observing reporter rituals abroad: "Some got a tailor to run up a safari jacket—Saigon tailors called it, a 'CBS jacket'—with matching trousers, which looked vaguely like a uniform, not, in most cases, out a sense of commitment, but so as to be less conspicuous in a military situation" (403). Perhaps more implausible than the maintenance of Janssen's look was the wardrobe of Linda Kozlowski playing an American *Newsday* reporter in *Crocodile Dundee*. There is an ever-so brief glimpse of her wearing a bush jacket as she travels by Jeep in the Outback but most of the time she is seen in sundresses, shorts, thong bathing suits and skirts all pulled from a supposedly regulation-size backpack.

By the time of the release of a trilogy of films about American journalists covering events in Latin America, studios could order wardrobes from mail order clothiers such as Banana Republic, founded in 1978 by former journalists Mel and Pat Ziegler who turned military surplus into a peacetime bonanza described as "New Age Abercrombie & Fitch" (Grossberger F87-93). In the 1982 *Missing*, set in Chile, Sissy Spacek takes to wearing her husband's bush jacket (actually a parka-like jacket with hood and tiny pockets on the upper sleeve) when he disappears. It's as if she put on the mantle of journalism to find the missing reporter and remember his spirit. That jacket seems to exemplify the protection the husband thought he had as an American and the security that Spacek is seeking in trying to find out the truth.

A year later in *Under Fire*, Nick Nolte was cast as U.S. press photographer Russell Price who goes to Nicaragua from Chad in the same khaki attire suitable for all warm war zones. His bush jacket is less elaborate than the one worn by his friend Alex Grazier (Gene Hackman) who sports a multi-pocketed jacket with Norfolk belted back. Grazier, who switches from working for a newsmagazine to TV news, wears beige shirts with epaulets and flap pockets. The women reporters wear tan clothing and one has a subdued version of the safari jacket (with fewer pockets). The neutral colors help reflect the sun and symbolize their seeming detachment. Nolte, who endangers himself and his friends every time he leaves the safe haven of the hotel, insists "I don't take sides, I take pictures." Even his light-colored clothing can't seem to camouflage his camera and his eyes as unwelcome observers.

Salvador (1986) focused on the life of James Wood playing gonzo photojournalist Richard Boyle. Although the film begins in San Francisco, the shift in scenery is portended by the movie's title and visually by the safari jacket hanging on the back of the apartment door. The man who is about to evict Boyle sarcastically refers to him as a war hero, and the viewer knows Boyle has not seen his last battle. He ends up in jail over traffic violations and, once released, the gray attired anti-hero drives to El Salvador where he soon dons a bush jacket with epaulets, wears a kerchief around his neck, and meets with news colleagues. His photographer friend John Cassady (John Savage) idolized war photojournalist Robert Capa and wears what Banana Republic would call the consummate photojournalist's vest with a shirt and cargo pants with huge bellows pockets at the thigh, seemingly big enough to act as a portable darkroom. While the safari suit establishes his link to journalism, Boyle's wardrobe of retro-tropical print shirts is perhaps the most symbolic statement of his character. He is distinguished from his fellow American journalists, other Westerners and even Salvadorans, whom he claims to love, by the shirts. It does not seem accidental that he wears a gaudy print shirt featuring Schlitz beer labels and Milwaukee pennants and baseballs to a cocktail party welcoming the new U.S. ambassador. His fellow Americans are in suits or, at least, more formal shirts while he chooses rather loud, casual attire which sets him apart from everyone else—both natives and foreigners. He and his shirts don't seem to fit in.

John Malkovich played an American photographer in Cambodia in the 1984 *Killing Fields*. He is differentiated from the print journalists by his rag-tag looking costume of camouflage pants, T-shirts, vests, and sometimes bandanas worn gypsy-style around his perspiring head. He physically goes out in the streets and climbs all over every object to get the right shot while the Sydney Schamberg character tends to blend in with the crowds, despite his height, look, and western-style rolled-up long-sleeved shirts and light-colored pressed trousers. He seems more at the mercy of his translator and guide than the photographer who tries to capture the truth through pictures alone.

Whether movie journalists are portrayed by themselves or in packs with other reporters, there seems to be a sense of "outsider" about them. They are all individuals with particular prejudices shrouded in a sense of professional objectivity and neutral-colored coats and jackets. They reflect the heat, but they sometimes absorb it too. During the Operation Desert Storm airwar in 1991, *People* magazine asked "aren't war correspondents supposed to be safari-suit-rumpled, like CNN's Peter Arnett, rather than bomber jacket-rakish like NBC's Arthur Kent?" (Wilhelm 99). Kent, who covered the conflict from Saudi Arabia, bucked the established dress code for journalists by appearing on air night after night in a dark leather jacket (to keep him warm against desert winds) and perhaps, unconsciously, to show his affinity with the Allied flying aces overhead. Fashion design assistant Douglas Erwin admired Kent's courage in clothing: "Most reporters have safari jackets or the most awful suits. But he's a very '90s correspondent—the open neck says he can get dirt under his nails but still come up looking good" (Harris 40). However, the trend to darker duds for reporters did not impress columnist Michael Killian who noted:

As was true before Desert Storm, the wartime fashion I find the most odious is the wearing of leather replica bomber and other flight jackets, invariably with military-looking khaki pants, by trendy civilian swells who have never even pulled K.P., let alone climbed into a cockpit. (15)

If, in fact, the brown leather jackets complete with regulation snap-down collar, shoulder epaulets, snap close pockets above the knitted waist band and cuffs, do catch on in movie portrayals, it will be just another example of the British military influence on American journalists both on and off-screen. It turns out that even the ever present journalistic tool and frequent film prop—the standard issue reporter's notebook: pocket-sized spiral bound sheaf of paper that looks like a stenographer's pad cut in half vertically—was adopted in the U.S. from British World War II surplus (PoKempner 22). But, more important than the origins of American journalistic fashion may be the symbolic shift from light-colored, neutral-looking outerwear to a shorter, darker jacket that bulks the upper body but covers less than the trench coat or safari jacket. Does it mean that journalists have chosen up sides and will be cast as headline-seeking heavies or does it simply mean that dark leather wears like iron and requires less maintenance than uniforms of the beige brigade? Only time, and the spate of films about the Persian Gulf war and other global hot spots featuring journalists working outdoors, will tell.

Notes

[1]Stanford University drama professor Douglas Russell is quoted as saying: "I think some women want to look rather geometric, simple and clean-cut because that suggests efficiency. Our capitalist business world depends on efficiency to succeed; our whole culture is based on that" (Beckett 156). Other references to the first female Hildy include Gaines and Herzog 232-46; Haskell 130-35; Kael 68-69; Larkin 94; Mordden's *Movie Star* 167-68; Powers 25-27 and Rosen 212-13.

[2]Mander describes how new technology and trench warfare created the modern occupational stereotype about reporters (95-107). Hillmer comments that the trenchcoat, among other clothing classics, "pass(ed) across the movie screen and into the realm of our desires" (12). Good descriptions of the origin of the coat style can be found in Dutt 104-05; Berendt 32; Schoeffler and Gale 150-56, 684 and Byrde 138-39.

74 Beyond the Stars III

[3]Lurie discusses the transformation of an actor's "temporary disguise...becomes part of the everyday wardrobe of some members of the public" and notes that what starts out as a costume convenience—a means to "instantly and clearly indicate age, class, regional origin and if possible occupation and personality" is stored in viewer memories and later imitated (25). Feminist scholar Angela McRobbie refers to the "interdependency marked by continual 'cross-referencing' which goes on between viewers as consumers and fictional characters portrayed on the screen" (qtd. in Gaines and Herzog *Fabrications* 17). Hollander too discusses reciprocity: "Both men and women began to dress and behave and respond to each other as they saw the people in the movies dressing and behaving, who were in turn purporting to represent reality. The copying done by audiences, with the help of clothing manufacturers and merchandisers, has taken the form of references and allusions of those crystallized images. And so again artistic style, when it is the vessel for the acceptable look of reality, becomes natural style" (344-50).

[4]While Theodore Roosevelt, who was known for his love of hunting, is credited with popularizing the style in the United States, the "British roots are well-illustrated in Knotel and Seig 264, 275-76. Also style details are described in Berendt 36; Schoeffler and Gale 62-63, 70-71, 141, 458, 650 and O'Hara 218-19.

Works Cited

Beckett, Kathleen. "What our clothes say about us." *Vogue* Aug. 1986: 156, 162.
Berendt, John. "The Trench Coat." *Esquire* May 1982: 32.
_____."The Safari Jacket." *Esquire* Nov. 1983: 36.
Bisplinghoff, Gretchen. "Hildy Johnson—A Question of Gender." *Film Reader* 5 (1982): 227-31.
Buchanan, Edna. *The Corpse Had a Familiar Face*. NY: Random House, 1987.
Byrde, Penelope. *The Male Image: Men's Fashion in Britain, 1300-1970*. London: B.T. Batsford, 1979.
Dutt, Robin. "The Trenchcoat." *Esquire* (Brit. ed.) Mar. 1991: 104-105.
Gaines, Jane Marie, and Charlotte Cornelia Herzog. "Hildy Johnson and the 'Man-Tailored Suit': The Comedy of Inequality." *Film Reader* 5 (1982): 232-46.
_____.*Fabrications: Costume and the Female Body*. NY: Routledge, 1990.
Grossberger, Lewis. "Yes, Do We Have Bananas!" *Esquire* Sept. 1986: F87-93.
Harris, Mark. "Arthur of Arabia." *Entertainment Weekly* 15 Feb. 1991: 40-41.
Haskell, Molly. *From Reverence to Rape: The Treatment of Women in the Movies*. NY: Holt, Rinehart and Winston, 1974.
Head, Edith. "Dialogue on Film: Edith Head." *American Film* 3.7 (1978):36.
Herr, Michael. *Dispatches*. NY: Avon, 1978.
Hillmer, Melanie. "The Cinema in the Wardrobe: A Stroll Through Seven Decades." *Fashion in Film*. Eds. Regine and Peter W. Engelmier. Munich: Prestel-Verlag, 1990. 12-17.
Hollander, Anne. *Seeing Through Clothes*. NY: Viking Press, 1978.
Kael, Pauline. *The Citizen Kane Book*. NY: Bantam, 1971: 68-69.
Killian, Michael. "If they dress like soldiers, they must want to see action, right?" *Chicago Tribune* 6 Feb. 1991: 14-15.

Press Dress 75

Knightley, Phillip. *The First Casualty: From the Crimea to Vietnam: the War Correspondent as Hero, Propagandist, and Myth Maker*. NY: Harcourt Brace Jovanovich, 1975.

Knotel, Herbert Jr., and Herbert Sieg. *Uniforms of the World: A Compendium of Army, Navy, and Air Force Uniforms, 1900-1937* Rev. ed. NY: Charles Scribner's Sons, 1980.

Larkin, Rochelle. *Hail Columbia*. NY: Arlington House Publishers, 1975: 94.

Lurie, Allison. *The Language of Clothes*. NY: Vintage Books, 1981.

Mander, Mary. "The Journalist as Cynic." *Antioch Review* Winter 1980: 95-107.

Mordden, Ethan. *The Hollywood Studios: House Styles in the Golden Age of the Movies*. NY: Simon & Schuster, 1988.

_____. *Movie Star: A Look at the Women Who Made Hollywood*. NY: St. Martin's, 1983.

O'Hara, Georgina. *The Encyclopedia of Fashion*. NY: Harry N. Abrams, 1986.

PoKempner, Marc. "The Nonpareil Notebook." *Quill* 70.5 (1982): 22-23.

Powers, Tom. "Screwball Liberation." *Jump Cut* 17 (April 1978): 25-27.

Rosen, Marjorie. *Popcorn Venus*. NY: Avon, 1973.

Schoeffler, O.E., and William Gale. *Esquire's Encyclopedia of 20th Century Men's Fashions*. NY: McGraw-Hill Co., 1973.

Wilhelm, Maria. "With Fan Clubs Lifting Off Like Patriot Missiles, NBC's Arthur of Arabia is the New Rising Star in the Gulf." *People* 18 Feb. 1991: 98-100, 105.

Filmography

Year	Title	Director	Costume Designer
1912	*The Old Reporter*	E.J. Montagne	
1914	*Making a Living or A Busted Johnny*	Mack Sennett	
1916	*His Picture in the Papers*	John Emerson	
1929	*Big News*	Gregory LaCava	
1931	*Front Page*	Lewis Milestone	
1932	*Is My Face Red?*	William Setter	
1932	*Roadhouse Murder*	J. Walter Ruben	
1933	*Headline Shooter*	Otto Brower	
1933	*I Cover the Waterfront*	James Cruze	
1934	*It Happened One Night*	Frank Capra	Robert Kallock
1936	*Bride Comes Home*	Wesley Ruggles	
1936	*Libeled Lady*	Jack Conway	Dolly Tree
1936	*Mr. Deeds Goes to Town*	Frank Capra	Samuel Lange
1936	*Next Time We Love*	Edward H. Griffith	Vera West
1936	*Wedding Present*	Richard Wallace	
1937	*I Cover the War*	Arthur Lubin	
1937	*Last Train from Madrid*	James Hogan	
1937	*They Wanted to Marry*	Lew Landers	Edward Stevenson
1939	*Cafe Society*	Edward H. Griffith	

1939	*Stanley and Livingstone*	Henry King	Royer
1940	*Arise, My Love*	Mitchell Leisen	
1940	*Foreign Correspondent*	Alfred Hitchcock	I. Magnin
1940	*Philadelphia Story*	George Cukor	Adrian
1942	*Berlin Correspondent*	Eugene Fords	
1942	*Woman of the Year*	George Stevens	Adrian
1943	*Guadalcanal Diary*	Lewis Seller	
1944	*It Happened Tomorrow*	Rene Clair	
1944	*Passage to Marseille*	Michael Curtiz	Leah Rhodes
1945	*Objective Burma*	Raoul Walsh	
1948	*Big Clock*	John Farrow	Edith Head
1948	*Call Northside 777*	Henry Hathaway	Kay Nelson
1948	*Conspiracy in Tehran*	William Freshman	
1948	*State of the Union*	Frank Capra	Irene
1952	*Deadline—U.S.A.*	Richard Brooks	Eloise Jenssen Charles LeMaire
1956	*You Can't Run Away From It*	Dick Powell	Jean Louis
1968	*Green Berets*	John Wayne	Jerry Alpert
1974	*Front Page*	Billy Wilder	Burton Miller
1974	*Parallax View*	Alan J. Pakula	Frank Thompson
1976	*All the President's Men*	Alan J. Pakula	
1978	*Superman*	Richard Donner	Yvonne Blake, Barney's
1979	*China Syndrome*	James Bridges	Donfeld
1979	*Electric Horseman*	Sidney Pollack	Bernie Pollack
1981	*Absence of Malice*	Sidney Pollack	
1982	*Missing*	Costa-Gavras	Joe I. Tompkins
1983	*Under Fire*	Roger Spottiswoode	Cynthia Bales
1984	*Killing Fields*	Roland Joffe	
1985	*Mean Season*	Phillip Borsos	Julie Weiss Linda Benedict
1986	*Broadcast News*	James Brooks	Molly Maginnis
1986	*Salvador*	Oliver Stone	Kathryn Greko Morrison
1987	*Full Metal Jacket*	Stanley Kubrick	Keith Denny
1987	*Street Smart*	Jerry Scatzberg	Jo Ynocenio
1988	*Switching Channels*	Ted Kotcheff	Mary McLeod

You Are What You Wear:
The Role of Western Costume in Film
Philip Skerry and Brenda Berstler

The opening segment of the David Miller/Kirk Douglas film *Lonely are the Brave* crystallizes the concerns of the following study of Western costume. The film begins with a long shot of a Western range. The camera pans to the left to reveal a campfire and then moves slowly to the right, showing a pair of boots on a reclining figure. The camera slowly pans the length of this figure and comes to rest on his head, propped on his saddle, his hat covering his face. The cowboy is smoking. At this point, the audience hears a noise that at first is unidentifiable, but soon reveals itself as the scream of a jet engine. The cowboy looks up, and the audience sees what he sees: the smoky trail of a jet plane roaring across the sky. The audience immediately becomes disoriented in time since the setting and costume have served to point it toward a "traditional" Western film. This scene's effectiveness is accomplished mainly through subverting audience expectation of the film's story based on an interpretation of the meaning of the Western costume. The costume communicates one idea, but the jet plane communicates another. In effect, the meaning of the costume changes as the scene develops.

As Cumming and Ribeiro point out in *A Visual History of the Costume*, "Personal adornment is one of the most immediate forms of communication" (12). The ways Western costumes communicate have made themselves felt not only in the Western genre but in non-Westerns as well. For the following discussion, we should like to examine the ways selected films use Western costumes to add dimension and resonance to their themes.

I

It is possible to consider Western costume as a kind of sign, using the terms of semiology. The logician Charles Sanders Peirce devised a taxonomy that classified signs; one aspect of this taxonomy is what Peirce called "the second trichotomy of signs," which classifies a sign into an icon, index or symbol. Of the three, the index is the most accurate term to describe the role of the Western costume, the index being a sign that creates an existential connection between itself and its object. Peirce states, "I see a man with a rolling gait. This is a probable indicator that he is a sailor. I see a bowlegged man in corduroy, gaiters, and a jacket. These are probable indicators that he is a jockey or something of the sort" (Wollen 122-123). In relation to *Lonely Are the Brave*, one might say, using Peirce's style, "I see a man on a Western plain wearing a cowboy hat and cowboy boots. These are a probable indicator that he is a cowboy and that the film is a Western." The key idea here is that a connection exists between the signifier and the signified that goes beyond mere resemblance (icon) but that is not totally arbitrary (the symbol). In this sense, Western costume is similar to Eisenstein's theory of "typage," which he developed from his ideas about the *commedia dell' arte*, with its seven stock types, immediately identifiable through audience conditioning (Leyda 9).

The traditional (or classic) Western depends to a great extent upon the immediately identifiable aspects of Western costume, which provide for the audience indices that are frequently as fixed and immutable as those of the *commedia dell' arte*. John Ford's *Stagecoach*, for example, with its eight stock characters, identifiable partly by their costumes, is a veritable *commedia dell' arte* of the Western: Doc Boone, the drunken, well-educated doctor; Dallas, the whore with the heart of gold; Hatfield, the Byronic gambler; Mrs. Mallory, the upper class snob; Curly, the reliable sheriff; Buck, the clownish sidekick; Peacock, the Eastern dude; and Gatewood, the corrupt banker/businessman; and of course, the Ringo Kid, the outlaw hero. All of these characters are immediately identifiable through the costumes they wear. A vivid example of this immediacy is the scene in which we first see Dallas being "escorted" out of town by the outraged ladies of the Law and Order League of Tonto. Dallas' "saloon girl" gaudiness contrasts sharply to the severe bonnets and dresses of the outraged women of the law and Order League. Gatewood, too, reflects in his costume the role of the respected town businessman, whose hypocrisy we discover later on in the film, an hypocrisy underscored and amplified by the contrast between the respected costume of the businessman and the thievery and corruption of the person hiding *behind* that costume.

A significant aspect of costume as index in the Western film is that Westerns are actually morality plays in which the forces of good and evil do battle. Even as early as *The Great Train Robbery*, the audience witnesses good triumphing over evil as the train robbers are caught with the loot. What makes the Western a complex morality play, however, is that the conflict between good and evil is played out in the context of a national epic: the trek west and the defining of a national identity. Hence, the traditional color symbolism of white and black, signifying good and evil, becomes associated with the moral positions of the hero and villain. But these moral positions are imbedded in additional layers of meaning connected to the Western as epic. These layers are frequently expressed as bipolars: civilization vs. wilderness; technology vs. nature; machines vs. animal; Indians vs. whites; survival of fittest vs. law and order; homesteader vs. rancher. The meaning of Western costumes, then, is almost always contingent upon the interplay between the epic and moral configurations of a particular Western film.

The interplay of epic and morality play functions in the Western costume as index of the bifurcation between town and frontier. Characters who function in the *place* of the town are frequently dressed differently than the characters who belong in the *space* of the frontier. Townspeople, for example, especially town officials and businessmen, frequently wear formal attire, such as buttoned frock coats and matching trousers, ties and buttoned vests. They don't usually sport guns; if these characters do have guns, the weapons are usually concealed, such as the vest or boot derringer. Frontier characters, on the other hand, usually wear Stetsons, neckerchiefs, open-collared shirts and unbuttoned vests, dungarees or chaps, boots, spurs, and the ubiquitous six-shooter, slung low on a cartridge belt. Such characters are intimately associated with their horses, since the horse is the means of traveling the large distances of the frontier, range, or plains. In *Stagecoach*, for example, Doc Boone, Gatewood, and Peacock clearly belong to the town; Curly, Buck and the Ringo Kid, to the frontier. In fact the Ringo Kid is intimately associated with the *space* of the frontier, for he is picked up by the stagecoach, not in town, but rather on the range where his costume seems adapted to the outdoor spaces of the frontier. Sitting within the coach, Ringo seems misplaced; it is more natural for him to ride on top, in the open space of the coach, than in the coach itself, where characters associated with the town ride. In fact, when the Indian attack occurs, Ringo immediately assumes his rightful position outside the coach and helps fight off the attack. The townspeople's outfits, conversely, seem more suited (no pun intended) to the restrictions of civilized *place*. One such character—Hatfield, the gambler—presents a special use of costume in the traditional Western. Frequently, gambler's costumes have a flashy, self-conscious gaudiness about them, emblemizing the gambler's trafficking in money and more importantly in illusion. For the gambler is frequently not what he appears to be; like Melville's "Confidence Man," the gambler plays on people's inability to distinguish appearance from reality. Beneath the surface is a reptilian coldness and deadliness; behind the vest or within the fancy boot lies a derringer waiting to strike out at an unlucky victim. In *Stagecoach*, Hatfield's costume, complete with cape and cane, gives him a kind of antebellum appearance; and his exaggerated, obsequious, and courtly manner towards the effete Mrs. Mallory belies the deadly coldness of his character.

In a related way, those characters who represent civilization (farmers, "sodbusters"), even though they may live on the fringes of the frontier, or on the border between town and frontier, dress differently than the cowboys (good or bad guys) who inhabit the wide-open spaces of the range. John Ford's later Westerns again are exemplary in their use of costume as index. Ford's lawmen frequently express through their costume the ambivalent role they play in his films, for these sheriffs and marshals frequently blend frock coat with six-gun, bandannas with store-bought breeches, to suggest their roles as arbiter between town and frontier. Wyatt Earp in *My Darling Clementine* first appears in cowboy dress in the beginning of the film. Yet after his brother James is killed by the ruthless Clanton family, Wyatt becomes marshal of Tombstone and thus dons the more formal attire associated with that position. In the memorable church dedication scene, Wyatt wears the frock coat and string-tie of a town official as he performs the civilized ritual of formal dance with Clementine. In like manner, the Reverend-Captain Clayton in John Ford's *The Searchers* wears a bizarre combination of top hat, bandanna, frock coat and dust jacket to suggest the ambivalence of his role as lawman *and* preacher.

George Steven's *Shane*, like *Stagecoach*, presents characters whose costumes underscore the themes of the film. Shane first appears on horseback, riding out of the space of the mountains and into the place of the Starret ranch. His role of Western knight-errant is highlighted by his Western garb of fringed buckskin and low-slung six-gun. This outfit seems to take on magical and epic dimensions, for when he removes the outfit, he seems bereft of power. For instance, Shane seems somehow shorn of power when he first appears in "sodbuster" clothes while he is in town picking up supplies for the Starrets. Shane is immediately typed by the toughs in the bar as a hated homesteader who will fence off valuable grazing land. He is humiliated by Chris, who throws whiskey on Shane's shirt, symbolically staining the outfit of the homesteader. Later in the film, Shane dons his magically charged fringed buckskin, his hat and his gun belt to do battle with the evil gunslinger Wilson and the Stryker Bros. He thus saves the Starrets, while getting wounded symbolically, at the same time as he redeems his image of himself as a hero, a point Robert Warshow makes in his essay on the Western. The act of putting on a costume contributes to the legendary quality of the Western as epic; the act connects the Western hero with an heroic past and identity. Even in Western spoofs like *Cat Ballou*, the transformation of Kid Shalleen from drunkard to gunfighter is accomplished through the ritual of putting on a costume.

In classic Westerns like *Shane* and *Stagecoach*, the "bad guys" usually have distinctive dress that sets them apart from the "good guys" in the film. The trend towards highly stylized dress for the hero and villain began early in the evolution of the Western film. As the Western developed its shape as a purveyor of America's national epic, costume provided immediately recognizable moral and epic indices for characters. In the classic Western, which developed during the forging of America as a world power, white becomes associated with the forces of good in the morality play of the Western. In epic terms, the heroic represents those facets of the American character that make up a national identity: individuality, personal courage, integrity, sympathy for the "little guy," and democratic values. The villain represents the perversion of these values; although he might be courageous, the "bad guy" is bad because his courage is used to further his own selfish ends, or those of the people who employ him, usually wealthy, "aristocratic" landowners. As the western evolved into a film genre, the dress of both hero and villain became more stylized. Television Westerns further encoded the costume stereotypes that had begun earlier in the Saturday matinees and Western serials.

Yet not all Western films employed costuming in this obvious way. In Ford's *Stagecoach* and *My Darling Clementine*, the villains are identified more through what they do than through what they wear. In *Stagecoach*, the Plummer Brothers, whom Ringo meets in Lordsburg for the final shootout, certainly look menacing, but their outfits are not really distinctive. The same can be said for the Clantons in *My Darling Clementine*. In *Shane*, however, the evil gunfighter Wilson looks very much the role of the hired killer, with his black hat, dark clothing, and reptilian movements. As it turns out, the Westerns made in the 1950s seem pivotal in the development of the villain's costume, especially that worn by the "hired gun," or professional killer. It is the recognition of clearly identifiable clothing for the hero and the villain that would later be employed in ironic or revisionist Westerns, especially in the "spaghetti westerns" of Sergio Leone, in which the anti-hero, the "Man with No Name," dresses very much like the villain of the classic Western. Conversely, the villain appears to be a hero. This subverting of audience expectation is used brilliantly in Leone's *Once Upon a Time in the West*. Henry Fonda, identified in the audience's mind with heroic characters, plays the villain, Frank, who dresses like a traditional Western hero but who guns down an entire family.

II

It is when irony takes place in the Western film that costume takes on a more complex role, for the interplay between epic and morality play becomes complex. Martin Ritt's *Hombre*, for instance, is a revisionist Western, in one sense, because it, like *Lonely are the Brave*, gives additional meaning to costume by deliberately violating audience conditioning to a continuum between epic and morality play. Ritt's film revisits Ford's *Stagecoach* 30 years later, during a time when Americans were examining their guilty consciences concerning mistreatment of Indians and reevaluating their attitudes toward a national identity. In *Stagecoach*, Geronimo is simply a plot device to add suspense to Ringo Kid's journey of vengeance. In *Hombre*, though, the outlaw hero John Russell becomes a kind of deconstruction of the Ringo Kid; in parts of the film, Russell dresses like a cowboy, but he is actually an Indian by upbringing. An early shot in the film, for example, features a tight close-up of Russell's face. He appears to be an Indian because of his braided hair and headband. This apparent identity, though, is subverted by his Anglo looks, including deep-blue eyes. Unlike Ringo, he does not fight Indians; he *is* an

Indian. Unlike Ringo, he does not get the girl and his freedom at the end; instead he dies protecting his white coach mates. His outcast state and his Christlike sacrifice at the end provide a commentary on the injustices done to Native Americans by the white imperialist/capitalist class, symbolized by Gil Favor, the crooked Indian agent, himself a reworking of *Stagecoach's* corrupt banker Gatewood. Both characters wear the frock coat, trousers, vest and ties of characters identified by affiliation with the town rather than the frontier.

The difference between the two films, in fact, says a great deal about the way the Western changed over 30 years. In *Stagecoach*, Gatewood's hypocrisy is highlighted by his costume. The moral paradox of his action—the respectable banker who absconds with the bank's receipts—is developed through the audience's realization that Gatewood is indeed not what he appears to be. Ford thus uses costume as a traditional moral index. *Hombre*, though, adds a social commentary to the moral index by presenting Gil Favor not as a banker but as an Indian agent who steals money that was originally intended to go to the Indians on the reservation. Thus Favor's moral corruption is intensified and deepened since he has not only stolen, thus violating the moral trust of society, but he has stolen from the Indians, who are thus doubly victimized. The ironic, or revisionist, Western, typified by films like *Hombre*, adds additional meaning to Western costume.

Ford's *Stagecoach* creates a dichotomy between town and frontier in order to establish the epic notion that the unspoiled characters of the frontier represent the goodness of nature and that the jaded and intolerant characters of the town represent the limitations of civilization. The revisionist Western adds additional meaning to the indices of Western costumes by suggesting that the epic ideals of the Western frontier have somehow been lost or perverted, or perhaps have never really existed at all. *Hombre* presents its viewers with the paradox that Indians, the traditional savages/villains of the classic Western, represent the true ideals of the space of the frontier and that white men, even those dressed like traditional Western heroes, are nothing more than the corruption of civilization imposing itself on nature. In this way, the morality play's axes of meaning shift as the questioning of the American epic becomes increasing critical and revisionist.

III

Other revisionist Westerns use the setting of the contemporary West and the costume of the traditional cowboy to comment on the loss of traditional cowboy values. In *Lonely Are the Brave*, for example, Jack Burns tries to be a "traditional" cowboy in the contemporary West. In a scene reminiscent of the opening of *Shane*, Burns rides in from the open range to the "homestead" of his friend Paul, who, it turns out, is in need of help. Unlike Shane, though, Burns finds himself in the modern West, which has been disfigured and corrupted by industrialization and commercialization; there's no place for Burns, a "real" cowboy, in this ugly, sterile, depersonalized world. We first see Burns' estrangement from the contemporary West when he encounters the wire fence of a power company, which has carved up the wide-open range for profit. Burns cuts the fence and enters an alien territory of freeways, gas stations, junk yards–and the ubiquitous automobile. In a scene that prefigures Burns' ignominious end on a rainy highway, he tries to cross the freeway, but his horse Whiskey panics at the sound and confusion of the roadway. Jack barely escapes, but his days are numbered, for it turns out that in the "modern" West, one does not have an identity unless one carries an identification card of some type, but Jack's identity is reflected in his costume—shirt, cowboy hat, boots. In the contemporary West, though, these, alas, are not enough to ensure identity. In fact, this costume subjects the wearer to harassment and unmotivated aggression, borne out by Jack's being viciously attacked by the one-armed man in the Mexican bar. The film culminates in a bizarre chase through the mountains as Jack tries to "escape" into the free spaces of the frontier, much the way the Ringo Kidd escapes in *Stagecoach*. However, the epic frontier of Ford's film no longer exists in the contemporary West. Jack is run down, as he attempts to escape into the illusory frontier, by a toilet-hauling semi, a blatant symbol of the mechanization of modern life.

In a related way, Sonny Steel in *Electric Horseman* is exploited by a cereal company, which is emblematic of the bastardization and corruption by big business of our traditional Western values of individualism and integrity. The glittering, garish costume of steel is a mocking commentary on how we desecrate out heritage in order to sell "things." And Steel's constant inebriation is a moral reflection of his self-hatred in betraying the "ideals" of the Western epic.

Joe Buck in *Midnight Cowboy* is also a pathetic imitation of the western epic. Unlike Jack Burns or Sonny Steele, Joe Buck has nothing truly Western about him; he lacks the integrity and honor that have always been aspects of the Western hero. The film begins with a white-out and slowly zooms back from a blank drive-in screen while the sound track mysteriously plays the ghost-like sounds of a cowboy and Indian fight. Next we see Joe Buck donning Western garb with intercuts of Joe's co-workers from the restaurant asking, "Where is that Joe Buck?" The question reverberates, like the evanescent sounds of cowboys and Indians on the soundtrack, as the meaning of the question becomes clear. In the contemporary West, there are no heroes—only cheap imitations, or only movie cowboys. It is significant that Joe's journey in the film is from West to East, a reversal of the epic movement that created heroes for the Western morality play.

IV

In the revisionist and ironic Western, costume therefore comes very close to Peirce's notion of the symbol; the role of accoutrement serves to emblemize the loss of national identity and ideals. In the more bitter revisionist Westerns like *Little Big Man*, costume symbolizes the lies that underlay the Western epic. In effect such films become reverse morality plays, with good and evil changing places. Jack Crabbe's retrospective narration turns traditional Western mythology on its head. The dandified Custer, constantly primping and posing, a parody of the cavalry heroes of John Ford, is in reality a psychopathic megalomaniac. Other Western heroes, like Wild Bill Hickock and Buffalo Bill Cody, are also exposed as neurotics or environmental terrorists. One memorable shot shows Buffalo Bill riding along with thousands of buffalo hides stacked high. The view had a mental picture of the thousands of rotting carcasses littering the plains, carcasses that could have been utilized by the Indians. Jack Crabbe, himself, goes through a catalogue of traditional Western dress, from gun fighter to drunk, as if to provide an ironic backdrop for the subversion of expected connections between costume and character.

In Kevin Costner's *Dances With Wolves*, the reversal of traditional moral values is closely associated with the symbolic function of costume. Lt. John Dunbar symbolically sheds his cavalry blues as he begins to realize that the values of the Sioux nation, typified by Kicking Bird and Wind in His Hair, are superior to the cultural and environmental destructiveness of white society. Throughout the film, costume emblemizes key stages in the evolution of Dunbar. Dunbar first meets Kicking Bird as Dunbar emerges naked from the pool of water near the deserted post. This ritualistic rebirth is accompanied by the gradual exchange of Dunbar's cavalry uniform for the clothing of a Sioux warrior. Dunbar first enters the Sioux camp in full-dress uniform; later he is given the traditional buffalo robe by Kicking Bird; still later he exchanges his cavalry jacket for Wind in His Hair's tribal vest. Finally, Dunbar wears the costume of a Sioux warrior. He becomes a true Sioux when he states after the battle with the Pawnees: "As I heard my Sioux name being called over and over, I knew for the first time who I really was." This discovery of a new Sioux identity is confirmed when Dunbar returns to his outpost for his journal and is mistaken by cavalry members as an Indian. He is brutally beaten but eventually escapes back to the Sioux, his true home.

V

Western costume can also function in non-Western films as well. In other words, the setting of the West disappears, but the costume of the Western appears in unexpected places. The Western costume is usually employed in these films to make a moral comment, the significance of which extends beyond the meaning of the West itself to include American values. Wim Wenders' *The*

American Friend takes great liberties with its novel source, Patricia Highsmith's *Ripley's Game*. In Highsmith's novel, Ripley is an urbane, but amoral, American living in Paris. But Wenders makes his Tom Ripley an ersatz cowboy, a satire on the American character and on the corruption of Europe by American commercialism and vulgarity. Ripley, sporting an anomalous cowboy hat and a pair of boots, draws the German framemaker, Bruno, into his nefarious plot to kill an international gangster. Bruno, suffering from a rare and incurable blood disease and thus eager for money to care for his family after his death, is easy prey for Ripley and agrees to do the killing. Wenders transforms Highsmith's novel about an American expatriate into a metaphorical condemnation of the American character and of American popular culture, shaped by the anarchical trek West and thus still searching for imperialist frontiers. In the same way, in Stanley Kubrick's *Dr. Strangelove*, Major Kong dons his cowboy hat when the bomber receives the "go code" to initiate an atomic attack. Kubrick's black comedy thus equates the suicidal and maniacal thrust of America's "nuclear deterrence" with the violent nature of the traditional Western character, symbolized by Kong's cowboy hat.

VI

As the Western film has evolved, so has the role and meaning of the Western costume changed. The shifting relationships between morality play and national epic enable the Western to reflect moral, political, and historical attitudes. Costumes are intimately connected to such attitudes. Cowboy garb has entered popular culture consciousness in much the same way as, say, the costumes of the Frankenstein monster and Count Dracula have become imbedded in sitcoms ("The Munsters") cereals (Frankenberry) and public television (The count in "Sesame Street"). The major difference, though, between these obvious iconic signs and the indexes and symbols of Western costume is that the Western, whether alive or dead as a genre, has been our great national epic, our *Odyssey* and *Iliad*, and we cannot escape the great trek West and its moral meaning in our lives.

Works Cited

Cumming, Valerie and Aileen Ribeiro. *A Visual History of the Costume*. London: B.T. Batsford, 1989.

Highsmith, Patricia. *Ripley's Game*.

Leyda, Jay. *Kino, A History of the Russian and Soviet Film*. NY: Collier Books, 1960.

Wollen, Peter. *Signs and Meaning in the Cinema*. 3rd ed. Bloomington: Indiana UP, 1972.

Selected Filmography

Year	Title	Director
1903	*The Great Train Robbery*	Edwin S. Porter
1939	*Stagecoach*	John Ford
1946	*My Darling Clementine*	John Ford
1953	*Shane*	George Stevens
1956	*The Searchers*	John Ford
1962	*Lonely Are the Brave*	David Miller
1964	*Dr. Strangelove*	Stanley Kubrick
1965	*Cat Ballou*	Elliot Silverstein
1967	*Fistfull of Dollars*	Sergio Leone
1967	*Hombre*	Martin Ritt
1968	*Once Upon a Time in the West*	Sergio Leone
1969	*Midnight Cowboy*	John Schlessinger
1970	*Little Big Man*	Arthur Penn
1979	*The Electric Horseman*	Sidney Pollack
1982	*The American Friend*	Wim Wenders
1991	*Dances With Wolves*	Kevin Costner

Art and Media

Desperately Seeking Meaning: "Personals" in American Popular

Linda K. Fuller

It is a rare and wondrous occurrence when we cinema scholars can point to a particular aspect of a particular movie in a particular year and claim that its star(s), or its director(s), or its underlying theme(s), or event(s), or some part(s) of it serves as a benchmark for studying the symbiosis between film and the popular culture.

Desperately Seeking Susan neatly fits this epiphany. When Susan Siedelman's surprise hit appeared in 1985, no one could have predicted that a sweet, silly PG-rated story about a bored woman who enlivens her life by following the personal love columns would have earned rave reviews and box office notice. Even though Madonna played a major role in the film, her appearance in it pre-dated what would become her later, legendary popularity. For our purposes is the more relevant consideration that *Desperately Seeking Susan* treated the personals in film not from the perspective of a sexual connotation, but as a means for finding excitement, companionship, acceptance of self.

Recall: 1985 just about pinpoints when the media was discovering AIDS as a valuable news story. It was no accident that self-advertisement personals became more "safe-sex" oriented around this time, both in the newspaper and magazine columns and also in film. This essay attempts to document the phenomenon of the personals historically, economically, and psycho-sociologically in their context as media mirrors.

Personals

Known as "the agony column," the personals were for a long time featured on the front pages of the London *Times* in the 19th century (Harkison 196). In the early days of this country, mail-order brides and matchmakers were commonplace means of arranging companionship. Yet, mainstream print media has been slow to incorporate them. While the personals have appeared as a staple of alternative publications like *The Village Voice* for more than a half-century, it is only within this last decade or so that they have become a more acceptable, more frequent means for meeting people of similar interest.

"In the middle of the social ferment of the 1960s and the self-actualization movements of the seventies, personal ads started making a comeback," writes

Susan Block in her book *Advertising for Love: How to Play the Personals* (29). "With skyrocketing divorce rates and fewer opportunities to find mates within the traditional church and small-town social structures, people had to start making matches for themselves. Gradually, the socially stigmatized 'advertising for it' become transformed into an acceptable way to find new friends."

Labelling the personals "an odd and compact art form, and somewhat unnatural...like haiku of self-celebration," essayist Lance Morrow has observed, "The sociology of personals has changed in recent years. One reason that people still feel uncomfortable with the form is that during the 1960s and early 1970s, personal ads had a slightly sleazy connotation. They showed up in the back of underground magazines and sex magazines, the little billboards through which wife swappers and odd sexual specialists communicated. In the past few years, however, personal ads have become a popular and reputable way of shopping for new relationships" (Morrow 74). Citing a dramatic increase in the number of singles in today's society, Steinfirst and Moran state:

In the 1980s, when leisure time is at a premium for today's working young people, personal ads have become an acceptable and comfortable alternative to the conventional methods of meeting persons (generally) of the opposite sex. Instead of going to a singles' bar or arranging for a blind date, individuals, both male and female, can compose an advertisement describing themselves and their desires and sit back and wait for a response. (129)

As of about the mid-1980s, emphasis in those descriptions has been less on seeking sex, more on seeking traditional, long-time relationships. *Advertising Age* claims the personals have gained new respectability because of our "efficiency-minded" times: "Readers and advertisers reply to whom they choose; cool selectivity is the name of the game" (Wallach 44).

By their nature, of course," writes media critic Caryn James, "personals reflect not only the writer's sense of humor, but also how he or she wants to be seen" (C19). D. Keith Mano has called the personals columns:

sub-pornographic: voyeur and exhibitionist maintain their anonymity. And their control. Society has discouraged perversion by isolating it. Personal columns unstring our social fabric by allowing isolated men and women to find each other without risk across a wide circulation. (52)

Whether they represent an escape into the fantasy world, a symptomatic undercurrent of loneliness in the United States, and/or "the natural outlet of the discreet, the sincere and the sensitive, all seeking kindred spirits for meaningful relationships" ("TLC" 65), the personals increasingly spell economic success. Although there are wide variations on censorship and taboos, the overwhelming majority of outlets for classified love advertisements—including print, telephone and computer dating services—find them extremely lucrative. More and more mainstream sources are including the personals, even upscale publications like *The Washington Post, New York* magazine, *The Chicago Tribune, The New York Review of Books, National Review,* even *The Law Journal* (Margolick B5). Clearly, personals are no longer simply the province of the raincoat trade.

Elizabeth C. Hirschman, a professor of marketing at New York University, reported on a "People as Products" study using the personals as examples of marketing exchange. While location (New York and Washington) didn't appear to make a difference, she found men more frequently seeking physical attractiveness resources from women, offering monetary resources in exchange, while women were the reverse: seeking monetary resources and offering physical attractiveness.

Calling personal advertising "the quintessential free-market instrument," an offshoot of yuppie pragmatism, D. Keith Mano considers personal advertising "a class phenomenon. Historically the middle and upper middle classes brokered their passion. Now they have to act as both agent and flack. Blue-collar people have a greater sense of either insecurity or shame" (52). Geoffrey Sheridan talks of how the lonely hearts search breaks traditional barriers of relationship testing:

You *know* that your contact is available (generally speaking). You *have* to be personal, even if you are in the habit of keeping up a front, of image-making... You meet as equals, and the compulsion to be open means that no holds are barred on the questions that can be asked. It can make for an unusual intimacy. (22)

In addition to the fact that a number of current books deal with the topic of the personals,[1] they have also been the subject of *New Yorker* cartoons, newspaper editorials, academic studies, stand-up comedians' fodder, and, as well next be discussed, a number of motion pictures. Caryn James has pointed out how a number of the words used in personal advertisements also reflect the movies (C19). Whereas the film *Desperately Seeking Susan* stole from the personals, advertisers often use expressions and names like Indiana Jones, Vicki Vale, Peter Pan, Valmont, the Bear, Woody Allen, Harry wanting to meet Sally, or someone wanting to *Cross Delancey,* join a *Dead Poets Society,* or get *A Little Mermaid.*

The Personals in Film

Although the personals may have appeared in movies prior to Leonard Kastle's *The Honeymoon Killers* of 1970, it marked the first filmic convention in which the personals figured prominently in a plot. Based on a 1947 true crime story about two lovers who became known as the "Lonely Hearts

Killers," who befriended and then murdered more than a dozen vulnerable women, they were an odd couple: he (Raymond Fernandez) is described as a sleazy grifter, she (Martha Beck) an overweight nymphomaniac. They met through the personals. Coming with a warning that this film is not for the squeamish, it is described as "simultaneously a love story gone terribly wrong and a tale of murder for profit, showing how the pair preyed on gullible widows (he married them for their assets and, with her help, murdered them). Tony LoBianco and Shirley Stoler play the pair (who were convicted of murder and executed at Sing Sing prison in 1951) as victims of romantic delusion—self-styled star-crossed lovers driven to hideous extremes to preserve their passion—without excusing the viciousness of their crimes" (McDonagh 22-23).

Still, it wasn't until the 1980s that a rash of personals-related movies appeared. In 1982 came the riotous film noir *Eating Raoul*. Co-written, directed and starred in by Paul Bartel, it was a low budget film that drew an audience to what became something a cult classic. The story centers around Paul and Mary Bland—who, as we meet them, live up to their name. In the midst of wild parties all around their Hollywood apartment, we see a sedate, happily married couple who work by day (he in a liquor store, as a wine connoisseur, she as a nurse), and at night talk of their dream about opening a country restaurant, before they retire in similar pajamas, to separate beds. When a soused swinger from down the hall inadvertently enters the Bland's place and attempts to attack Mary, Paul hits him over the head with a frying pan. They soon find out that the would-be rapist is not only dead, but is rich. The Blands keep his money, call in their banker for a loan toward their dream, and decide to get the rest of the cash they need by collapsing their morals and advertising kinky sex through the personals. "We do anything...whatever your fantasy," the lure reads. Call the number, set up a date and time, and come to our place—with cash. The first victim wants to be disciplined by a mommy, another comes dressed as a Nazi and wants to be tied up. Paul and Mary then begin to worry about being robbed, and call in Raoul's Lock Service. It turns out that Raoul himself had seen their ad. He confesses to considering answering it, but when he discovers their plan, wants a deal in exchange for his knowledge: he gets cash for bodies at Doggie King, a burger joint, and wants the cadavers. Through a number of amusing contrivances, the couple eventually manages to murder Raoul, then decide to grind him up to serve as "something special" for their banker. It's a Mexican dish, and they gloat on the compliments: "It's amazing what you can do with a cheap piece of meat."

Sex was also being advertised in the personals in 1983s teen comedy sensation *Risky Business*. A clean-cut teen who's only thinking about getting into Princeton, played by Tom Cruise (Joel), is entrusted with the house while his parents are off on vacation. As a lark, his friends respond to an ad that reads,

"For a good time in the privacy of your home, call Jackie," and have a hooker sent over to him. The door bell disturbs Joel and his homework: "She" is a black transvestite who charges $75, but reconsiders that Lana would be better under the circumstances—"It's what every white boy off the lake wants." Forget concentrating on homework; instead, Joel begins studying the personals, and of course ends up calling Lana. She charges $300, which he can't afford, but the two end up with a crazy scheme of inviting over his friends and her friends, and make $8,000 in one wild night.

But now we reach mid-decade, and the personals theme changes. Classified self-advertisements begin a gain in both actual and movie popularity and presence. Their content in both also changes. *Desperately Seeing Susan* is unquestionably the ultimate personals film, and the clearest one from which to examine the tenor of the times. Made from the feminist perspective of director Susan Siedelman, its plot has already been delineated: a housewife with ennui (Rosanna Arquette as Roberta) wants to add some excitement to her life, and so follows the personal love columns. We see her in the opening shot, sitting in the beauty parlor, reading the newspaper and startling at the message, "Desperately seeking Susan," signed Jim. She begins following the players, intrigued at first to know what they look like, then what they are up to, and why. Through a number of unlikely plot convolutions involving mobsters, hit men and identity crises, we film viewers are drawn in as voyeurs.

The next year, we also become engrossed in Michael Mann's thriller *Manhunter*, where we're introduced to the psychopathetic psychiatrist Dr. Hannibal ("The Cannibal") Lecter, who later figures in Jonathan Demme's *Silence of the Lambs*. It turns out that the man being hunted is in contact with the jailed Lecter—through the personals. Their codes need to be deciphered for the case to be solved.

Classified Love a 1986 made-for-cable quickie, focuses on three co-workers who decide to improve their social lives by placing ads in a magazine's personals column. Although the movie didn't get wide play, it serves as a representative reminder of how the television film industry is quick to pick up on "in" themes.

The comedy *Perfect Match* (1987) centers on a couple who get their due from falsifying claims about themselves in the personals. Jennifer Edwards is a nice girl, a dreamer, an aestethete—and although she's cute enough, she just doesn't get asked out much on dates. Her best friend reminds her she's 29, and a "mush," too bookish. She suggests the personals. "Do you think I'm low enough to stoop to that?" our heroine exclaims. But a lot of people do it, she's told, and an advertisement with her telephone number is placed. Marc McClure, meanwhile, is a classic couch potato, who's enticed to respond to her message. But each one thinks the other is much more outdoorsy and active than they are. The couple try a number of different sports, like skiing, horseback riding, tennis and hiking—all with disastrous but funny results. Predictably, though, romance blossoms once they discover other, more similar interests.

Part of the primary message more recently in the personals has been the suggestion of their use for finding romance, commonality, a blending of similar interests without the perquisite sexual involvement. Films also began to reflect this trend, graphically demonstrating that the traditional use of self-advertising columns could, in fact get you in trouble. Even murdered.

Witness the 1989 hit *Sea of Love*, where Al Pacino plays the role of a NYPD detective in search of a serial killer whose male victims have all played the personals, seeking members of the opposite sex. While the song of the movie's title plays on the turntable, yet another man's naked body is found, and next to his bedside table are 31 unopened letters responding to his ad. One woman hadn't been able to resist his poetry in the *New York Weekly* ("Silver balloons/endless Junes/old rock tunes/let me put it in your moons"), and tracked him down. "Fate sucks, I swear," she states at the crime scene, balloons in hand. Pacino is Frank Keller, a divorced, degenerating cop of 20+ years, who runs a poetic ad and, with comic relief from a partner played by John Goodman, checks out a number of potential suspects via a rendezvous in a restaurant. One partner talks to the Lonely Hearts respondents, some kinky and some straight, while the other plays waiter, gathering fingerprints from their glasses. Ellen Barkin stars as Helen Cruger, a particularly seductive suspect who arrives at her appointed hour, but gets jumpy and won't stay, saying Pacino has cop's eyes. Yet, he is very attracted to her. They meet later, have a steamy affair, and the tension mounts: is she the killer? Pacino nearly freaks out when he sees a gun in her purse, when he finds out that she subscribed to *Singles Magazine*, when he sees a number of personals plainly pinned to her refrigerator—including some of the victims. Do you already know what happened? There is a pivotal confrontation, followed by a wonderful twist in the crime drama, and we're left wondering what will happen next in the sea of love.

Citing a clear reversal of the romantic optimism in classic screen stories, Caryn James notes a trend toward gimmicky and cynical love stories: "Now, characters often hope for the best and discover the worst" (H1). Such is certainly the case in Woody Allen's *Crimes and Misdemeanors* of 1990. It is only a side story, but Woody's character, ever searching for romantic love, entreats his sister when he hears she got some action on the ad she placed in the personals. What she got was humiliation of the first degree. "I'm a wreck," she confesses, feeling sick and shaking for days. The story then unfolds: he was very attractive. They had gone out on three dates, and he'd never been fresh—a perfect gentleman. When she took him back to her place, he wanted to tie her up to the bed post and tear her dress off. Then he defecated on her. "I'm so lonely,' she sobs. "You don't know what it's like to be alone. My whole life is passing me by. It's so lonely out there." Yet, we certainly can't consider the personals as an option out of loneliness.

This retribution theme also appears in the 1990 made-for-cable *Personals* starring Jennifer O'Neill as Pamela, who develops fatal attractions for the men she meets in the classified columns. A staid librarian named Heather by day, she self-advertises in the *Village Daily*, using as her signature yellow roses— "beautiful and delicate, like women," she claims, but also "thorny and painful," she is reminded by her therapist. One of her victims is a happily married journalist who wants to write a series on loneliness. He places ads for dates, reporting to his wife, "They talk, I listen. So far I've had one fox and one dog. Are they desperate? No, lonely." They are all pictured as vulnerable, with interlocking stories of woman as victim. Heather/Pamela responds to the writer's ad saying he was an attractive married man looking for an uncomplicated sexual relationship with "I am blond, beautiful. Wear the flower." His wife (Stephanie Zimbalist) finds the note and follows him, but too late—for now.

Another film of 1990 deals with the personals, but in yet a different way—as a password to enter a high-priced—"den of inquity," complete with drinks, drugs, bare-breasted beauties, and the implicit message of trouble. Rob Lowe, playing the title character in *Bad Influence*, mutters "Gay white male" once to the bouncer so that he and James Spader can enter. Later, when the latter is trying to get retribution against Lowe, he peruses the personals column of "The Reader" tabloid for the current password: "Fun-loving couple seeks petite wrestling fan." It works, but it inevitably means mayhem.

Most recently, Barbet Schroeder has directed *Single White Female*, a film he labels as a "Hitchcockian relationship of codependency." Positioned as a thriller for late-summer in 1992, it featured Bridget Fonda as a woman desperately seeking a roommate for her New York apartment. She gets more than she bargained for in Jennifer Jason Leigh, who answers the SWF ad, then becomes "dangerously—even murderously" obsessive with her new best friend" ("Entertainment Weekly" 45).

And so, for now, the warnings are there, both in real-life media and in film: watch for and watch out for the personals.

Notes

[1] For example, Mary Higgins Clark's *Loves Music, Loves to Dance* (Simon and Schuster, 1991), John Lutz's *SWF Seeks Same* (St. Martin's, 1990) and Paul Theroux's *Chicago Loop* (Random House, 1991).

Works Cited

Block, Susan. *Advertising for Love: How to Play the Personals*. NY: Quill, 1984.

Harkison, Judy. " 'A Chorus of Groans,' notes Sherlock Holmes."*Smithsonian* Sept. 1987.

Hirschman, Elizabeth C. "People as Products: Analysis of a Compex Marketing Exchange." *Journal of Marketing* 51 (Jan. 1987).

James, Caryn. "Lovelorn hope movies have just the right words." *New York Times* 30 November 1989: C19.

"Love With Improper Strangers." *New York Times* 22 April 1990.

McDonagh. "All About Evil: Capturing killers on film." *Entertainment Weekly* 29 March 1991.

Mano, Keith D. "Getting Personal." *National Review* 31 December 1987.

Margolick, David. "At the Bar." *New York Times* 29 Sept. 1989.

Morrow, Lance. "Advertisements for Oneself." *Time* 2 Sept. 1985.

Sheridan, Geoffrey. "Clever, handsome, witty man seeks." *New Statesman* 15 Aug. 1986.

Steinfirst, Susan and Barbara B. Moran. "The New Mating Game: Matchmaking Via the Personal Columns in the 1980s." *Journal of Popular Culture* 22:4 (Spring, 1989).

"Summer Preview." *Entertainment Weekly* 22 May 1992.

"TLC for DWMs and SWFs: Classified love ads are a booming business." *Time* 10 January 1983.

Wallach, Van. "Monitoring the personal touch." *Advertising Age* 25 July 1985.

Filmography

Year	Film	Director
1970	*The Honeymoon Killers*	Leonard Kastle
1982	*Eating Raoul*	Paul Bartel
1983	*Risky Business*	Paul Brickman
1985	*Desperately Seeking Susan*	Susan Siedelman
1986	*Manhunter*	Michael Mann
1986	*Classified Love*	Made-for-cable television
1987	*Perfect Match*	Mark Deimel
1989	*Sea of Love*	Harold Becker
1990	*Crimes and Misdemeanor*	Woody Allen
1990	*Personals*	Steven H. Stern
1990	*Bad Influence*	Curtis Hanson
1992	*Single White Female*	Barbet Schroeder

"Saying It With Pictures":
Alfred Hitchcock and Painterly Images in *Psycho*

Erik S. Lunde and Douglas A. Noverr

Throughout his adult life, Alfred Hitchcock was a collector: he collected fine wines, good books, tidbits of gossip, and, most significantly, works of art. From the time of his youth,when he took classes in drawing and painting at the University of London, Hitchcock nurtured a deep appreciation and love of fine arts; according to biographers John Russell Taylor and Donald Spoto, Hitchcock, once he achieved wealth, gradually purchased a small but important collection of paintings, including paintings by his favorite artist, Paul Klee (Taylor 20, 142). One must recall that in his years of apprenticeship in filmmaking at the Famous Players-Lasky (Paramount) in London in the early 1920s, Hitchcock was first employed as a designer of title cards and subsequently as an art director (Spoto, *The Dark Side* 59). Indeed, he was first hired on the basis of a portfolio of drawings he presented at the studio in 1920. In his catalogue of notable art directors and production designers in film history, Elliott Stein includes Alfred Hitchcock. When he achieved celebrity status some years later, Hitchcock drew a silhouette of himself that became justifiably famous. And as he matured as a filmmaker, he depended heavily on storyboards, composed by himself at first and later by others. This great interest in the fine arts strengthened the cinematic vision displayed in countless brilliantly conceived photographic images in his films, but his films were also permeated with quite specific visual references to paintings and statues placed in his sets. In this fashion, Hitchcock transformed homes, resorts, and even business offices into virtual mini-museums, displaying all kinds of art, from sculpture, to prints, to photographs, to paintings. Hence, in such films as the much underrated *Rope* (1948), the paintings on the walls of the main set, a large urban apartment, reinforce themes of life and death so central to the story. In the masterwork *Vertigo* (1958), the hero Scottie (James Stewart) becomes obsessed by a beautiful portrait of the legendary figure of the past, Carlotta, a painting he has seen the heroine Madeleine (Kim Novak) admiring at the Palace of the Legion of Honor in San Francisco. During the making of *Spellbound* (1945), Hitchcock utilized the services of the world renowned artist Salvador Dali to create the sets for the famous dream sequence in the film. Nowhere do the print and painterly images have a more direct impact on the thematic content of the story than in Hitchcock's masterwork, *Psycho* (1960). In this film, Hitchcock, with the aid of art director George Milo and set decorators Joseph Hurley and Robert Clatworthy, brilliantly integrates the static images of paintings and statues with the dynamic images of the cinema.

Psycho, based on Robert Bloch's 1959 novel and on Joseph Stefano's fine screenplay, relates the story of a young woman, Marion Crane (Janet Leigh), who in her late twenties feels a desperate need to escape the entrapment of a life confined to the position of a secretary in a Phoenix, Arizona real estate firm where, under her boss Mr. Lowery (Vaughn Taylor), she has labored for ten years with no hope of advancement. She pins her dream of private fulfillment on marriage to her divorced boyfriend, Sam Loomis (John Gavin), who also feels imprisoned in an economically insecure position as the owner of a less than prosperous hardware store in a northern California town called Fairvale. On a Friday afternoon in December, after a rendezvous with her lover in a downtown hotel, Marion, acting on an irrational impulse, steals $40,000 from a client of the firm, a Mr. Cassidy (Frank Albertson), and flees in her car toward Fairvale, where she hopes to persuade Sam to marry her. On the second night of her journey, she becomes disoriented during a severe rainstorm and ends up off the main highway at an apparent refuge called the Bates Motel, only 15 miles from her destination. There the young proprietor, Norman Bates (Anthony Perkins), greets her. Later, Norman, dressed up as his dead mother, slashes Marion to death in the most celebrated shower scene in film history. The second half of the story concerns the ultimately successful efforts of Sam and Marion's sister, Lila (Vera Miles), to discover what happened to Marion and to unmask the culprit.

In the sets of Marion's office, of the rooms in the Bates Motel, and of the rooms of the famous Bates house situated on a hill and looming threateningly above and behind the motel, works of art reinforce the major characters' own feelings of confusion about their self-worth and ultimate destiny. Images of paintings in print form appear in the outer office of the real estate firm which Marion enters on a Friday afternoon after her meeting with Sam during a "lunch break." As would be typical of a realtor's office, there are landscapes hanging on the walls, each illustrating the variation of topography in Arizona, from the desert to flourishing greenery. Furthermore, these painterly representations underline three psychological realities: Marion's emotional despair, her dream of escape, and her fear of insecurity. The very details of these visual selections help propel the story forward and to tie together characters and settings.

Behind Marion's desk is a picture of a bright desert scene in which the sands toward the bottom of the picture look like waves raked onto the surface. Behind the neighboring unoccupied desk to her left hangs a print of a darker, tranquil mountain lake landscape located significantly next to a water cooler. And to the side of the desk, directly opposite her and occupied by her office mate, Caroline (Patricia Hitchcock), hang two landscapes, of which the most noticeable is overflowing with vegetation, a mature tree in the foreground and a mountain range in the background. As Marion enters the office, she first passes quickly by the water landscape, which has a menacing presence; of course, it will be the abundance of too much water which will steer her off course and into the clutches of the Bates compound. Also, she will die while being washed by the warm water of her shower, and she and her white car will be buried in a black, water-laden bog behind the motel. The threat of water is clearly anticipated here. Just before and as she seats herself at her desk, her head is positioned in front of the desert image. This representation, of course, is the direct opposite of the lake scene, as it depicts a scene with too little water present. While the lake image represents the threat of too much water in the future, the desert image, as Donald Spoto indicates, suggests the reality of her immediate present, which has become an emotional desert of emptiness and "no exit" (*The Art* 362). Also, the contrast between the treatments of the two landscapes further accentuates the distinction between Marion's outward appearance and internal frenzy; during the office sequence, Marion seems tranquil and calm on the outside like the cool, twilight lake scene, while internally, she is nervous and tense like the hot desert wavelets that move in a zigzag pattern just above her head. Indeed, Marion complains of a headache to Caroline. Later, Marion will spend her first night on her journey to California alongside a road in just this kind of setting.

In contrast, opposite Marion, Caroline's head is positioned in front of the Edenic land image. The viewer soon learns from Caroline's commentary that, in contrast to Marion, her private life is apparently more fulfilling, as she is married to a man called Teddy. Therefore, the image here suggests the hope for a fulfillment Marion has been denied. It is the reality of the contrast between the empty desert and the fruitful land that drives Marion to the compulsive need to flee with the money that she thinks will bring her happiness.

As Marion enters Mr. Lowery's inner office to ask if she can go home early, the camera eye now views her from the inside of this office, and, as she walks through the doorway, she is again visually linked with the water image as her head passes in front of the lower portion of the painting. Here, as earlier, the body of water featured in the painting figuratively floods the foreground as if to almost flow out of the print and thereby engulf Marion in a threatening fashion. In the inner office, on the wall behind Mr. Cassidy, hangs a painting resembling the work of Henri Matisse; in Matisse's modern style, there is a playfulness. an electric charge. In another nice verbal to visual reference, Cassidy says to Marion that what she needs is a "weekend in Las Vegas—the play-ground of the world!" (Anobile 31).

When Marion appears in the outer office again, her head is once more positioned in front of the desert scene as she says to Caroline that one "cannot buy off unhappiness with pills" (Anobile 31), suggesting her emotional panic.

Once again, as she exits, she goes by the water cooler, and the upper part of her body passes in front of the ominous water scene.

After Marion leaves Phoenix, several long sequences trace her journey to Fairvale. When she is caught in the blinding rain, Marion is attracted by the lighted sign, "Bates Motel." In a sense, the sign serves as "bait" for her encounter with the youthful proprietor, Norman. Marion stops just outside the Bates Motel office; when looking for the manager, she sees the large Victorian house perched on a hill behind the motel. In an upper window, she notices the dark silhouette of what appears to be an old woman, apparently Mrs. Bates. Then Norman appears, promptly registers her, and shows her to her room, which is located next to the office, including the parlor behind the front desk. Inside Marion's room, in addition to two images featuring flowers, three of the prints adorning the walls introduce the first fully visual references to birds in the film. There are two prints featuring single small birds with sharp beaks, situated to the right side of Marion's bathroom door, and two prints featuring two ducks swimming in water, located both behind the main door and over the bed. Earlier, visual and verbal references to birds had been introduced in the film. There are the names of Phoenix and Crane and the image of the Bates house resembling a birdhouse perched on the hill from which Norman will swoop down to attack Marion later; there are visual linkages between Marion and birds, as close-ups of her face suggest a bird-like profile, as dissolves of her face against the skyline during her journey imply a "bird in flight," and as her hands gripping the steering wheel resemble talons; the camera movement at the beginning of the film also introduces the idea of flight, as in a panning motion the camera "flies" over the skyline of Phoenix and then "perches" on the windowsill of Sam and Marion's hotel room.

Several times during the sequences when Norman is in Marion's room, his shadow passes over the images of the single birds, implying his potentially violent side, which could erupt at any moment. Also, the profiles of the two birds are exactly opposite: the "lower" bird's beak points to the right side of the frame, identifying it clearly with Marion's profile when Norman sees her undressing through a peephole in the office parlor. Later, when Norman enters the room after the murder and sees what his "mother" has done, his profile, with his face looking toward the left side of the frame, identifies him with the "upper" bird, whose beak points toward the bathroom door. There should be no surprise that Norman accidentally and yet prophetically knocks off the picture of the "lower" bird, clearly identified with Marion, whom he as "mother" has just savagely murdered. Furthermore, after he cleans up Marion's room, he restores the "fallen" bird to its proper position on the wall, just as he had played the role of the "restorer" of order after the chaos generated by his "mother."

More bird references and the most significant painterly images in the film are present in Norman's parlor, where he invites Marion to have a dinner of his own making and where he and she have a confessional "heart-to-heart" discussion about private traps, emotional pitfalls, and irrational behavior. Of the distinguishing features in the parlor, the viewer is first struck by the number of stuffed birds mounted on the walls and standing on the small buffet in the corner. In the ensuing conversation, Norman comments rather humorously that his hobby is taxidermy, "stuffing things." One of the most notable birds is the owl in the corner, with which Norman is visually identified in several shots. Both the owl's wings and claws are spread out, as if it is about to attack, and, of course, it is a bird of night. As well, there is another owl located directly above Norman's head. Also, Norman comments that Marion "eats like a bird," and that one has to "scratch" and "claw" to try and get out of private traps (Anobile 79-80). The scene description in the original screenplay located in the Motion Picture Academy Library states that the parlor "is a room of birds. Stuffed birds, all over the room, on every available surface...The birds are of many varieties, beautiful, grand, horrible, preying" (Stefano 43).

Of the several painterly images adorning the walls, three of them are most visibly emphasized: the scene of angels in flight located in an oval frame situated next to a stuffed raven on a perch, jutting from the wall behind the seated Marion as she eats; a painting of a nude woman standing before what appears to be a young man in a rendition of the classical story of "Cupid and Psyche," hanging on the wall to Norman's right; and the most important, a representation of the Biblical story of *Susannah and the Elders,* located in a higher position on the same wall immediately to Norman's right. The screenplay's reference to these paintings as having a "vaguely religious overtone" further implies the Biblical connection (Stefano 43).

This latter painting's significance has been specially noted by such scholars as Donald Spoto, James Naremore, Peter Van Gelder and William Rothman precisely because it covers the peephole through which Norman peers at Marion. Indeed, a close reading of the Biblical story from the thirteenth chapter of the Book of Daniel reveals several themes elucidated in *Psycho*: voyeurism, wrongful accusation, corrupted innocence, power misused, secrets, lust and death. This story, which appears in the Apocrypha in the Catholic version of the Bible, tells the tale of two elderly voyeurs who spy on the innocent, naked Susannah as she is about to bathe outdoors, then pounce upon her and, after she refused her favors, wrongfully accuse her of adultery. Eventually, she is cleared by Daniel, and the two guilty accusers are executed. While the scene in this painting in the motel parlor, that of the two elders grasping each of the sides of the nude Susannah, does not literally depict a rape scene, it certainly suggests the aroused desires of the two men as they accost the hapless and vulnerable woman. This scene foreshadows the figurative rape of Marion in the shower sequence, as "Ma" Bates plunges the knife repeatedly into her naked flesh.

And just as the two elders wrongfully accuse Susannah of adultery, so too from her motel room window Marion overhears the fictitious mother, enacted by Norman in the house, wrongfully accuse Marion of arousing and tempting her son. In this scene, Norman, influenced by his "mother" side, sees Marion as being guilty of hiding the truth about some wrong she had committed, especially after he discovers she had registered with a fake name, Marie Samuels, possibly signifying her wish to "marry Sam." And like the two elders, Norman's "mother" condemns the heroine.

Also in the painting, much is made of the invasion of privacy as the two men visually and then actually violate Susannah's private moment of relaxation. In the film, voyeurism is the "guilt trip" from which the audience does not escape, as, reinforced by the camera movement, the viewers constantly invade the private moments of others. Hence the painting prepares the viewer for Norman's own voyeuristic action as he removes it to spy on the charming, attractive Marion. She is dressed in black lingerie when he first views her undressing, a marked contrast to her outer appearance in a white blouse and skirt.

For, like Norman, the two elders felt lust for Susannah, but were "ashamed" of it. And while Marion is by no means innocent, unlike Susannah, she is innocent of having invited such a savage attack upon her. Of course, Susannah, unlike Marion, is already married, and also, unlike Marion, she had a savior in Daniel. Sadly, Marion's savior, Sam, is too late, and she is in a sense beyond redemption. And also, the youthful Norman, unlike the elders, cannot declare his desire for Marion directly.

A closer look at the details of the painting reveals other parallels. The unclothed Susannah about to bathe anticipates Marion's act of undressing as she is about to shower. Furthermore, Susannah is looking toward the heavens, as if she is appealing to the Lord for salvation. Similarly, before Marion is attacked, she thrusts her head upward into the water jetting out from the showerhead. Again, Susannah is relaxing just before the attack, just as the intruder interrupts Marion as she is enjoying the soothing and cleansing warmth of the shower. Just before her shower, Marion had checked her savings book and decided she had enough money to make restitution for the money she had spent. Furthermore, Susannah's position, as the two men touch her, suggests that she has no chance to escape, just as Marion is trapped in the shower. Susannah's right hand, which reaches helplessly and imploringly toward the heavens, reminds one of the dying Marion's hand as it clutches the shower curtain in a last, futile attempt to remain standing. Also, the painting is a study of contrasting light and shadow, as the elders emerge from the darkness of the forest in the background into the light of the foreground; similarly, the attacker in *Psycho* is a figure of darkness who intrudes upon the sanctum of light, the bathroom. The power of the painting and of the subsequent shower sequence is matched.

As William Rothman suggests, the "Cupid and Psyche" image of the nude before the young man hints at Marion's dilemma, as she virtually "unmasks" herself before Norman. This image, a scene from the tale out of classical mythology, is positioned on the same wall with *Susannah and the Elders* because it also refers to a story full of themes central to *Psycho*: themes of love, blindness, murderous impulses, jealousy and temptation. The real distinction is that this classical narrative ends with an optimistic tone, suggesting another unfulfilled destiny for Norman and Marion, that of triumphant love. Rothman correctly notes that when Marion is eating her sandwich, her left arm, in an upraised position, mirrors the left arm of the nude in the painting, presumably Psyche, whose name, interestingly enough, is the Greek derivative of the prefix "psycho" (Rothman 283). This could be the moment, when, according to Edith Hamilton's account drawn from Ovid in her *Mythology*, Psyche awakens and lays her eyes on her lover, who has come to rescue her from his envious mother, Venus. Her Cupid (or Eros), the young man in the painting, could resemble Norman, who, like Cupid's mother Venus, also has a jealous "mother." Psyche has first "known" Cupid only in darkness; she had brought troubles upon herself when she had broken her pledge not to look upon him. But in the "Cupid and Psyche" story, Zeus resolves Psyche's dilemma by making the mortal Psyche into a goddess and thereby forcing Venus to accept Psyche as her legitimate daughter-in-law. According to Hamilton's account, "all came to a most happy end. Love [for Cupid] and the Soul (for that is what Psyche means) had sought and, after sore trials, found each other, and that union could never be broken" (Hamilton 134). Sadly, such a happy ending, also implied by the statue of Cupid in the Bates house, would be denied to Marion and Norman; indeed, a shadow of the raven, reminding one of Hitchcock's interest in Edgar Allan Poe, and forecasting doom, appears on the wall to the viewer's left of the painting. Here again, the relationships depicted in this pair of paintings indicate a contrast between a delicate, sensitive, restrained love affair and one that is disruptive and potentially violent.

In the painting behind Marion, the images in ascent imply Marion's predicament of being a "bird in flight" and her wish to rise to a more heavenly and fulfilling life. The Cupid images suggest her frustrated search for love. She is totally wounded in her pursuit of love. In contrast, the screenplay describes Norman "as unable to fly as are the many still, stuffed birds" (Stefano 123).

In this parlor sequence, Hitchcock's deep love of painting, combined with his Catholic religious sensibility, adds a dimension of special power. For, like Hitchcock, Norman is a collector, a collector of birds he loves to stuff, of phonograph records, of books, of "dead" bodies, of paintings. And Norman's own collection of paintings underlines the darkness not only of his own heart, but of us all.

Later in the film, after Norman disposes of Marion's body, and his "mother" kills an inquiring private detective, Marion's sister Lila and Sam

Loomis undertake the full investigation of the matter by registering as man and wife at the motel. Several water images are identified with Lila, apparently threatening her as well. When she and Sam are discussing tactics in their motel room, there is a nautical image of a great rigged sailing vessel on a lampshade. Later, when, according to their plan, Lila is searching through "Ma" Bates' room in the house while Sam diverts Norman in the motel office, on the far wall there is another landscape with a river, which is positioned behind Lila's head at one point. When she enters Norman's room on the third-floor landing, there are two other seascapes with sailing vessels hanging on adjoining walls: these are described in the screenplay as "silhouettes of…sailboats" (Stefano 121).

These nautical images have other implications: they suggest the sense of flight, of pushing out, of a voyage of discovery which Marion inadvertently undertook, and on which Norman, in his better moments, might wish to embark. Also, the turbulence of the sea reflects the undulating pattern of Marion's and Norman's disturbed emotional lives.

In "Ma" Bates' room and on the landing outside the door, there are other notable painterly images. Over the headboard of Mrs. Bates' bed, where there is a zigzag imprint made by her body, hangs a painting of the head and shoulders of a Victorian youth. Similarly, at the top of the stairs on the first landing hangs another Victorian image, a full figure of an elegantly dressed young lady, suggesting the mother in full flower. Again, this aristocratic image contrasts sharply with the "shabby" conditions of the house, which seems caught in the past, almost in its death throes. Indeed, this wistful painting serves as a stark contrast to the gloomy nature of the house, a lighter side to the darkness within, a tenderness inside the terror. For this is a story about the conflict between tenderness and toughness, the battle between compassion and resentment—a tension brought to rest, when Lila, upon finding the skeleton of Mrs. Bates in the fruit cellar, is saved by Sam from an avenging Norman again dressed as his mother.

All these images associated with the Bates compound underline one of the most enduring themes in Hitchcock, the theme of loss rendered in the conflict between the "classical and the romantic." The details in the office parlor and the rooms of the house suggest a kind of former beauty, appreciation for the fine arts, and luxury and extravagance. For instance, the screenplay describes the contents of "Ma" Bates' room as "ollapodrida of mismated furnishings and bric-a-brac of the last century" (Stefano 119). In one sense, Norman bemoans the loss of this past and tries to restore its "classical" order and emotionally security. When his mother took on a lover, she betrayed her devotion to her son, and when his mother's friend persuaded her to invest family money in the motel, Norman broke trust with the old order by inviting "strangers"—outsiders and intruders like Marion and two other young women—onto the premises, a "Romantic" or uncontrolled violation of the safety and security attached to the

Victorian house. In one sense, Norman killed his mother and lover ten years before and attacked Marion, detective Milton Arbogast (Martin Balsam), and Lila in order to protect this earlier and lost world in which he had been nurtured as a child and where he, as he tells Sam, had been quite happy. To a sensitive if warped spirit like Norman, the contemporary twentieth-century world of 1959 was commercial, vulgar, crass; the finer things, like Cupid's passion for the lovely Psyche, were vanishing, leaving only the savagery behind. The beast was consuming beauty, not the other way—hence the sadness and bleakness of *Psycho*. It is a kind of modern day version of Poe's "The Fall of the House of Usher," which Hitchcock read and appreciated (Spoto, *The Dark Side*, 40-42).

Hitchcock often emphasized that cinematic art was a matter of telling a story with "pictures." He was referring to photographic images, but, in another sense, he was saying that the historical source of the power of film comes from the long heritage of brilliant drawing and painting that preceded the invention of the camera, a source he acknowledged and exploited with the carefully chosen pictorial scenes with which he decorated his sets.

Works Cited

Anobile, Richard, ed. *Alfred Hitchcock's Psycho*. NY: Avon Books, 1974.

Bloch, Robert. *Psycho*. NY: Simon & Schuster, 1959.

Hamilton, Ruth. *Mythology*. Boston: Little, Brown and Co., 1942.

The Holy Bible Containing the Old and New Testaments and the Apocrypha. 14 vols. Boston: R.H. Hinkley Co., 1904.

Naremore, James. *Filmguide to Psycho*. Bloomington: Indiana UP, 1973.

Rothman, William. *Hitchcock—The Murderous Gaze*. Cambridge: Harvard UP, 1982.

Spoto, Donald. *The Art of Alfred Hitchcock: Fifty Years of His Motion Pictures*. NY: Hopkinson and Blake, 1976.

_____.*The Dark Side of Genius: The Life of Alfred Hitchcock*. Boston: Little, Brown and Co., 1983.

Stefano, Joseph, screenwriter. *Psycho*. Los Angeles: Margaret Herrick Library, Academy of Motion Picture Arts and Science, general collections.

Stein, Elliott. "Filmographies of Art Directors and Production Designers." *Calgari's Cabinet and Other Grand Illusions: A History of Film Design*. Boston: Little, Brown and Co., 1976.

Taylor, John Russell. *Hitch: The Life and Times of Alfred Hitchcock*. NY: Pantheon, 1978.

Van Gelder, Peter. *That's Hollywood: A Behind-the-Scenes Look at 60 of the Greatest Films of All Time*. NY: Harper Collins, 1990.

Reel Art:
Excursions into the Biopic, Mystery/Suspense, Melodrama and Movies in the Eighties
Brooks Robards

When Director Vincente Minnelli began filming *Lust for Life* in 1956, he decided to use a real artist's hands instead of actor Kirk Douglas's in scenes of Van Gogh at work. Painter Robert Andrew Parker was chosen for the part, and MGM flew him to the set in France, along with Douglas.

"No one knew whether to treat me as one of the film's big guns or a humble technician" (58), Parker reported. Instead of having his hands filmed, though, Parker found himself copying Van Gogh's most famous works, including "The Sower," and "Crows Over a Cornfield." Minnelli, who had hoped to photograph the originals and have them transferred to canvas for use in the film, instead found himself stonewalled by Van Gogh's estate. So he put his real-life artist to work making replicas. Parker's hands never appeared in the movie.

This page out of film history helps define a number of the issues that emerge from the way fine arts like painting and sculpture are represented by the movies. Particularly in its early years, reel art mirrors the ambivalence and competitiveness film feels toward its more respected sister arts. It also provides a focus for cinematic explorations of the relationship between reality and illusion. As part of film's material world, reel art sits squarely at the nexus of two contradictory cinematic impulses. On one hand, the inclination towards concreteness and realism pushes movies toward as authentic as possible a representation of a painting, sculpture or other type of art. On the other, the medium's metaphoric impulses drive it toward representations of art that attempt to be expressionistic and transcendental.

Most of the conventions involving the use of art objects in movies were established well before 1930. In its early, pre-sound days, when the medium still relied almost exclusively on images for story and meaning, movies seemed to reflect a certain reverent fascination for the world of fine art, and the use of reel art tended to be realist in approach. As signs of the artist and his/her world, art objects can convey a variety of functions and values that are frequently bipolar.

Money and wealth, for instance, combine with the frequent impoverishment of the artist him/herself and make the art object an analogue for metaphysical values. Early reel art frequently combines with themes of mystery and intoxication, and the connection occurs both in the broader sense of lifestyle and quite literally through drugs or alcohol. Religious motifs are often counterbalanced with those of lust and hypocrisy. Art objects may also combine with adventure and travel, taking moviegoers to foreign places or exposing them to exotic cultural traditions. Art objects are perennially lost or left unfinished, and they evidently lend their creators a romantic aura, since artists in early movies always seem to be falling in love.

The subjects for painting and sculpture in Silent films are rarely male, and early reel art provided an important way of defining women or talking about them. In addition to providing a culturally acceptable way to objectify women, reel art conveys a deep ambivalence about them. As art objects, women can be a source of inspiration, lust, beauty or evil. The Pygmalion myth, for example, provides the classical plot device for *The Marble Heart* (1915), where an artist who dislikes the flaws of real-life women dreams that he is Phidias and his statues come to life.

Female nudity in reel art takes on a special significance, suggesting roles for art as both idealizing and sensational in the representation of female sexual identity. *The Hypocrites* (1915) uses a painting of Truth as a naked woman as a source of inspiration for a minister bent on exposing his congregation's hypocrisy. In a case of life imitating art, the nudity in this film by Lois Weber, one of the important women directors of the Silent era, caused a scandal. The Mayor of Boston demanded that clothes be hand painted onto the nudes before the film was to be shown there. In Edwin Porter and Hugh Ford's *Sold* (1915), starring silent movie queen Pauline Frederick, an idealistic artist destroys his painting of a nude rather than have people leer.

Artistic renditions of female nudity usually allowed the filmmaker to sidestep social propriety and issues of voyeurism, exhibitionism and male-inspired objectification of women. The prurient potential of nudity was often compensated for with religious allusions, à la eighteenth century French painting. In *The Painted Soul* (1915), the model for a painting of the Resurrection is inspired to mend her dubious ways and subsequently refuses to pose for a second painting, entitled "The Fallen Woman."

The dual characterization of women as saints or whores is an extension of reel art's preoccupations with the female body. A sculptor abandons his work in *Inspiration* (1915), until he finds a pure-hearted country girl to be his model. The "good" women who work as models for reel art are frequently forced by reduced circumstances to pose in the nude and then are threatened with rape—as in *Her Mad Bargain* (1921). Their portraits or sculptures often inspire the artist's love, as in *The Girl O'Dreams* (1916) and *Purity* (1916). In other cases, reel art exposes not only the model's body, but her identity, to a rival—as in *The Primrose Path* (1915) and *Wife Against Wife* (1921), or to a lover, as in *Sold*.

Reel art may become a means for "purifying" fallen women. In *My Madonna* (1915), the model for an artist's portrait of the Madonna is a prostitute who is reformed by the artist's vision of her, as in *The Painted Soul*. In *The Devil* (1915), however, a former artist's model ends up in hell, after she returns to the studio with her husband to have her portrait painted and revives a now-adulterous romance with the artist.

If the art object in early films is usually a woman, its creator is most often a man—although, interestingly enough, there is less gender typing in the Silent era than in any of the years that follow. Reel art may help to signify a variety of character traits in the artist him/herself. It is evidence of success in *The Great Adventure* (1921), where a famous painter seeks anonymity by assuming the identity of his valet but is discovered when he begins to paint again. It provides the measure of true worth in *The Banker's Daughter* (1914) when the artist is at first rejected as a suitor because he is too poor. It can also provide evidence of a debauched lifestyle, however, as it does in *Absinthe* (1914), or the motive for madness, such as in *The Hidden Menace* (1925).

In addition to suggesting deprivation as a source of creativity, varying degrees of blindness in early movie artists provide some of the first and most literal avenues for reel art to explore distinctions between reality and illusion. This is the case in *When Love was Blind* (1917) and *The Trouble Buster* (1917), both of which involve blind characters who "see" in a new way after their vision is restored. The blindness motif was reprised in a different form in William Wellman's talkie *The Light That Failed* (1939), where Ronald Colman struggles to finish his portrait of Ida Lupino before he goes blind.

As well as having gender associations, reel art often signifies great value. It is visually more interesting than cash and certainly classier, as in Vitagraph's silent version of *Arsene Lupin* (1916), which concerns the theft of valuable art. John and Lionel Barrymore starred in the 1932 sound version. Sometimes the issue is destruction of a valuable work. Theda Bara, who played a variety of artists' wives and models during her career in Silent pictures, poses for a sculptor's statue in *The Devil's Daughter* (1915) and then tries vengefully to destroy his work. The artist's work also may serve as a personal signature, becoming a way of tracking her/him down in *Through Dante's Flames* (1914).

One recurrent reel art convention, suggesting the difficulty of distinguishing between reality and illusion, involves substitution of a copy or forgery for the real thing. The artist in *Stolen Honor* (1918) is framed for the theft of the valuable Italian painting she's been copying. *Barriers Burned Away* (1925) is a melodrama in which a stolen Old Master is tracked down by the copy being made of it.

When the focus is broadened to considerations of the larger world of the film, early reel art functions conventionally as part of an exotic or foreign setting. The most common locales are Greenwich Village and Paris, with their suggestions of adventure and freedom, but a number of early motion pictures also incorporate an oriental context, adding intrigue and mystery. Particularly popular was the Cecil de Mille production *The Cheat* (1915), starring Sessue Hayakawa, in which museum-quality Chinese carved furniture figures prominently—along with love, blackmail and murder. When shown in Los Angeles, the movie generated a protest by the Japanese Association of Southern California, but it was remade anyway—in 1923 with Pola Negri and in 1931 with Tallulah Bankhead. The statue central to *The Fox Woman* (1915) is that of a Japanese god, and in *The Soul of Kura-San* (1916), an artist's portrait of his lover stops him from avenging her death.

Sometimes reel art seems to acquire magical power. In Maurice Tourneur's *Trilby* (1915), an artist's model is mesmerized and transformed by Svengali but finally falls and dies in front of her master's portrait. The popularity of the movie's theme is attested to by the fact that it was reissued in 1917 and 1920; remade in 1923, in 1931 as *Svengali* with John Barrymore and again in 1955. In King Vidor's *The Woman of Bronze* (1923), a sculptor's work does not acquire "soul" until after he smashes and then restores it. In *The Devil's Double* (1916), the artist animates his rendering of Lucifer by insulting his model and then recreating the "Lucifer-like hardness" in his eyes.

The realist contexts out of which most of these early plot machinations involving reel art emerged find their natural extension in art biopics—movies about famous artists. One of the prototypes for American art biopics may have been Alexander Korda's *Rembrandt* (1937). Described by film critic Leslie Halliwell as "Perhaps the most satisfying film ever produced about a painter," it was made in England, featured a painterly mise-en-scene and starred Charles Laughton with Gertrude Lawrence in one of her few film appearances. The first film of writer-director Albert Lewin was the faithful adaptation of Somerset Maugham's novel based on the life of Paul Gauguin. *The Moon and Sixpence* (1942) did well at the box office, but art biopics hit their stride in the 1950s.

In those days Hollywood still tended to reserve black and white for its "artier" and more realistic genres, but the art biopic belonged among those subjects singled out for color treatment, like westerns, Biblical epics, musicals and such travel adventures as *King Solomon's Mines* (1950). The apparent contradiction was understandable and disappeared as the technology of color film improved, removing some of the aesthetic distinctions between black and white and color. *Moulin Rouge* (1952), John Huston's dramatization of Toulouse Lautrec's life, won Oscars for Art/Set Direction and Costumes.

Vincente Minnelli's art biopic, *Lust for Life*, won three Oscar nominations in 1956, including one for Best Color Cinematography,[1] and an award for

Anthony Quinn as Best Supporting Actor in his role as Gauguin. Although Ronald Neame's *The Horse's Mouth* (1958) was neither American-produced nor a true biopic, it should be mentioned because of its obvious connection to the popularity in the 1950s of films about artists' lives. Sir Alec Guinness, who played the amiable and eccentric painter Gulley Jimson, had won an Oscar for Best Actor in *Bridge on the River Kwai* (1957) the year before. Unlike Robert Andrew Parker in *Lust for Life*, John Bratby, the artist responsible for creating the fictional Jimson's works, received screen credit in *The Horses's Mouth*

   After another appearance in *The Naked Maja* (1959), a half-baked Ava Gardner vehicle about the Spanish painter Goya, art biopics went out of fashion. Except for Carol Reed's *The Agony and the Ecstasy* (1965), the subgenre all but disappeared until the late 1980s, when the world of art became a popular source of Hollywood movie material in many forms. Starring Charlton Heston and Rex Harrison, *The Agony and the Ecstasy* tells the story of Michelangelo in terms of his conflicts with Pope Julius II. It won Oscar nominations for Best Color Cinematography and Best Art/Set Direction, but lost in both cases to *Dr. Zhivago* (1965).

   Two movies outside the art biopic subgenre are appropriately grouped there. Vincente Minnelli's musical *An American in Paris* (1951) uses artist Gene Kelly's Parisian studio and paintings to provide the backdrop for romance, song and dance. Victor Saville's Biblical epic *The Silver Chalice* (1954), about the artist who designs the cup for the Last Supper, is best remembered as Paul Newman's film debut. Newman didn't have much enthusiasm for the epic, though; he placed an ad in *Variety* apologizing for his appearance in the film. As excursions beyond the biopic, these two "artist" films suggest some of the possibilities for reel art that lay outside Hollywood's carefully predetermined treatments.

   When it appears in art biopics, reel art is usually overshadowed by the artists who produce it. It often had no particular filmic impact of its own because the realist impulse behind reel art conventions tends to confine it to the artistically literal. In the 1940s and 1950s, however, reel art appears frequently in mysteries and melodramas, particularly in the form of portraits, and starts to assume a more expressionist function. The pattern may have been set by Alfred Hitchcock, who made regular use of painted portraits, beginning with *Rebecca* (1940).[2]

   Hitchcock's use of portraits can be seen as a variation on the Pygmalion myth. There are echoes of the demonic, as in the mesmerizing hero and portrait of the Silent film, *Trilby*. Hitchcock's use of portraits also suggests how the director enjoyed turning his characters into objects and making a joke out of it.

   The painting of Maxim de Winter's first wife in *Rebecca* functions on the surface as a conventional sign of de Winter's wealth and position. It also contributes to a mise-en-scene that fairly drips with romance and nostalgia. The second Mrs. de Winter's father was a painter, establishing his daughter as particularly receptive to the power of her predecessor's portrait. The portrait's depiction of the dead Rebecca's beauty dominates the atmosphere at Mandeley.

On a less obvious level, the portrait functions to reify a recurrent Hitchcock theme, the power of the dead to affect the living. As a painting, Rebecca's portrait is quite conventional. Its almost supernatural role in the plot, however, gives it a special power.

A portrait figures prominently again in one of Hitchcock's next films, *Suspicion* (1941). This time, however, it is a painting of the heroine's father, General McLaidlaw, who starts out very much alive in the movie. The portrait's power to affect the movie's characters is no longer confined to its function as a stand-in for a ghost. Lina McLaidlaw's irrepressible suitor, Johnny Aysgarth (Cary Grant), talks to the portrait as if it were human, and his marriage proposal to Joan Fontaine's Lina literally "knocks the General's portrait off the wall.".

While critics tend to prefer *Rebecca* to *Suspicion*, Hitchcock's manipulation of mise-en-scene in *Suspicion*, as demonstrated by the way he uses General McLaidlaw's portrait, is less sentimental and more psychologically complex. Once Lina and Johnny are married, Hitchcock also utilizes their reactions to the General's wedding gift, two museum-quality chairs that are family heirlooms, to delineate the differences in character between husband and wife.

Disappointed in his daughter's choice of husband and as mistrustful of Johnny's motives as Lina is, the General leaves only his portrait to the couple when he dies. Hitchcock has played a sophisticated Oedipal joke not only on them, but on the audience as well. He continues the fun at the end of the movie through two dimwitted police inspectors, who stare uncomprehendingly at an abstract painting in the Aysgarth home.

In *The Paradine Case* (1947), Hitchcock explores the capacity of a painting to allow the director quite literally to remove the mask of personality and probe it. Hitchcock balances scenes in which Keane (Gregory Peck) confronts first his wife Gay (Ann Todd), and then Maddelena Paradine (Alida Valli), through the positioning of their portraits. While Mrs. Keane's is hung in traditional fashion on a wall in her husband's study, Mrs. Paradine's is part of the elaborate bedstead in her bedroom. The association of her portrait with sexual passion is clear.

Both the female characters in one of Hitchcock's greatest films, *Vertigo* (1958), have reel art associations. Midge (Barbara Bel Geddes), is a friend of James Stewart's Scottie and a would-be painter who makes a living drawing ladies' underwear for ads—a perfect parody of reel art. While Midge may provide the movie's "normal" point of view, she is successful neither as an artist nor a lover. Hitchcock's Pygmalion-like hero remains a man—the criminal investigator Scottie.

The portrait of Carlotta Valdes plays a prominent role in *Vertigo*, but it is a McGuffin. Instead, Hitchcock makes Scottie's obsession a real woman, Madelene (Kim Novak), rather than a work of art. The movie's real concern is the investigation of the nature of film rather than of painting or other such classical art forms.

Despite his more profound explorations of reel art, Hitchcock was typical of many directors of the period. The quality of the portraits used in his movies was poor and, no doubt, irrelevant as far as he was concerned. Much like his use of rear screen projection and studio sets, the obviousness of the artifice didn't matter and could even be considered part of the point. Discrepancies in visual power between real and reel art, however, detract from the illusion, which was often the reason for the art in the first place. Until the 1980s, movies tend to limit reel art to highly reductive, almost banal representational formats that emphasize their static nature in contrast to the dynamic film medium. A number of mystery/suspense movies and melodramas illustrate how the medium struggled with this limitation.

In *The Maltese Falcon* (1941), director John Huston discovered a unique way to exploit the evocative power of art in film without reducing it to a comic simulacrum. He treated the 16th century statuette known as the Maltese Falcon, which private eye Sam Spade (Humphrey Bogart) refers to as "the Bird," the same way monsters are treated in horror movies. In other words, he never lets the audience actually see it.

The titles roll over a dark likeness of the statuette, followed by the falcon's history. The jewel-encrusted gold statuette, intended as a tribute to King Charles V of Spain, was stolen by pirates and has been sought after ever since. The audience, whose fantasies about this magnificent piece of art are allowed to proliferate as Spade and his opponents search for it, never suffers the disappointment of reality. "The stuff that dreams are made of," Spade tells the ignorant cop who asks what the statuette is, and the movie ends. The crude facsimile shown at the very beginning of the movie is the closest any of the characters gets to the real Maltese falcon, while the elusive original retains its magnetic powers for them as well as for the audience.

Reel art finds more conventional uses, as established by early Silent films, in several other 1940s mystery/suspense movies. Bogart plays a murderous artist who paints his wives as angels of death and then kills them in *The Two Mrs. Carrolls* (1947). Madness is the motif in Jacques Tourneur's *Experiment Perilous* (1944), while a philandering husband figures in *A Woman's Vengeance* (1948). Implicit in such genre applications is the more expressionist and transcendental function that reel art may serve. For films of the era, art itself is a bit of a mystery.

Taking his cue from Hitchcock perhaps, Otto Preminger capitalizes in *Laura* (1944) on the power of a portrait to evoke the presence of its subject. As in *Rebecca*, the portrait is of a mesmerizingly beautiful woman, supposed to be dead, and the camera hovers over Laura's portrait as if it were a spectral presence. Laura, however, turns out to be alive. Harking back to such silents as *The Devil's Daughter*, Preminger sharpens the focus on the beautiful woman as deceitful temptress, until the movie becomes a litmus of 1940s attitudes towards women and their changing social roles.

Like *The Maltese Falcon*, the film opens with the titles over Laura's portrait. The camera dissolves to a statue of Buddha and pans across other objets d'art in a lavishly furnished apartment. The painting—like Laura—is just one of many objects in a world of art, money and status. Laura's mentor Waldo Leideker reinforces the point later, when he ironically complains that the artist who painted Laura's portrait and was in love with her failed to capture her true warmth and vibrance.

The movie's play with art objects is integral to the plot. A commercial artist, Laura has cultivated a successful career through Leideker. She has been surrounded by adoring men who are now the suspects in her murder. After Laura's death, Leideker, who has been generous in sharing his art collection with her, is quick to try to take back the pieces he has given his protégée, since one of them conveniently hides the murder weapon. The audience watches a tug of war between him and the detective investigating the case,

While Laura may be a promising professional as well as a decorative object, the movie is ambivalent about her career—implying that it has been built on beauty more than talent. In death Laura becomes interchangeable with another young woman, reinforcing her status as *objet d'art*. Her motives are compromised throughout, and although the movie implies that she will find happiness with the detective who solves the mystery, Laura herself says of Waldo, "I'm as guilty as he is."

In *The Picture of Dorian Gray* (1945), social corruption becomes pervasive, and the women, doll-like innocents in its 19th-century world, are not the cause. Based on a story by Oscar Wilde, the plot concerns a man who gets his wish that his portrait age instead of him. The emphasis in the setting, reminiscent of *Citizen Kane* (1941) in its Wellesian lushness, is, as in *Laura*, on a home filled with *objets d'art*.

This time, though, the handsome young Victorian gentleman Dorian Gray (Hurd Hatfield) provides the focus, along with his portrait, shown in color sequences inserted in the black and white film. Dorian's friend, painter Basil Hallwell, tries to prevent him from meeting the other principle character, the decadent Lord Henry (George Sanders), but the two meet while Dorian is having his portrait painted.

In terms of reel art, it is as if director Albert Lewin had combined elements of *Rebecca* or *Laura* with *The Maltese Falcon*. The mysterious quality of Dorian's portrait, which causes Basil to say it has "a life of its own," is tied in with a statue of an Egyptian cat, which may or may not have magic powers. At Lord Henry's prompting, Dorian corrupts a young singer, Sibyl Vane (Angela Lansbury), who then commits suicide. Dorian seems to remain untouched, but his portrait undergoes its first change.

One decadence follows another with no visible evidence to mar Dorian's youthful features. The painting, however, deteriorates from a conventional, illusionist portrait into a Kokoschka-like grotesque, revealed in vivid color in an otherwise black and white film, after Dorian murders its creator. At the end of the movie, when Dorian tries to destroy the painting by slashing it with a knife, he falls to the floor—killed by the painting. The portrait is immediately restored to its original, pure state, and the lifeless Dorian's face disintegrates.

At the narrative level, Dorian's picture functions to signify Faustian ambition and the corrupting power of wealth, motifs that become increasingly important in 1980s movies. Lewin dramatizes the point by balancing scenes at Dorian's art-filled and palatial home with those of the elegantly dressed Dorian moving in the rough world of working-class taverns.

As hokey as the film is from both narrative and technical standpoints, its thematic concerns and mix of black and white with color make sense in terms of the larger preoccupations of the medium with reel art. If film as a medium cannot actually animate reel art, it comes as close as possible to it in the transformations Dorian Gray's portrait undergoes. Cinematographer Harry Stradling, who also photographed *Suspicion*, won an Oscar for his work in *The Picture of Dorian Gray*.

Reel art operates in a more realist framework for Fritz Lang's melodrama *Scarlet Street* (1945). Edward G. Robinson plays against type as cashier and Sunday painter Christopher Cross. Aspiring to the pleasures of his wealthy boss, Cross, who is unhappily married, acquires a mistress of sorts in Joan Bennett's Kitty, who mistakes him for a successful painter and plans to con him. The timid painter's work, represented as a crude form of Magic Realism, becomes a big success after Kitty's boyfriend (Dan Duryea) secretly hocks it and it is bought by an art critic. In the ironic final scene of the movie, Cross, who has been reduced to a street bum, walks past the gallery where one of his paintings has just been sold for $10,000.

When the audience is asked to take reel art seriously, as it is in a film like *Scarlet Street*, its lack of authenticity is reductive and becomes much more obvious. Perhaps when stymied by the static nature of painting, sculpture and other forms of reel art, films like *Scarlet Street* must necessarily fail in their representation of it as anything more than narrative cipher.

Making almost no realist claims whatever, William Dieterle's *Portrait of Jennie* (1948) is one of the more successful movie explorations of art. The painter Eben Adams, played by Joseph Cotton (who portrayed another disturbed character for Dieterle in *I'll Be Seeing You* in 1945 and the evil Uncle Charlie in

Hitchcock's *Shadow of a Doubt* in 1943), is unsuccessful until he meets up with a mysterious young girl in the park. Jennie (Jennifer Jones), seems to come from another era. Siren-like, she vanishes and reappears mysteriously but inspires Adams' work so that he becomes successful. When he tries to track her down, Adams meets with tragedy. The film ends with school girls observing his legacy, the now-legendary portrait of Jennie that hangs in a museum.

As improbable as the plot is, *Portrait of Jennie* manages to capture something of the metaphysical allure that painting has in its ability to articulate an artist's vision and transform the particular into the universal. The final reel of the Selznick production, which won an Academy Award for Special Effects, is tinted green, ending with a Technicolor insert of Jennie's completed portrait.

Not until nearly the 1980s does reel art break out of the generic confines that limit its earlier use. As Norden points out, Carol Reed's *The Agony and the Ecstasy* (1965), in which Michelangelo struggles to paint the Sistine Chapel ceiling, is visually stunning but suffers from the static plotting that is a problem in most biopics. Hitchcock uses a portrait again in *The Birds* (1963), but it lacks the resonance of his earlier uses of reel art. While Vincente Minnelli makes Elizabeth Taylor an artist in his Taylor-Burton vehicle, *The Sandpiper* (1965), reel art plays no significant role in the film. Stolen art periodically provides the plotting linchpin for such movies as John Frankenheimer's *The Train* (1965) and Sydney Pollack's *Castle Keep* (1969), but Paul Mazursky's *An Unmarried Woman*, released in 1978, marks the first major change in how Hollywood used reel art.

Before this period, reel art tended to provide an exotic but undigested presence in the material world of the movie, perhaps reflecting the ambivalence and inherent sense of rivalry of the newer medium towards its more traditional sister arts. Its presence in *An Unmarried Woman* marks a more natural incorporation of the art scene into the movie's fictional world.

Jill Clayburgh plays Erica Benton, a happily married woman who works at a downtown art gallery, and the plot moves easily through a world of artists and gallery openings. After her husband leaves her for another woman, Erica becomes involved with a painter (Alan Bates), and much of this part of the movie takes place in his Soho loft, a setting *Art in America* describes as "the right combination of exotic and domestic" (14). The camera observes him in close-up pouring acrylic paint onto canvas to create abstract paintings, which are actually those of artist Paul Jenkins, whose loft provides the movie's setting.

Although the movie's central character is never presented as much more than a bystander in the predominantly male world of serious art, the final scene leaves Erica standing on a New York street with a painting given to her by Bates that is easily three or four times as big as she. It is a clever sight gag and a satisfying tribute to the concerns on which the movie is based. In contrast, the less successfully realized world of James Toback's *Fingers* (1978) plays artist

Tisa Farrow as a variation on the stereotypical "refined" artist, and the reel art supposed to be hers is, in fact, a hodgepodge of different artists' work.

An Unmarried Woman and *Fingers* are important in the way they extend the focus in reel art beyond one specific art object in movies that are not art biopics. They also begin to break down the respectful distance maintained toward reel art in movies before the 1980s. Woody Allen's ode to New York, *Manhattan* (1979), provides another appropriate transition. Its central character Isaac (Woody Allen) is a television writer who makes clear his loyalty to populist art. As a director Allen uses reel art to establish contrast. The characters' visits to art exhibits allow him to make fun of their cultural pretensions. Mary (Diane Keaton) finds one photograph at an exhibit "very derivative. Diane Arbus with none of the wit." She also claims a sculpture has "a marvelous kind of negative capability." Both statements infuriate Isaac. Later, he hears weird noises—apparently behind the abstract painting in his bedroom while he is seducing Mary, and reel art becomes another sight gag, poking fun at the incomprehensibility of modern art.

Once the price tags on works by Van Gogh, Picasso and other artists began making headlines in the 1980s, film lost its reverence for its sister arts, and reel art started to function like any other secular status symbol. Robert Benton's thriller *Still of the Night* (1983), for example, uses an art auction as the setting in its denouement. Nor are paintings the only props, since real-life Pace Gallery Director Arnold Glimcher plays one of the bidders competing against fictional gallery employee Meryl Streep. Erotic drawings by Soho artist Jac Applezweig (played by real-life artist Larry Rivers) provide a sight gag for Marshall Brickman's *Lovesick* (1983).

In James L. Brooks' *Terms of Endearment* (1983), the Renoir hanging in the bedroom of Shirley MacLaine's Aurora is her "nest egg," giving her the pretext for inviting an aging astronaut (Jack Nicholson) into her boudoir. Later, when her daughter Emma (Debra Winger) is hospitalized with incurable cancer, Aurora has the Renoir, the portrait of a young girl, hung in Emma's hospital room. Although the camera never comes close enough to the painting to confirm its authenticity, it successfully establishes the illusion of authenticity. That authenticity is an extension of Aurora's world.

Once Hollywood learns how to capitalize on a blurring of reality and illusion, it has domesticated reel art. By 1983, critic Raymond Durgnat calls attention to Hollywood's new interest in the painterly, whereby films like *Superman* (1978) "quote" specific works of art—while others, like *Blue collar* (1978), evoke a particular artistic current. The connection was not exactly without precedent; for example, former painter John Huston borrowed from de Chirico for the opening of "The Asphalt Jungle" (1950). Critics in general become tuned into a new rapport between art and the movies, however. Director Sidney Lumet, for example, is referred to as having studied Caravaggio's paintings in preparation for filming *The Verdict* (1982). The implication in the 1980s is that Hollywood has co-opted the art world's sensibility as well as its artifacts.

Hollywood's increasingly relaxed approach to reel art is reflected in *Beverly Hills Cop* (1984). The movie popularizes a new kind of villain, the evil art dealer, who in this case uses the Hollis-Benton gallery, which he owns, as a front for drug smuggling. Eddie Murphy's Axel plays the typical neophyte who does a double take when he enters the gallery, which has Segal-esque white heads spinning on a table set with dinner plates. During the final shoot-out in the dealer's home, paintings as well as people are the casualties.[3]

At the same time that Hollywood grows more comfortable with reel art in the 1980s, it continues to use many of the conventions established in the early days of film. Reel art represents lifestyles of debauchery and kinky sex in *After Hours* (1985) and *9 1/2 Weeks*(1986). Ivan Reitman's *Legal Eagles* (1986) works harder to contemporize the art world. The movie uses the apparent destruction by fire of the works of fictional artist Sebastian Deardon in an insurance fraud as the basis for its suspense plot. Pace Gallery Director Arnold Glimcher, who served as Associate Producer, helped establish the film's art credibility, filling its fictional gallery with $12 million worth of original Miros, Calders, DuBuffets and de Koonings.

The fictional Deardon's work is never shown because, according to Glimcher, "Portraying the art world in the most accurate manner we could, there was no way that we could fabricate this great artist, Deardon" (C13). The characters are established in conventional clichés. Assistant D.A. Robert Redford is unable to recognize a Picasso when standing in front of it; Deardon's daughter Chelsey (Daryl Hannah) is a kooky performance artist; and one of the bad guys is a gallery owner.

In Oliver Stone's epic on greed, *Wall Street* (1987), art dealers are not the only villains. Reel art has come to represent a decadence that permeates modern society and is not muted by being set in an earlier era, as it was in *The Picture of Dorian Gray*. As Darien, Daryl Hannah is demoted from the performance artist she played in *Legal Eagles* to interior decorator, and she talks about the art owned by financier Gordon Gekko (Michael Douglas) in investment terms. An Etruscan vase in Gekko's apartment is interchangeable with other symbols of money and power, like an expensive rug and a robot that serves drinks. When Darien decorates up-and-coming Charlie Sheen's new apartment, it is with fake brick and mouldings as well as trendy Caribbean art and Beckman-esque death head paintings.

The motif of decadence continues in Alan Rudolph's *The Moderns* (1988), where Keith Carradine plays a 1920s art forger, and real-life convicted art forger David Stein produces real forgeries for the film. Both Rudolph and *Legal Eagles* director Reitman call attention to the affinities between

Hollywood and the art world, which, according to Reitman, "has become part of fashion, nightclubs and music" (20).

In addition to the popularity of the art world as a fictional milieu, the life of the artist as eccentric generates a revival of the art biopic in the 1980s. *The Wolf at the Door* (1987), which features Donald Sutherland as Paul Gauguin, revives the convention of the model who destroys the artist's work. The film's decor is coordinated with that of Gauguin's painting. Bruno Nuytten's *Camille Claudel* (1989)—depicting the life of the sculptor who was Auguste Rodin's model, lover and collaborator—is the first halfway feminist entry in the genre. Robert Altman deconstructs the artist as hero in *Vincent and Theo* (1990).

Reel art continues to represent the world of high style in such movies as James Ivory's *Slaves of New York* (1989), which portrays the New York art scene, and Martin Scorsese's "Life Lessons" segment for *New York Stories* (1989), which follows the middle-aged trials of successful painter Lionel Dobie (Nick Nolte). Although it plays a less prominent role, reel art also figures in *Ghost* (1990) in the form of Demi Moore's amateurish sculpture, in *L.A. Story* (1991) as part of the museum backdrop for Steve Martin's roller skating and as mall decor in Paul Mazursky's *Scenes from a Mall* (1990). So much a part of movies had reel art become in the late 1980s that Eddie Murphy easily parodied it (and *The Bill Cosby Show*) in *Coming to America* (1988) with black versions of classic Impressionist paintings on the walls of one of the character's homes.

Gone were the reverent awe for fine arts and the reductive literalism that characterized reel art in the Silent era. While many of the conventions established in those early days—the sense of art's magical powers, its aura of the romantic and adventurous, its power as a symbol of status and money—others disappeared by the eighties. Reel art had long since lost its association with religious motifs, and its role as a signifier of male-defined female sexuality was—understandably in terms of the times—muted. Nor was it confined to particular genres like the biopic, mystery/suspense or melodrama. Liberated from a static, literalist function and domesticated as a secular status symbol, reel art in the eighties became a comfortable part of the apparatus of modern life. Once assimilated into the world of film, it was free to take on a much broader range of meanings.

Notes

[1]Michael *Anderson's Around the World in Eighty Days* won the Oscar for Best Color Cinematography in 1956.

[2]See Eric Lunde and Doug Noverr's essay in this volume for a more extensive discussion of Hitchcock's use of art.

[3]Destruction of a painted portrait is also central to Stanley Kubrick's *Lolita* (1962).

Works Cited

Dowd, Maureen. "Experts Set and Torch *Legal Eagles* Art Scene." *New York Times* 30
    June 1986: C13.

Durgnat, Raymond. "Art for Film's Sake." *American Film* May 1983: 41-45.

Halliwell, Leslie. "Rembrandt." *Halliwell's Filmgoer's and Video Viewer's Companion.*
    9th ed. NY: Charles Scribner's Sons, 1988.

Norden, Martin. "Film and Painting." *Film and the Arts in Symbiosis.* Ed. Gary
    Edgerton. NY: Greenwood P, 1988.

Parker, Robert Andrew. "The Hand-In."*American Film.* Nov. 1985: 58ff.

Ratcliff, Carter. "Arty Movies, Locus Soho." *Art in America* Oct./Nov. 1978: 14.

Rickey, Carrie. "Great Artists of the Past Leave Their Imprint on the Movies of Today."
    New York Times 31 July 1983: II 15-16.

Taylor, Paul. "Lights! Camera! Easel!" *New York Times* 21 Feb. 1988 II 1 & 20.

Filmography

Year	Film	Director
1915	*The Hypocrites*	Lois Weber
1915	*Sold*	Edwin Porter/Hugh Ford
1915	*The Cheat*	Cecil De Mille
1915	*Trilby*	Maurice Tourneur
1919	*The Homebreakers*	Thomas Ince
1923	*A Woman of Paris*	Charles Chaplin
1923	*The Woman of Bronze*	King Vidor
1923	*While Paris Sleeps*	Maurice Tourneur
1924	*Cheap Kisses*	John Ince
1925	*Barriers Burned Away*	W.S. Van Dyke
1936	*Rembrandt*	Alexander Korda
1939	*The Light That Failed*	William Wellman
1940	*Rebecca*	Alfred Hitchcock
1941	*The Maltese Falcon*	John Huston
1941	*Suspicion*	Alfred Hitchcock
1942	*The Moon and Sixpence*	Albert Lewin
1944	*Experiment Perilous*	Jacques Tourneur
1944	*Bluebeard*	Edgar G. Ulmer
1944	*Laura*	Otto Preminger
1945	*The Picture of Dorian Gray*	Albert Lewin
1945	*Scarlet Street*	Fritz Lang
1947	*The Paradine Case*	Alfred Hitchcock
1947	*The Two Mrs. Carrolls*	Peter Godfrey
1948	*A Woman's Vengeance*	Zoltan Korda
1948	*Portrait of Jennie*	William Dieterle
1951	*An American in Paris*	Vincente Minnelli
1952	*Moulin Rouge*	John Huston

1954	*The Silver Chalice*	Victor Saville
1956	*Lust For Life*	Vincente Minnelli
1958	*Vertigo*	Alfred Hitchcock
1958	*The Horse's Mouth*	Ronald Neame
1962	*The Chapman Report*	George Cukor
1963	*The Birds*	Alfred Hitchcock
1964	*What a Way to Go!*	J. Lee Thompson
1965	*The Train*	John Frankenheimer
1965	*The Sandpiper*	Vincente Minnelli
1965	*The Agony and the Ecstasty*	Carol Reed
1966	*Gambit*	Ronald Neame
1966	*The Group*	Sidney Lumet
1966	*How to Steal a Million*	William Wyler
1967	*Guess Who's Coming to Dinner*	Stanley Kramer
1969	*Castle Keep*	Sydney Pollack
1978	*An Unmarried Woman*	Paul Mazursky
1978	*Fingers*	James Toback
1979	*Manhattan*	Woody Allen
1983	*Still of the Night*	Robert Benton
1983	*Lovesick*	Marshall Brickman
1983	*Terms of Endearment*	James L. Brooks
1984	*Beverly Hills Cop*	Martin Brest
1985	*After Hours*	Martin Scorsese
1986	*9 and 1/2 Weeks*	Adrian Lyne
1986	*Caravaggio*	Derek Jarman
1986	*Legal Eagles*	Ivan Reitman
1987	*Wall Street*	Oliver Stone
1987	*The Wolf at the Door*	Henning Carlsen
1989	*Coming to America*	Eddie Murphy
1989	*Slaves of New York*	James Ivory
1989	*"Life Lessons"* (*New York Stories*)	Martin Scorsese
1990	*Scenes from a Mall*	Paul Mazursky
1990	*Ghosts*	Jerry Zucker
1991	*L.A. Story*	Steve Martin

Tools and
Weapons

The Mary Ann, The Ruptured Duck and The Enterprise: Character Relationships with Air and Space Craft as Metaphors for Human Affinities

Ralph R. Donald

...Kirk loves the "Enterprise" more than he ever would any woman; loves her passionately and to the exclusion of all else. But she is a harsh mistress as well...So why such a great love for a starship? Kirk is in love with being *captain of the "Enterprise."* It is the position and the power—and the responsibility—which excites, motivates, and consumes him.

Walter Irwin
"Love In Star Trek," in *The Best of Trek*

One of the most recognizable characters in popular culture, *Star Trek's* Captain James T. Kirk and his epic love affair with the starship *Enterprise* are well known. But a man/machine relationship such as this is by no means as unique as one might think.

Virtually throughout the history of aviation and space flight pictures, flyers and flight crewmembers are conventionally portrayed as possessing a special affinity with their flying machines. In much the same way that a cowboy displays a special (and sometimes unnatural) affection for his horse, or a sea captain cherishes his ship, flyers can exhibit an unusual bond with the vehicle that propels and sustains them in flight.

The ways male, and occasionally female, protagonists in these films interact with their ships are usually complex, sometimes loving, sometimes lustful, sometimes irresponsible, sometimes Platonic and occasionally in mortal conflict. In short, they are metaphors for human interaction, especially those occurring between the sexes. The aim of this article is to examine and describe the conventions created by these character/airship thematic relationships, and to characterize them in terms of human relationships.

The Mother Ship

The first and most elemental of relationships between characters and their ships is that of mother-child. A mother gives life to her young, sustains them, nurtures them, and acts as an anchor and safe-haven for her children. For example, everyone's first reaction to "Mother," the computer that runs the space vessel "Nostromo" in the film *Alien* (1979), seems to fit this description. The ship's crewmembers are all tucked away in their uterus-shaped beds, sleeping in suspended animation under Mother's watchful eye. She disturbs her children's sleep only when a distress signal causes them to stray from their mission to investigate and render aid. When Captain Dallas requires advice or analysis beyond the capability of his crew, he enters a womb-like computer module, and communicates intimately with Mother.

Mother ships in aviation films often simulate the act of giving birth—but some mimic the birth and development of marsupials more than humans. This is because in these films, baby ships proceed out of the belly of mother ships, but then later return to the pouch. In *Close Encounters Of The Third Kind* (1977), an alien spacecraft referred to as the mother ship was the base from which tiny scout craft came and went. Likewise, in *Star Wars* (1977), the malevolent mother ship, nicknamed the "death star," served as home base for swarms of the Empire's fighter spacecraft.

That hybrid of ship and plane—the aircraft carrier—is also a source for studying the mother ship theme in action. In carrier films such as *Wing And a Prayer* (1944), *Bridges of Toko-Ri* (1954), and *Midway* (1976), coming home to the carrier after flying a combat mission is likened to "putting a baby to bed"— pilots find safety and security in a return to the womb.

In other pictures, the mother ship symbolically gives birth but once. In *When Worlds Collide* (1951), a Noah's ark of humans and animals is spared the destruction of the Earth caused by a runaway star. The ship, now the repository of all that remains of Earth's inhabitants, rockets off to another habitable planet, lands, and unloads its precious cargo, there to begin life anew, As well, in countless science fiction films during the 1950s and 1960s, malevolent alien mother ships land on Earth, spewing out space monsters intent on starting their lives over on our planet—usually with little or no regard for Earth's indigenous population.

The mother ship is also sometimes characterized as an umbilical cord between characters and home. In *Outland* (1981), a mining colony located on Io, one of Jupiter's moons, has only one substantive link with Earth: the shuttle. This is a spacecraft that populates the colony by transporting workers back and forth, and provides everyone with food and supplies. Everyone marks time by the arrivals and departures of the shuttle: Affixed on walls throughout the colony are clocks displaying the time remaining until the next shuttle arrives.

In other films, such as *The Last Starfighter* (1984) and *Star Wars*, the air/spacecraft portrays a less obvious symbol of motherhood. In films like these, the ship performs the difficult parental task of releasing its young from home, and launching its children into independent lives. In *The Last Starfighter*, both the con man Centauri's spacecraft and the gunship provide the means by which young Alex can leave the nest and begin his adult life. It is interesting to note that Centauri's spacecraft was automobile-like, subtly mimicking the emancipating role played by the automobile in American society—mobility serving as the teenager's first step toward independence. Likewise, in *Star Wars*, Luke already owns a hovercraft jalopy, but he eventually trades it in for passage on the "Millennium Falcon," the ship that will catapult him skyward to adventure, glory and adulthood.

Sometimes the mother ship's apron strings are tied too tightly, and affection for the ship and an unwillingness to leave it can retard a protagonist's natural development. In recent episodes of the television series *Star Trek: The Next Generation*, second-in-command Will Riker passes up opportunities to command his own vessel rather than leave the *Enterprise*, which has become his home, the very place where he ironically developed his potential for command. In that same series, young Wesley Crusher also has great difficulty deciding whether or not to leave the "Enterprise" to attend Star Fleet Academy. Whether it is by plot manipulation, fear of the future, or the young man's unconscious intent, Wesley always finds a way to delay his departure—and his transition to manhood. He helps a student succeed in an academy entrance test, but as a result, that student out-scores Wesley, and goes to the academy in his place. On another occasion, Wesley misses his ride back to earth, and yet another opportunity to attend the academy, because he stays behind to solve an engineering dilemma on board the ship.

The Wife Ship

The second conventional man/machine relationship is portrayed as less filial, more resembling that of a husband and wife. In some cases, this relationship actually becomes a substitute for spouse and family. Certainly Captain Kirk and the *Enterprise* come to mind in this context. Kirk, the son of a Star Fleet captain, grows up in Iowa with his lonely mother. If they're lucky, they see his father every six months or so, when he comes home on shore leave. So when Kirk grows up and becomes a starship captain, he chooses the unmarried—if not celibate—life, devoting himself to the Lady called "Enterprise." One of the major wolves of the galaxy, Kirk has amorous adventures with dozens of females from many different humanoid species. But no matter how much (or how often) he is attracted to other women, Kirk ultimately returns to—and recommits his faithfulness to—his ship.

A generation later, Jean-Luc Picard, captain of the current Starfleet vessel carrying the name "Enterprise," is also unmarried, and similarly wed to his ship. Since he was commissioned in star Fleet, Picard has made a conscious effort to avoid romantic entanglements. Nearly celibate, unsure with many women, and uncomfortable around children, confirmed bachelor Picard permits himself only one all-encompassing affection: his vessel.

But both captains possess one thing in common: Marriage to their ships is their outlet for expressing their love and fidelity for a deeper, more abstract object. In reality, each man's ship represents a concept that is the true object of their affections: Walter Irwin interprets Kirk's love of the *Enterprise* as really his love for the adventure, power and prestige that comes with being a starship captain. Employing the same logic in analyzing Picard, one could state that his affection for his vessel is Picard's way of personifying his love for space exploration and discovery.

Cut from the same cloth, but created a decade earlier than *Star Trek* creator Gene Roddenberry's characters, is *Forbidden Planet's* (1956) Captain J.J. Adams, commanding the United Planets starship with the unimaginative name of "C-57D." Like Kirk, Adams is a certified "space wolf" with the women and, also like Kirk, he seems to be wed to his vessel. However, in typical 1950s movie fashion, it is suggested that he may soon succumb to the charms of Alta, the young woman he rescues from the doomed planet. At the film's conclusion, the two stand on the bridge of the starship, holding each other, as they fly off into hyperspace.

As a human attempts to shield and keep his/her spouse from harm, characters also act protectively toward their ships. For example, in *Midway* and many similar movies, pilots refuse to bail out of badly damaged planes, and instead attempt to "bring them in." Aside from pilots' ego, their only motivation can be to save these ships. But it is often difficult to separate ego from genuine affection and attachment for their aircraft. To do so, we must look within each film for evidence of which factor provides protagonists with greater motivation. In the case of Capt. Matt Garth in *Midway*, it's clear that flying and the Navy are his entire life. Wounded at Pearl Harbor and beached, Garth performs his shore duties with skill and competence, but he's impatient for his damaged hand to heal, so he can fly once again. Later in the film, he's assigned duty as an operations officer on an aircraft carrier. Toward the end of the climactic battle for Midway Island, Garth gets his chance: His carrier has more aircraft than pilots, so he volunteers to "fly one off." Returning from his bombing mission, Garth's plane has been badly shot up, but he stubbornly refuels to ditch in the ocean. He tries to bring his plane in for a carrier landing, but his still-weak hand fails him, and he crashes in flames.

In *Rocketship X-M* (1950), Dr. Ekstrom devotes his life to developing a rocketship capable of journeying to the moon. Not willing to abandon the space craft to others, Ekstrom leads the first expedition. When technical difficulties develop in flight, he becomes defensive and blames the fuel mixture rather than the spacecraft. Ekstrom then slavishly devotes himself to solving the fuel problem, and resuming their adventure.

The reverse also occurs, in which the aircraft is portrayed as the devoted spouse caring for its mate. *The Memphis Belle* (1991) is an example. Based on the World War II documentary of the same name, the film provides a semi-factual account of the 25th and last mission of the first American B-17 to complete a tour of duty in the daylight bombing campaign against Germany. Although the Belle's pilot, Capt. Dearborn, named his aircraft after a girlfriend who lived in Memphis, his attitude toward her can best be described as that of a faithful, loving husband. The night before this last mission, Capt. Dearborn unburdens his heart to his Belle. He thanks her for helping him and his crew through 24 missions, and says he's confident that together the two of them will make it back from mission number 25. Although in real life the Belle's 25th bombing raid was not that difficult, Hollywood's version of this last flight could be subtitled "The mission from hell." Between unrelenting Luftwaffe attacks, flak hits, having to make two passes over the heavily-defended target, wounded crewmen, damaged engines and landing gear, only luck—or, as Capt. Dearborn would put it, the Belle's intervention—gets them back alive.

The Soul Mate Ship

Some relationships between pilots and their planes are more mystical than the husband-wife convention, and lend themselves more to a "dream lover" state. In this relationship there is more of a spiritual linking than a concrete relationship. In *A Guy Named Joe* (1943) and its remake, *Always* (1990), the protagonists, skilled flyers, like nothing more than to nose their trusty twin engine bombers up among the clouds and "listen the the music" of high flight. Both films' protagonists experience this, but have great difficulty explaining it to others, even other pilots. Both also die unusually early in these pictures. But then they become what amounts to aeronautical "guardian angels" for rookie pilots—and ectoplasmic advisors for their former girlfriends, who also are pilots. At the end of each film, with the help of these unseen spirits, each girlfriend successfully flies a dangerous and difficult mission, and the women, too, experience their own high flight ecstasy.

Similarly, in *God Is My Co-Pilot* (1945), Col. Scott, a World War II Flying Tiger in the China-Burma-India theatre, initially has no relationship at all with his aircraft. Rather, as the antithesis of the pilots in *A Guy Named Joe* and *Always*, he is convinced that nothing exists beyond his field of view. But during the course of the film, Scott discovers a mystic link between himself, his airplane, and God. Again, as in *A Guy Named Joe* and *Always*, Scott has great difficulty articulating this metaphysical joining, but through the magic of motion picture techniques (principally close-ups of pilots' glazed eyes, smilingly content faces, and choirs of heavenly angels on the sound track), audiences understand.

In *Dive Bomber* (1941), every pilot, from generals to flight cadets, is "crazy in love" with flying, and with aircraft. In the middle of arguments, parades, and conversations, pilots stop what they're doing to stare at a formation of planes flying over, or gaze with envy and longing at a lone plane overhead—all with the understanding that when they're on the ground, they want nothing more than to fly again—soon.

Dive Bomber, Ceiling Zero (1936), *Only Angels Have Wings* (1939) and *Flying Tigers* (1942) all share a recurring plot convention: a veteran flyer finds that, for one reason or another, he is physically unfit, and must be grounded for his own safety. Each pilot is so in love with airplanes and flight that he ignores his grounding and flies again—dying in the attempt. But regardless, audiences understand that if these men had to choose their method of dying, they would prefer to "check out" behind a stick and rudder. So in these cases, we see the aviation equivalent of two star-crossed lovers leaping to their deaths rather than live apart.

The Sister Ship

But not all such relationships suggest romantic love. Certain relations between flyers and their ships, although warm and caring, can be better described as fraternal and Platonic. Certainly the prototype of this relationship is the love between the crew of the "Mary Ann" and their bomber in the classic World War II saga, *Air Force* (1943). The film tells the story of a bomber crew that arrives at Pearl Harbor during the Japanese attack on December 7, 1941. Within a few days they find themselves in the middle of the first American counterattack in the Pacific against the Japanese. In a series of adventures as the bomber island-hops its way to the Philippines, the crew displays a love for the airplane that can only be described ad that of a protective big brother for his sister. At more than one point in the film, the crewmen risk their lives, staying behind to repair the plane, so it won't be destroyed along with the others. When the men speak about the "Mary Ann," they use reverent terms, and vow that "this girl" won't fall into enemy hands.

Although Capt. Ted Lawson didn't name his bomber after a girl, the crew of the "Ruptured duck" in *Thirty Seconds Over Tokyo* (1944) still reveres their aircraft in the same affectionate way as does the crew of the "Mary Ann." They brag about her as a proud sibling might, boasting that she's the finest ship in the squadron, and are convinced that "The Duck" will bring them safely home again. Unfortunately, after taking part in the Doolittle raid on Tokyo, their bomber barely makes it to the Chinese seashore, and then crashes. The aircraft is destroyed, its pieces scattered in the surf. The crew, and especially Lawson, although seriously injured, takes a moment to grieve "The Duck's" passing as they would a close relative.

The Combative Sibling Ship

In contrast to the foregoing conventions is a relationship best described in terms of two combative siblings, in which each attempt at any given task by one sibling is thwarted by the other. For example, in *The Right Stuff* (1983), Chuck Yeager's relationship with the jets he tests fits this description (although it could also be described as that of a cowboy breaking a wild horse). Yeager assumes that whenever he climbs into the cockpit, he will test his skill as the greatest living pilot against an aircraft that may malfunction at any moment.

Clint Eastwood's character also has great difficulty interacting with his stolen Soviet fighter plane in *Firefox* (1982). The aircraft is designed so that the pilot has only to look at the target he wants the aircraft to destroy, and tell the plane what he wants it to do. The aircraft's fire control computer does the rest. Unfortunately, he tends to forget that the aircraft is designed for pilots who speak Russian. In the final aerial battle with another similarly-armed Firefox, his missiles won't fire. Just before he is shot down, he remembers that he must tell the computer his commands in Russian. He does so, and the enemy is destroyed.

Sometimes this dysfunctional relationship displays itself in scenarios in which the human is ashamed of his sibling, and wants nothing more than to be disassociated from it. Such was the case of Lt. Col. Gately in the World War II Film, *Twelve O'Clock High* (1949). Because of his cowardice, laziness and malingering, Gately's new group leader assigns him command of an aircraft called "The Leper Colony." This plane is the bomber group's equivalent of the proverbial "dog house," to which every foul-up, goof-off and malingerer in the group is assigned. Because Gately can count on having the worst crew in the bomber group, flying in the "Leper Colony" was much riskier than in a normal bomber—and membership in that bomber's crew was a distinction to avoid at all costs. In this film, as is the case with many individuals, Gately chooses to rise above his dysfunctional family relationship. Although he has sustained an agonizingly painful back injury, Gately distinguishes himself by continuing to fly hazardous missions. Finally the pain becomes too excruciating, and he must be carried from his plane to the base hospital. When his group leader discovers this, he visits Gately in the hospital, and forgives him.

The "One-Night Stand" Ship

Some lovers use the opposite sex as if they were Kleenex: they use them and discard them, or, as the saying goes, "love 'em and leave 'em." In a number of aviation pictures, this "one-night stand" relationship is portrayed. For example, in *The War Lover*, (1962), bomber pilot "Buzz" treats his aircraft and girlfriends with equal disdain. He uses women, conquers them with a fury, and throws them away when he's used them up. Likewise, he pursues his role as an extremely successful bomber pilot with the same abandon and skill. But ultimately, both in love and war, he extends himself too far. First, to prove his sexual prowess, he attempts to steal his friend's girl—but he fails. His luck as a pilot runs out, too. On previous missions, no matter how damaged his B-17 had been, Buzz had always brought his ship home. But this time his aircraft is too shot up. They're trying to get back to their base, are over the English channel, but the bomber is swiftly losing altitude. Although Buzz orders his crew to bail out, his enormous ego prevents him from also parachuting to safety. But unlike the pilots of the Memphis belle or the Mary Ann, his insistence on bringing the B-17 home isn't due to love or loyalty—to Buzz the ship is just a tool to bomb Germans. He tries to bring the ship in just to prove that he can still do the impossible, that he's the best. But the aircraft is too badly damaged, and there's no magic between ship and pilot to help Buzz gain the needed altitude. So in attempting to clear the cliffs at Dover, he instead crashes into them.

Most pilots displaying this relationship don't fly bombers: Perhaps it's the cavalier, devil-may-care attitude of the fighter pilot, or perhaps it's because he only has himself to worry about. Regardless, in most of these films, many more fighter jocks prefer the one-night-stand than any other kind of pilot. In *The Hunters*, (1958), a Korean War film, Maj. Cleve Seville is characterized as a ruthless, Mig-killing machine, a fighter ace who also has no use for his aircraft except as a weapon. Because Seville seems to be emotionless, his commander calls him "the ice man." But later in the film, Seville performs a seriously unprofessional, emotional act: When his friend Lt. Abbott is wounded and shot down in enemy-held territory, Seville decides to intentionally crash-land his jet so that he can care for Abbott and help him escape. In this action, Seville certainly lays to rest the "Ice Man" label, but still shows his utter disregard for the million-dollar plane he destroys.

Likewise, in *Top Gun* (1989), Maverick appears to have no personal relationship at all with his aircraft. He's a talented pilot, perhaps the best there is, yet to Maverick, like to Buzz and Seville, his jet fighter is just a tool to be used, like a rifle. Unlike Buzz, Maverick is quite capable of sustaining relationships. He is in love with a female Top Gun instructor, and has a very close relationship with his co-pilot, Goose. When Goose dies in a plane crash, we see that Maverick is also capable of grief. But throughout the process of mourning for his friend and coming to terms with this tragedy, it's obvious that he doesn't extend this sense of loss to his multi-million-dollar aircraft. To Maverick it's simply a disposable item.

In the black comedy *Catch-22* (1970), the few sane pilots in the squadron spend most of their waking hours trying to figure out a way to survive the war. They couldn't refuse to fly without being court-martialed, and they couldn't claim they were too crazy to fly because that admission proves they're sane. That's the catch. The exception is Lieutenant Orr. He flies his missions gladly, so everyone assumes that he's crazy. Actually, Orr is planning his eventual escape to neutral Sweden in a life raft. He even rehearses being shot down, exposing his airplane to flak to test his theories of survival and raft navigation. At the conclusion of the film, after wasting a number of "rehearsal aircraft" like so many one-night stands, Orr pulls it off: he gets himself shot down, crash-lands in the water, and paddles his way to Sweden, where he can stay safely interned for the rest of the war.

Similarly, the pilots of *Air America* (1990) consider their CIA-owned aircraft mere toys to manipulate and throw away. One pilot, Gene Ryak, uses his planes to move contraband arms from place to place. Later, in a momentary fit of morality, Ryak off-loads and destroys his contraband guns to make room in his C-130 aircraft to rescue innocent villagers caught in a firefight. Since the cache of guns amounted to his CIA "retirement fund," Ryak decides to steal and sell the CIA's aircraft as repayment. Ryak also boasts, "I crash planes better than anyone I know." But another pilot, Billy Covington, is even more cavalier about his aircraft. Covington must escape from the villains of the film. To do this, he lands his plane, and to hide it, he taxies it inside the broken fuselage of a larger plane he crashed there the day before, breaking off the wings and tail of his new plane.

In both *Flying Leathernecks* (1951) and *Flying Tigers*, irresponsible rookie pilots are more interested in shooting down Japanese planes than in following orders designed to protect both their planes and themselves. The result: both pilots crash and destroy their own aircraft. Miraculously, both survive, but must face the terrible wrath of their commanders, in both films played by John Wayne.

But these flyers are the second generation of this type of "love 'em and leave 'em" pilot—James Cagney had written the book on the character in the previous decade. In such films as *Devil Dogs Of The Air* (1935), *Ceiling Zero*, and *Captains Of The Clouds* (1942), Cagney played the same irresponsible, selfish egotist who doesn't care about the planes he flies: they're just equipment. At one point in *Devil Dogs* he boasts, "I'll fly any plane, and the crates they come in." And in an impressive array of crashes in these pictures, Cagney's characters never once consider aircraft anything but disposable commodities.

Bruno Stachel, the Luftwaffe ace in *The Blue Max* (1966), is perhaps the coldest of these "users." Nearly emotionless after years as an infantry soldier in the trenches of World War I, Stachel is unable to enter into any relationship—male-female, pilot-to fellow pilot, or man-airplane, with any dedication beyond his own interests and ambitions. He uses, and disposes of, airplanes to kill allied soldiers with the same cold cynicism that he treats the love interest in the film. Poetically, his reputation as a pilot, obtained at the expense of these airships, is his undoing. He is killed testing a new aircraft on the very day that he receives his coveted Blue Max medal.

So, as mothers, wives, soul mates, sisters, siblings, and one-night stands, aircraft are portrayed as possessing truly unique, and amazingly human, attributes in the material world. There is something very special about Kirk's romantic love for his *Enterprise*, and the protective love of the *Mary Ann's* crew for their flying fortress. There is also something exceedingly similar to some male-female relationships in Bruno Stachel's and Cleve Seville's cold, pragmatic detachment from their fighter planes—relationships that often end up in divorce court.

Admitting the fact that many other material objects, such as cars, sporting equipment, motorcycles, etc., inspire their users to develop somewhat similar relationships, how then can one single out the character/aircraft relationship and call it unique? It is this writer's view that these man/machine relationships are special because no other interaction with objects in the material world permits humans to "slip the surly bonds of earth." And in these special relationships, filmmakers can portray character exposition in an environment that is at once exciting, inspirational and romantic. Since man first looked up and gazed with envy at birds in flight, he has yearned to fly. So it is not surprising that he might develop a truly special affection for the instrument used to achieve that end.

Filmography

Year	Film	Director
1935	*Ceiling Zero*	Howard Hawks
1935	*Devil Dogs Of The Air*	Lloyd Bacon
1939	*Only Angels Have Wings*	Howard Hawks
1941	*Dive Bomber*	Michael Curtiz
1942	*Captains Of The Clouds*	Michail Curtiz
1942	*Flying Tigers*	David Miller
1943	*A Guy Named Joe*	Victor Fleming
1943	*Air Force*	Howard Hawks
1944	*Thirty Seconds Over Tokyo*	Mervyn LeRoy
1944	*Wing And A Prayer*	Henry Hathaway
1945	*God Is My Co-Pilot*	Robert Florey
1949	*Twelve O'Clock High*	Leon Shamroy
1950	*Rocketship X-M*	Kurt Neumann
1951	*Flying Leathernecks*	Nicholas Ray
1951	*When Worlds Collide*	Rudolph Mate
1954	*Bridges of Toko-Ri*	Mark Robson
1956	*Forbidden Planet*	Fred M. Wilcox
1958	*The Hunters*	Dick Powell
1962	*The War Lover*	Philip Leacock
1966	*The Blue Max*	John Guillermin
1970	*Catch-22*	Mike Nichols

1976	*Midway*	Jack Smight
1977	*Close Encounters Of The Third Kind*	Steven Spielberg
1977	*Star Wars*	George Lucas
1979	*Alien*	Ridley Scott
1981	*Outland*	Peter Hyams
1982	*Firefox*	Clint Eastwood
1983	*The Right Stuff*	Philip Kaufman
1984	*The Last Starfighter*	Nick Castle
1989	*Top Gun*	Tony Scott
1990	*Air America*	Roger Spottiswoode
1990	*Always*	Steven Spielberg
1991	*Memphis Belle*	Michael Caton-Jones

Television Series: *Star Trek* and Star Trek: The Next Generation

Extra Innings:
Bats, Balls and Gloves
in Baseball Films of the 1980s
Howard Good

In contemporary baseball films bats, balls and gloves are more than playthings. They are significant objects, objects that glow with meaning, symbols. N. Roy Clifton, in *The Figure in Film*, listed some of the many ways in which "the mere things of a story" become symbols: by cultural context, by narrative, by convention, by lighting, by camera angle, by editing (29-50). When we ask, then, what the presence of a particular object or set of objects signifies in a film, we really are asking what is its relation to other elements of the film and to the culture beyond. The longer we ponder this question, the deeper the shadows on the screen seem. We begin to realize how immaterial— in the sense of "incorporeal," "spiritual"—the material world in popular American film is.

Baseball films are older than the World Series. What might charitably (very charitably) be called the first, Edison's minute-long *Casey at the Bat*, was produced in 1899. Since the turn of the century an estimated 200 films about baseball have been made—and mostly forgotten (Booth 45). Indeed, there is a Hollywood adage that baseball films are "box office poison" (Sayre 182). Producer Samuel Goldwyn expressed a version of it when *The Pride of Yankees* (1942) was first proposed to him. "If people want to see a baseball game," he said, "they should go to a ballpark" (Robinson 275).

Thus it is surprising, even puzzling, that baseball films staged a come-from-behind rally in the bottom half of the 1980s (Fuller 64). *The Natural* (1984) was followed to the plate by *Long Gone* (1987), *Bull Durham* (1988), *Eight Men Out* (1988), *Field of Dreams* (1989) and *Major League* (1989), to mention just the better known films. Suddenly such stars as Robert Redford, Kevin Costner and Tom Berenger were up there on the screen in the uniforms of the New York Knights, the Durham Bulls and the Cleveland Indians, making acrobatic catches, smashing out clutch hits. And the rally isn't over yet. At least a half-dozen baseball films were released or in production in 1991-92: *Talent for the Game*, *The Babe, Mr. Baseball, A League of Their Own* and *Comrades of Summer*.

The new popularity of baseball films obviously is bound up with the kind of stories they tell and the kind of images in which they tell their stories. Bats,

134

balls and gloves are a predominant part of the visual code, or iconography, of the films and serve various and often simultaneous functions within it. They serve as (1) a shorthand means of identifying a film as belonging to the category or class—I hesitate to use the much debated word "genre"—of baseball films; (2) a means of defining the status of characters; (3) a means of articulating or crystallizing an underlying theme; and (4) a means of conveying ideological values, particularly the conservative values of America's rural past. Whatever else baseball films are—and they have been criticized as being "either slapstick or schmaltz, bearing little relation to life within the baselines or beyond" (Booth 45)—they are complex, allusive, multi-layered works in which magic and religion, physical objects and psychological states, the myths of Hollywood and Cooperstown, converge.

A Means of Identification

"The idea and form of the Western," Richard Slotkin wrote in "Prologue to a Study of Myth and Genre in American Movies," "is [sic] inseparable from certain images—open space, horses, dust, false-front buildings, six-guns, and Stetsons; the idea and form of the gangster story is [sic] caught up in images of mean streets, slum boyhoods, the ambience of out-group ethnicity" (418). Similarly, the idea and form of the baseball film are linked to images of bats, balls and gloves. The presence of these objects visually distinguishes the baseball film from other types of films, as well as dictates many of the conventions or cliches by which the baseball film is known and recognized by filmgoers.

Through consistent usage from one baseball film to another, images of bats, balls and gloves have become charged with meaning and thus can serve filmmakers as a vivid, economical way to establish milieu. *Trading Hearts* (1987), for example, begins with a series of slow-motion, black-and-white shots of pitcher Vinnie Icona (Raul Julia) struggling on the mound. Even as the opening credits roll, we see him pick up a rosin bag and then toss it down; see him wearily remove his cap, wipe the sweat from his forehead with his sleeve, and wearily replace his cap; see him lean in toward the plate to get the catcher's sign while gripping the ball behind his back—the ball, now seen in close-up, coiled, potent, fateful. With a few suggestive visual strokes, the creators of *Trading Hearts* immediately identify the category or class to which the film belongs and evoke the corresponding set of audience expectations.

And what precisely are these expectations? That the setting for much of the film will be a ballpark and its environs...that the ballpark will be the focus of not only sharp physical contests, but also of mythical or magical events...that most of the characters will be male and members of a losing baseball team...that the team will be managed by a profane, overweight, somewhat futile father figure called "Pop"or "Skipper"...that eventually the team will unite around a veteran, battle-scarred player who is himself seeking legitimacy and renewal...that the first female lead will be a sort of fertility goddess and the second female lead her dark double, a siren allied with the forces of destruction and death (greedy team owners, oily gamblers, etc.)...that the theme will deal with time and change, beginnings and endings, the upheaval of passing from an old stage of life to a new one...that the ideology of the film will be nostalgic and conservative, opposed to the city and modern business and the values that underlie them.

Images of bats, balls and gloves introduce a pattern, a system of conventions and connotations, that will fully emerge over the course of the film. To a certain extent, they do even more than introduce the pattern; they actually determine it. The dynamic is similar to that of the Western, where six-guns are an essential—perhaps *the* essential—icon. As Thomas Sobchack pointed out, the guns impose on the characters who wear them a limited range of responses to situations, afford a limited range of plot options (45). It follows that the standard plot of the Western must inevitably climax with a final fatal showdown between the hero and villain.

The Western showdown has its counterpart in the baseball film, with bats, balls and gloves substituting for guns. *The Natural, The Slugger's Wife* (1985), *Chasing Dreams* (1986), *Long Gone* and *Major League* all culminate in the protagonist's last at-bat during a championship game. This is the tense, terrifying moment of confrontation toward which the protagonist has been propelled from his very first appearance with a bat or ball or glove in his hand. In *The Natural* "middle-aged rookie" Roy Hobbs (Robert Redford) clouts an epic home run with two outs in the bottom of the ninth. In *Long Gone* "Stud" Cantrell (William Peterson) goads a pitcher against whom he is batting less than .100 lifetime into hitting him with a pitch. In *Major League* Jake Taylor (Tom Berenger) beats out a surprise bunt despite bum knees. But is it the batter, or the stick that he holds, that really wins the game?

A Means of Defining Character

As the six-gun defines the cowboy in film, so bats, balls and gloves define the baseball player. They are the tools of his trade and the way he handles them reveals his character, his psychology. The pattern has been fixed ever since the mighty Casey struck out in Ernest L. Thayer's famous poem more than 100 years ago.

The players in contemporary baseball films tend to fall into two broad categories: promising youngsters and worn-out veterans. The first group has talent. What they don't have yet are the experience and discipline to use their talent constructively. As catcher Crash Davis (Kevin Costner) tells rookie pitcher Ebby Calvin "Nuke" LaLoosh (Tim Robbins) in *Bull Durham*: "You've got a gift. When you were a baby, the gods reached down and turned your right arm into a thunderbolt. You've got a Hall-of-Fame arm, but you're pissing it away."

Crash himself belongs to the second group of players. These have plenty of experience, but have seen their skills gradually diminish through injuries and age. Now they are struggling to hang on to the game they love, to have, as Jake Taylor puts it in *Major League*, "just one more good year in the sun." The struggle is slightly ludicrous: here, after all, are grown men who insist on continuing to play a boy's game, who refuse to acknowledge that boyhood ambitions—to make the "bigs," to be "the greatest that ever was"—are dead and gone, and that a new stage of life is upon them. Complains Jake's former fiancee (Rene Russo): "You'll always just be a little boy who wouldn't grow up."

But though they may seem to their frustrated wives and girlfriends to be cases of arrested development, the over-the-hill players are more than mere boys in tired men's bodies. They are engaged in a mythical quest, a quest for identity, continuity, their place and purpose in the scheme of things. Before they are forced out of baseball, they must, on the one hand, fulfill the dreams of the fading generation, represented by the grizzled old manager, and on the other, impart their know-how to the rising generation represented by the undisciplined rookie. The survival of the game—or of the team, the community, that best embodies the game's deepest, greenest values—depends on their courage and savvy and luck.

Generally the more immature a character is, the wilder he throws or the clumsier he bats. A good example is Nuke LaLoosh, described by the manager of the Durham Bulls as having "a million-dollar arm and a five-cent head." In his professional debut Nuke doesn't just walk 18—a league record—but also plunks a sportswriter, the PA announcer and the Bulls' mascot with the ball. His control problems on the mound are a metaphor for his control problems off it. "He fucks like he pitches," Millie, a baseball groupie, observes, "sort of all over the place."

Major League features a whole team of clods and clowns. There is pitcher and juvenile delinquent Rick Vaughn (Charlie Sheen), who earns the nickname "Wild Thing" when he loads the bases on 12 straight pitches and then gives up a grand slam. There is rightfielder and voodoo worshiper Pedro Serrano (Dennis Haybert), who believes he can't hit a curve ball because his bats are "sick." There is a third baseman and prima donna Roger Dorn (Corbin Bernsen), who declines to dive for ground balls. "I took one in the eye last year," he explains. "I'm not about to lose my sight." All are emotionally or morally flawed in some way, and their inept play reflects this.

Writer-director John Sayles' *Eight Men Out*, based on Eliot Asinof's revisionist history of the Black Sox scandal of 1919, offers the grimmest portrayal of sloppy baseball as moral corruption. The film opens with the

Chicago White Sox clinching the pennant behind the pitching of Eddie Cicotte (David Strathairn), the hitting of "Shoeless" Joe Jackson (D.B. Sweeney) and the fielding of Oscar "Happy" Felsch (Charlie Sheen again). But the victory sparks no raucous celebration in the clubhouse. The players are bitter over their cheap, abusive treatment by team owner Charles Comiskey. As much out of hate for Comiskey as out of greed, they conspire with gamblers to throw the World Series. They game they once played with pride and pleasure they now play with criminal intent. Their fall from grace is measured by the balls that roll off their gloves, the base hits that fly off the opposition's bats. It is all very sad and shabby. Fans and teammates are betrayed, careers and souls destroyed, for an untrustworthy promise of dirty money.

Sayles, as Frank Ardolino remarked in a recent article, is the "dissenter" among directors of contemporary baseball films, exhibiting an uncommon pessimism about the chance, in either baseball or life, for late-inning rallies, sudden and unexpected comebacks (45). Usually in these films a last-place team—the New York Knights in *The Natural*, the Tampico Stogies in *Long Gone*, the Durham Bulls in *Bull Durham*, the Cleveland Indians in *Major League*—miraculously becomes a first-place one. The catalyst for the transformation is a man with a checkered past and an uncertain future, but a beautiful swing.

He has many names: Roy Hobbs, Stud Cantrell, Crash Davis, Jake Taylor. No matter what he is called, he can be recognized by his confidence and self-control at the plate. "Homer, triple, single—anything he wants to hit, he hits," sportswriter Max Mercy (Robert Duvall) says with awe of Hobbs. Awe-inspiring blasts occur in film after film. Stud, coming up to bat in the bottom of the ninth in a tie game, tells his teammates, "Now, gentlemen, I'm going to show you how to be a hero." He promptly rips the first pitch to him clear out of the ballpark.

But there is more to being a hero than belting home runs. The heroic role requires an active conscience as well as an active bat. So long as Stud lives by his oft-repeated motto, "Fuck 'em if they can't take a joke," he is just another dumb ballplayer, drinking, philandering and riding the team bus to the next dinky town on the circuit. To be a real hero, Stud must develop a sense of responsibility for his world, a world gown cold and dark while he frolicked. "Who needs heroes?" mythologist Shirley Park Lowry asked, and answered: "The community does. Great insights keep getting lost, and only a hero, able to see behind a particular community's muddle, can retrieve them" (84).

A Means of Crystallizing Theme

Because it is an untimed game, baseball seems pecularily fit to serve as a basis or background for certain types of stories—stories about initiation, about rites of passage, stories about dying and being reborn. Unlike football or basketball, which are governed by the clock, baseball has its own pace and rhythms. A team's turn at bat can be long or short or, theoretically at least, endless. As Roger Angell, who philosophizes about baseball for *New Yorker* magazine, once wrote, "Since baseball time is measured only in outs, all you have to do is...keep hitting, keep the rally alive, and you have defeated time" (320).

Baseball bends linear time in another sense. For both adult players and spectators, it provides a chance to recapture lost youth. "One need not be a young man to cherish the game;" novelist George V. Higgins wryly noted, "one of the nicest things about it is the gentle way that it reminds you of what it was like to be eighteen, and have all your teeth" (113). Nostalgia has always been a source of baseball's appeal. Frank Pigeon, captain of the Eckford nine of Brooklyn in the 1850s, recalled that he and his teammates "would forget business and everything else on Tuesday afternoons, go out on the green fields, don our ball suits, and go at it with a rush. At such times we were boys again" (Lamoreaux 597-98).

Spatially as well as temporally, baseball is different from other sports. Football, basketball, hockey and soccer are organized into polarities; that is, the action oscillates between the goals. Baseball's movement is uniquely circular, around the bases and back to home. The circle is the most common mankind's symbols for God and eternity (Edinger 211). Is it accidental, Allen Guttmann wondered in *From Ritual to Record*, that the four bases correspond numerically to the four seasons of the year, the sacred cycle of birth, growth, death and renewal (107)?

And yet there remains a poignancy to the passage of time in baseball. The game may have eternity at its command, but individual players get old and weary and fade away. "...a ball player," sportswriter Roger Kahn observed, "must confront two deaths. First, between the ages of thirty and forty he perishes as an athlete.... At a point when many of his classmates are newly confident and rising in other fields, he finds that he can no longer hit a very good fast ball or reach a grounder four strides to his right. At thirty-five he is experiencing the truth of finality.... Mortality embraces him" (*Boys of Summer* xviii-xix).

The fact that baseball combines both the mythical and the mortal, the archetypal and the merely archaic, has, I think, rendered it attractive to filmmakers as a metaphor for human development. "This growth process," child psychiatrist Bruno Bettelheim explained, "begins with resistance against the parents and fear of growing up, and ends when youth has truly found itself, achieved psychological independence and moral maturity, and no longer views the other sex as threatening or demonic, but is able to relate positively to it" (12). The thematic pattern of most baseball films couldn't be described more succinctly.

Bettelheim argued that fairy tales can help children cope with the strains of growing up. The tales help, he said, by translating the hidden contents of the unconscious into visual images: witches, talking animals, deep, dark forests (14, 25, 94, 155). There is a possible link here to film, where inner states also are externalized as the figures and events of the story. Perhaps baseball films became popular in the eighties—an era marked, in the words of one commentator, by "greed, narrowness, and strange want of joy" (Shames 27)—because their iconography reflected the audience's search for a persuasive model of what a functioning adult should be. Of course, no baseball film contains a frog prince or spooky forest, but several do feature some rather unusual bats and balls.

Such as Roy Hobbs' bat "Wonder Boy" in *The Natural*. Hobbs made the bat from a special tree on the farm where he grew up. At the foot of the tree—the tree of life and the tree of knowledge in the Judeo-Christian heritage; the bo tree under which Buddha received his great revelation; the world-tree of the Norse—his father collapsed and died, and later the tree itself was knocked down by lightning. In folk belief lightning fertilizes the earth. Ancient Greeks regarded places and people struck by lightning as holy (Lowry 235). The barrel of "Wonder Boy" is engraved with the insignia of a lightning bolt.

Hobbs appears one day at the ballpark of the New York Knights, carrying the bat in a long black case. He had set out sixteen years earlier to be the best player ever, but had met the very beautiful and very crazy Harriet Bird (Barbara Hersey) on a train to Chicago. On reaching the city she had lured him to her hotel room and had shot and nearly killed him. Although the bullet is still buried in his left side—a Christ-like wound—Hobbs now has a second chance to fulfill his destiny. It is a symbolic version of our own, the discovery or achievement of adult values and responsibilities.

The Natural, like the novel by Bernard Malumud on which it is based, weaves together biblical allusions, Greek myths, Arthurian legends and baseball folklore. Knights manager "Pop" Fisher (Wilford Brimley), a surrogate for the Fisher-King of the grail legend, rules over a sterile land. His ballfield is hard and dry and scabby, his team is stuck in last place, his job is coveted by an evil owner and undermined by a crooked gambler. Hobbs can revive the land if he submits totally to the task. At one point he seems to forget why he joined the Knights and has an affair with Pop's treacherous niece, Memo Paris (Kim Bassinger). The result is a terrible batting slump. But when he stays deserving—alert, faithful, brave—supernatural aid comes to him through "Wonder Boy." He swings and literally tears the cover off the ball.

"Wonder Boy" meets a curious end. Hobbs breaks his beloved bat during the playoff game for the pennant. In Malamud's novel this is a sign of his ultimate unfitness to be the grail knight, but in the film it is a sign that he has matured and no longer requires outside support. He has absorbed the bat's magic, internalized its power. With two strikes on him, he borrows another bat and lifts the next pitch into the arc lights, which explode in a celebratory shower of gold.

Balls—"small, round, solid, and full of life" (Smith 15)—also help protagonists attain a meaningful identity. In *Chasing Dreams* (1986) a gawky farm boy named Gavin Thompson (David J. Brown) becomes the unlikely star of his community college baseball team, but is still dominated and derided at home by an ogrish father. Gavin's two biggest fans are his younger brother, who is dying and confined to a wheelchair, and an assistant coach with a heavy limp. Bettelheim noted that in fairy tales "physical malformation often stands for psychological misdevelopment" (70). The cripples are aspects of Gavin himself, reflections of his unwillingness or inability to leap from the parental nest. What he needs is a good knock on the head, and he gets one when he is beaned by a pitch in the final game of the season. He wanders through the rest of the film in a sort of visionary trance.

Joseph Campbell tells us that rites of passage in primitive tribes are "distinguished by formal, and usually very severe, exercises of severance, whereby the mind is radically cut away from the attitudes, attachments, and life patterns of the stage being left behind" (10). Gavin is launched on some such passage, retreating from the outer world to clarify his psyche. As it was a baseball that sent him off on his interior journey, so it is a baseball that brings him back. He finds an old scuffed-up ball lying under a bush and suddenly remembers playing catch with his now-dead brother. The memory reconnects him to history and family, but on a more positive basis than before. "Dad?" he calls in a groggy voice. Father and son embrace. The circle of the ball has dissolved into the circle of the generations.

Stealing Home (1988) is another film in which a ball both stimulates and symbolizes a character's coming of age. In this film, though, the ball isn't covered with cowhide and stitched with red thread. It is a gold charm on a chain, a gift to Billy Wyatt from his baby-sitter and spiritual adviser Katie Chandler (Jodie Foster). She insists that the boy always wear the necklace so that "You don't ever forget who you are. You're a baseball player." He later becomes a standout on his prep-school team, attracting the interest of major-league scouts. But growing up remains just as dangerous for him as for more ordinary teenagers. While home on spring break, he loses his virginity to the girl-next-door and commemorates the event by giving her the necklace. He forfeits, in effect, all protection when he strays over the border of adulthood.

The years that follow are dark, disorienting, a naked descent into the world's chaos. His father dies in a car crash; his baseball career founders; his good fairy, Katie, kills herself. The shock and hurt of her suicide causes the grown-up Billy (Mark Harmon) to retrace his steps—the film is a dizzying series of flashbacks within flashbacks—and try to figure out where he went wrong. Along the way he recovers the necklace from the girl-still-next-door, who has kept it like a promise. The last scene, set in a cozy, minor-league ballpark on a sun-drenched afternoon, shows him back in the right relation to fate. He bangs a triple in the bottom of the ninth and then steals home and wins the game.

By achieving psychological independence and moral maturity, Billy releases hidden powers in himself and is able, finally, to do what he was born to do. But what he was born to do wasn't only to score the winning run. It was also to create a family of his own. The typical baseball hero gets paired with a woman as he emerges from identity confusion: Billy with the girl-still-next-door, Roy Hobbs with Iris (Glenn Close), Crash Davis with Annie Savoy (Susan Sarandon), Stud Cantrell with Dixie Lee Boxx (Virginia Madsen). Growing up means answering the call to be fruitful and multiply.

Baseball is explicitly linked with sex, marriage and parenthood in *Bull Durham* and *Long Gone*. Annie Savoy, in the voice-over narration that opens *Bull Durham*, declares: "There's never been a ballplayer that slept with me that didn't have the best year of his career. Making love is like baseball—you've just got to relax and concentrate." She is the self-appointed high priestess of the Bulls—an animal, incidentally, that was a common fertility symbol in ancient cultures (Lowry 50)—whose job is to give chosen minor-league players "life wisdom" and help them reach the majors. This season she chooses hayseed Ebby Calvin LaLoosh for her bizarre rites. "When you know how to make love," she says, taking out a rope to tie him to the bed, "you'll know how to pitch."

But Ebby—or "Nuke," as she nicknames the fireballer—is only a boy, and a pretty unripe one at that. A more appropriate mate for her in terms of age and experience is veteran catcher Crash Davis. "Oh my!" she gasps when she first sees his long, smooth home-run stroke. His power complements or completes hers, and between them, they "mature the kid." At the end of the film Nuke is up in the majors and out of the way, and Annie and Crash are together, their union blessed by "the church of baseball." Crash has a good shot at becoming the manager in Visalia next year and father to a whole new brood of Nukes.

If it seems silly to suggest that the hero's bat is a phallus, then consider that the hero of *Long Gone* is named Stud, and that he is always saying things like "Kid, I'm going to tell you one of the great truths you're going to learn in a lifetime—all girls fuck." The recipient of this piece of information is Jamie Weeks (Dermot Mulrooney), second baseman for the Tampico Stogies, who proceeds to "knock up" his girlfriend Esther (Kathy Boyer). When Stud finds Jamie anguishing over the pregnancy and whether to marry the girl, he hastens to set the boy straight. "Son," he intones, "listen to the words of the master. Women only get pregnant if they want to. It's a goddamn trap."

Stud is the male principle, but undirected, incomplete, wasting itself in crude macho posturing. He needs a monster to slay, a war to fight, a woman to love, and in time he gets them. The monster is the business side of organized baseball; the war is the clash for the pennant; the woman is Dixie Lee Boxx. Dixie is in every way Stud's equal; even her last name, slang for the female genitals, is equal to his first name. After the monster is killed and the war won, Stud and Dixie and their young proteges, Jamie and Esther, are married in a double ceremony at the Stogies' home ballpark. The happy couples march to the altar between two rows of players, who hold aloft, in a sort of sexual salute, shining bats.

A Means of Conveying Ideology

Baseball films are conservative, and not just because one of their standard plots has a roughneck being housebroken by a woman. They are conservative because of their underlying ideology, which is anti-business, anti-city, anti-modern. This probably reflects the "primitive-pastoral elements" in baseball itself. As Allen Guttmann noted, the hitter who swats the ball over the fence and then trots around the bases is unconsciously imitating prehistoric runners whose exertions were intended to bring the dead land to life again (114).

All ball games played by teams originated in ancient fertility rites. "Egyptians combined sport with their spring ceremony," George Grella explained, "splitting up a group of priests into two teams which fought to move a ball across a designated line or through the doorway of a temple" (551). The ball may have represented the head of Osiris, the god of agriculture, or it may have been a sun symbol. In either case the ball was related to the idea of fertility, and the game was a ritual combat between the forces of good and evil, light and darkness, summer and winter (Henderson 8-9, 15, 19).

Guttmann and others have suggested that baseball draws on "whatever traces of primitive religion remain in modern man" (104-105). Grella called it "the nearest thing to a national Rite of Spring that all Americans can celebrate and enjoy," pointing out that "Even in cold climates we know that if Opening Day has come, Spring cannot be far behind" (551). But baseball's closeness to the rhythms of nature is only one dimension of its pastoralism. The very atmosphere of the sport—sunshine, high skies, grass—is firmly pastoral, or was until the advent of artificial turf and domed stadiums in the 1960s. Players used to refer to the ballpark as "the garden" or "the orchard" (Coffin 56).

It is out of this rich background that the quasi-religious, quasi-rural ideology of baseball films emerges. The ideology is expressed partly by bats, balls and gloves, which serve in a number of films as conductors of supernatural or occult powers, powers excluded from modern life, forgotten. "Wonder Boy," the sacred bat that Roy Hobbs made from a lightning-struck tree in *The Natural*, has been mentioned already. No less cosmic (though somewhat more comic) are certain bats and gloves in *Bull Durham* and *Major League*.

The Hispanic second baseman of the Bulls ritualistically rubs his bat with a chicken-bone cross. "Takes the curse off the bat and makes me hits," Jose confides to a teammate. We laugh, perhaps, at his superstitions, but later, when his girlfriend puts a hex on his glove, he commits three errors in a single game. Similarly, in *Major League*, Cuban-born player Pedro Serrano sets up a voodoo idol named Jo-Boo near his locker and leaves the ugly wooden gnome offerings of cigars and rum. One day Harris, a teammate who has scoffed at Jo-Boo in the past, drinks the sacramental rum, then calmly strolls out onto the field—and gets knocked unconscious by a thrown bat.

Although meant to be humorous, these incidents still reveal the existence of terrifying primal forces just beyond the margins of the known world. Of course, minor characters like Jose and Pedro cause mostly mischief by enlisting the forces. A central character like Hobbs, on the other hand, causes bitter upheaval. Once he begins to communicate with his gods, he precipitates crises, disrupts established patterns, releases unsuspected creative energies. He lives up to Joseph Campbell's description of the mythological hero as "the champion not of things become but of things becoming; the dragon to be slain by him is precisely the monster of the status quo..." (337).

In baseball films the status quo is represented by team owners—Judge Banner in *The Natural*, the Buchanans, father and son, in *Long Gone*, ex-Las Vegas showgirl Rachel Phelps in *Major League* who use their authority to corrupt and oppress. All of them seek, in a reversal of normal expectations and for a variety of selfish reasons, to keep their teams from winning the pennant. It is dark work, discussed in whispers and carried out with bribes and threats. The owners personify the worst features of modern society—routine violence, moral chaos, the steady deterioration of community.

Often opposed to them or to other evil figures are protagonists from rural America, a place identified in the films with everything good and true. We are introduced to Hobbs, "a natural" in more than one sense, through nostalgic vignettes of his farm boyhood: young Roy shagging flies in a chest-high field of wheat; young Roy throwing a pitch at the side of a barn and shattering the old weather-beaten boards; young Roy having a catch with his soil-stained father at day's end. These memories, revolving around the land and full of innocence and peace, haunt Hobbs down the years and define the goal of his quest. His struggle against the Judge's perverse rule is, at bottom, a struggle to return home, to restore a vanished world, to regain the condition of paradise. Significantly, when we last see Hobbs, he is playing ball with his own son in the same golden field where his father had played ball with him.

This isn't to say there aren't any rubes—or, for that matter, any urbane intellectuals—among the central characters of baseball films. Nuke LaLoosh of *Bull Durham* is pretty much the stereotypical bumpkin, while his mentor, Crash Davis, knows that the novels of Susan Sontag are "self-indulgent, overrated crap." But it does seem that baseball films have always idealized rural life to a considerable degree; the hero of *The Pinch Hitter* (1917), the earliest extant feature film with a baseball theme, is a lad from the Vermont backwoods who ultimately conquers the snobs at his college by cracking the winning home run in a championship game. Today the country boy still exhibits the virtues and values that Americans like to attribute to themselves, still incarnates a mythical national heritage of freedom, equality, initiative, and courage. In *Chasing Dreams* farm-bred Gavin Thompson grips the bat just as he would an ax, with hands spread far apart, a visual reference to his connection to the legendary frontiersmen who tamed the wilderness.

The conflict between country and city, between community and commerce, between traditionalism and modernism, is waged in baseball films with bats and balls. Roy Hobbs' bat "Wonder Boy" isn't only a totem and an occupational tool, but also a weapon, a war club. He smashes one ball through the window of the press box, scattering the vulturous sportswriters from their perch. He smashes another through the huge clock atop the scoreboard. His explosive hits bring about the collapse of a decadent society. Old confining patterns break into fragments, and the universe opens up and shows what is possible.

Players who wield bats as weapons do so to extend the range of the human over the inhuman. The Tampico Stogies of *Long Gone*, for example, use theirs to rout a lynch mob. As they are heading home after a victorious night game, their team bus is halted by Ku Klux Klansmen gathered in the middle of the road around a burning cross. The Klansmen demand that the team send out its fine black catcher, Joe Louis Brown (Larry Riley). Instead, Stud Cantrell shouts, "Batting practice!" and the Stogies grab their bats, charge off the bus, and put the Klansmen to flight. Brown then personally knocks down the burning cross with one vicious swing.

Bats again become instruments of liberation or extralegal justice toward the end of the film. Both Stud and Brown have accepted bribes to miss the playoff game for the pennant. Stud's bribe is the promise of a managing job in the minor league system of the St. Louis Cardinals and Brown's is a shiny new Cadillac, that well-recognized symbol of material success. But their loyalty to their teammates is too strong for them to stay permanently bought. Before hurrying to the ballpark to don their uniforms, they take turns beating the Cadillac into a pile of junk metal with Brown's bat. They are applying the democratic credo that Stud had expressed moments earlier in the hotel bar. "Baseball ain't nothing but a little boy's game played on some grass," he said. "It shouldn't matter who the pitcher's daddy is or how much money he makes. It shouldn't matter what color a fellow's skin is. You just go out there with a bat in your hands, hit the ball and run like hell."

Of all the baseball films of the 1980s, probably the most nostalgic for old American values is *Field of Dreams*, based on W.P. Kinsella's 1982 novel,

Shoeless Joe. Humorist Dave Barry irreverently described the film as "the heartwarming story of a man, played by Kevin Costner, who receives instructions from corn." More precisely, it is a film about second chances, about the eternal human desire to redo the past. Iowa farmer Ray Kinsella (Costner) breaks the bonds of chronological time by obeying a mysterious voice he hears in his cornfield and a la *The Natural* during a lightning storm. "If you build it," the voice says, "he will come." Ray plows under his corn and builds a baseball diamond.

Onlookers declare him a "damn fool" and predict he will lose his farm. And he almost does lose it to his brother-in-law Mark (Timothy Busfield), a generic capitalist obsessed with the bottom line and outraged by the creation of a "useless" ballfield in the middle of rich farmland. Against Mark and the mercenary corporate culture he represents, the film sets the counterculture of the Vietnam War era. Ray and his wife Annie (Amy Madigan) are both graduates of Berkeley. Officially Ray majored in English, but really he majored in the '60s. "I marched, I smoked some grass, and I tried to like sitar music," he recalls. The voice symbolizes or addresses the unfulfilled ideals of his "flower power" past; Annie even jokes after he hears it for the first time that maybe he had an acid flashback.

Ray's ballfield is a strange, hallucinatory place, a sort of sacred grove where wishes and memories take bodily shape. There he patches things up with his dead father; there long-silent author Terence Mann (James Earl Jones) recovers the urge to write and publish; there Shoeless Joe Jackson (Ray Liotta) and the other Black Sox who were banned from baseball for life play again; there Doc Graham (Burt Lancaster) gets the turn at bat he missed 50 years ago in his one inning in the majors. These instances of rejuvenation deeply touched audiences. Three years after the film was released, people still pilgrimaged to the ballfield used in it. The field lies on Don Lansing's farm a mile or so outside Dyersville, Iowa, and they came from Nebraska, from Arkansas, from Missouri, from California, to run around the bases, to stand on the pitcher's mound, to dig in at the plate—and, of course, to buy souvenir postcards and T-shirts (Stark 1B).

"Baseball's hold on American males," Roger Kahn pointed out, "has been traced by many...to the relationship of fathers and sons" (*Good Enough* 190). The many include poet Donald Hall, who lyrically wrote, "Baseball is father and sons playing catch, lazy and murderous, wild and controlled, the profound archaic song of birth, growing, age, and death" (42). One of Ray's great regrets is that in his rebellious teens he had refused to play catch with his father. He fixes this when his father appears on the field as a young ballplayer in the final scene. "Hey, dad, do you wanna have a catch?" Ray asks. "I'd like that," his dad says. They begin to toss the ball back and forth, back and forth, working up a rhythm. The soft, repeated plump of the ball into their gloves is the sound of America dreaming.

Conclusion

So why do we watch baseball films? It can't be because we are baseball fans. Most baseball films fail to give even a fleeting sense of what Christopher Lehmann-Haupt called "the entire ballet of baseball," the intricate interlocking movements of pitcher, batter and fielders (87). The fact is that baseball films and baseball games are two very different things. They have different casts, different settings, different rules, different functions. Samuel Goldwyn was right: if people want to see a baseball game, they should go to a ballpark.

Baseball films aren't really about baseball. They are about the perilous process of growing up. The stories they tell are mythical versions of our own life stories, our own trying passages through time and change. We discover on Hollywood's ballfield men who share our longing for reconciliation and order and for a past that can't return; who confront the unknown future equipped only with bats, balls and gloves and boyhood dreams of baseball glory; who suffer the same doubts and bewilderments we do, but who still undertake large quests and bring back boons that help make the world a safer and more just place.

These men are heroes, and we need heroes. Living in the dying moments of the twentieth century, surrounded by ghosts and abandoned gods, we face, individually and collectively, vexing questions about who we are and where we are headed. Baseball films offer an answer of sorts. They tell us that magic exists. They tell us that we can go home again. They tell us that, no matter what the calendar says, it is always baseball weather.

Works Cited

Angell, Roger. *The Summer Game*. NY: Popular Library, 1972.

Ardolino, Frank. "Ceremonies of Innocence and Experience in *Bull Durham, Field of Dreams*, and *Eight Men Out*." *Journal of Popular Film & Television* 18 (Summer 1990).

Asinof, Eliot. *Eight Men Out*. NY: Henry Holt, 1963.

Barra, Allen. "Hollywood Keeps Striking Out On Real-Life Baseball." *New York Times* 28 April 1991, sec. 2.

Bettelheim, Bruno. *The Uses of Enchantment: The Meaning and Importance of Fairy Tales*. New York: Alfred A. Knopf, 1976.

Booth, Stephen A. "Hollywood Goes to Bat." *Video Review* Sept. 1989.

Campbell, Joseph. *The Hero With a Thousand Faces*. Princeton, N.J.: Princeton UP, 1949.

Clifton, N. Roy. *The Figure in Film*. Newark, Del.: U of Delaware P, 1983.

Coffin, Tristram Potter. *The Old Ball Game: Baseball in Folklore and Fiction*. NY: Herder & Herder, 1971.

Edinger, Edward. *Ego and Archetype*. NY: Putnam's, 1972.

Fuller, Linda K. "The Baseball Movie Genre: At Bat or Struck Out?" *Play & Culture* 3 (1990).

Grella, George. "Baseball and the American Dream." *Massachusetts Review* 16 (Summer 1975).

Guttmann, Allen. *From Ritual to Record.* NY: Columbia UP, 1978.

Hall, Donald. "Fathers Playing Catch with Sons." *Baseball Diamonds.* Ed. Kevin Kerrane and Richard Grossinger. NY: Anchor P, 1980.

Henderson, Robert W. *Ball, Bat and Bishop: The Origin of Ball Games.* NY: Rockport P, 1947.

Higgins, George V. *The Progress of the Seasons.* NY: Henry Holt, 1989.

Kahn, Roger. *The Boys of Summer* NY: New American Library, 1971.

_____.*Good Enough to Dream.* Garden City, NY: Doubleday, 1985.

Lamoreaux, David. "Baseball in the Late Nineteenth Century: The Source of Its Appeal." *Journal of Popular Culture* 11 (1977).

Lehmann-Haupt, Christopher. *Me and DiMaggio: A Baseball Fan Goes in Search of His Gods.* NY: Simon & Schuster, 1986.

Lowry, Shirley Park. *Familiar Mysteries: The Truth in Myth.* NY: Oxford UP, 1982.

Malamud, Bernard. *The Natural.* NY: Farrar, Straus & Giroux, 1952.

Robinson, Ray. *Iron Horse: Lou Gehrig in His Time.* NY: W.W. Norton, 1990.

Sayre, Nora. "Winning the Weepstakes: The Problems of American Sports Movies." *Film Genre: Theory and Criticism.* Ed. Barry K. Grant. Metuchen, NJ: Scarecrow P, 1977.

Shames, Laurence. *The Hunger for More: Searching for Values in an Age of Greed.* NY: Times Books, 1989.

Slotkin, Richard. "Prologue to a Study of Myth and Genre in American Movies." *Prospects: The Annual of American Cultural Studies.* Vol. 9. Ed. Jack Salzman. Cambridge: Cambridge UP, 1984.

Smith, Robert. *Baseball.* NY: Simon & Schuster, 1947.

Sobchack, Thomas. "Genre Film: A Classical Experience." *Film Genre: Theory and Criticism.* Ed. Barry K. Grant. Metuchen, NJ: Scarecrow P, 1977.

Stark, Al. " 'Dreams' do come true on a diamond in Iowa." *Poughkeepsie (NY) Journal* 16 April 1991.

Selected Filmography

Year	Film	Director
1917	*The Pinch Hitter*	Victor Schertzinger
1942	*The Pride of the Yankees*	Sam Wood
1984	*The Natural*	Barry Levison
1985	*The Slugger's Wife*	Hal Ashby
1986	*Chasing Dreams* ·	Sean Roche and Therese Conte
1987	*Long Gone*	Martin Davidson
1987	*Trading Hearts*	Neil Leifer
1988	*Bull Durham*	Ron Shelton
1988	*Eight Men Out*	John Sayles
1988	*Stealing Home*	Steven Kampmann and Will Aldis
1989	*Field of Dreams*	Phil Alden Robinson
1989	*Major League*	David Ward

Lethal Weapons:
The Gun as Icon in the
Popular Urban Vigilante Film
Gary Hoppenstand

One of the more popular types of crime motion pictures to have surfaced in recent years is the urban vigilante film. These movies have not only become star vehicles for some of the most famous male names in Hollywood—actors who frequently look better delivering a punch or karate chop than a line of dialogue—they have also provided their producers the opportunity to make low budget, high profit pictures, films that seem to find perpetual release both in the local movie theater and on home video. Yet despite its obvious popularity at the box office and in the video store, the critical reception given to the urban vigilante film has, at best, been extremely negative, or has, at worst, not existed at all. This essay aims to draw attention to this much neglected cinematic genre, and it specifically intends to do this by focusing upon a particular thematic element: the icon. First, though, a definition of the urban vigilante film will be advanced, including its placement within the larger spectrum of the crime/detective genre and a brief history of its development in the film mass media. Then, a definition of the term "icon" will be presented, and along with this definition, a recognition of the importance of the gun as icon in both American culture and in the popular urban vigilante film will be outlined. Finally, a discussion of two important urban vigilante films—*Dirty Harry* (1971) and *Death Wish* (1974)—will be offered that specifically illustrates the metaphoric function of the gun as iconic symbol.

Before addressing the particulars of the urban vigilante film, or the gun as significant icon in these movies, a recognition of the importance of audience response needs to be addressed, a discussion that doesn't rely as much upon audience response theory as upon personal observation. During every film showing at the local motion picture theater, there are two performances: one on the silver screen and one in the theater's audience. I first realized this truth several years ago. When a colleague learned that I was researching the popular urban vigilante hero in film and fiction, he suggested the next time I view the latest release in the urban vigilante genre (and the films of this genre are produced more frequently than what most people think) that I keep an eye on the audience as well as the movie. Immediately following this conversation, I went to see *Cobra* (1986), directed by George P. Cosmatos and starring Sylvester Stallone, and my very informal, unscientific observation of people's reactions during *Cobra*'s showing revealed an intensity of emotional response that was, quite frankly, surprising. The theater was full, since the movie was in its first day of release, and very few empty seats were evident. No doubt capitalizing upon his notoriety from his past two blockbuster series, the "Rambo" and "Rocky" films, Sylvester Stallone had packed the house for his latest cinematic effort. Even though the intellectual content of the movie left a great deal to be desired, during those frequent instances of intense violence, the audience gasped, cheered, and, interestingly, laughed. During one particular scene when the vigilante hero, Cobra, confronts a rather nasty grocery store terrorist with the statement, "You're the disease, and I'm the cure," and then promptly guns down the terrorist, a number of the people in the crowd hollered an intense whoop of glee. And when the leaders of the cult serial killer biker gang receive their just, grim punishment at the conclusion of the story, the audience cheered and hooted their obvious joy. I had realized even before the final credits made their appearance that what I had witnessed was a truly cathartic moment, an instance when movie and movie audience were united in a powerful grip of emotion, and subsequent emotional release.

Indeed, sometimes what happens with the film's audience is much more interesting than what's happening artistically with the film. Undeniably, *Cobra* is a "bad" movie: it is overacted, lacks subtlety, and contains too much gratuitous violence. But then, most urban vigilante movies are bad, if one's standards are cinematic art. If, however, the viewer were to gauge audience interaction with a motion picture as a measure of success, then a great number of bad vigilante films are actually rather good at what they do. They flood the senses of their audience with powerfully symbolic images, archetypal characters, and highly ritualized myth-narrative action. Their simple goal is emotional involvement. Urban vigilante films are one of two movie genres—the other being horror films—that are *not* interested at all in intellectual reflection. Both horror and urban vigilante films are laden with powerful emotional baggage, material that lacks narrative subtlety, but that packs a puissant wallop when viewed (most probably because of their lack of subtlety). Each of these two genres first seeks to shock its audience, then emotionally resolves the effects of that shock, either in a negative (the horror film) or a positive (the urban vigilante film) fashion. The less either of these two types of popular motion pictures involves intellectual reflection, the better. But this does not deny the fact that both of these film genres are very skilled in what they do. They are sophisticated because of their denial of sophistication.

The urban vigilante protagonist can be defined simply as a middle-class hero who takes the law into his or her own hands in order to counteract the vicious threat of crime and the terrible acts of evil, violence-loving criminals.

During the process of fighting crime in the city streets, the urban vigilante becomes judge, jury, and executioner, circumventing the "law" (which is frequently portrayed as either being inefficient or corrupt) in order to save society and preserve the ideological concept of law and order from those who would subvert it at the expense of the weak and innocent. The urban vigilante originated in the popular Western story, and descended from the literary cowboy/lawman figure, a protagonist who employed his impressive skills with six-shooter or Winchester rifle to tame the old West. The vigilante hero from this tradition is not to be confused with vigilante gangs, often portrayed as a group of mindless "red-neck" killers hell-bent on senseless hangings, and who are even more anarchistic than those they intend to "string up." The urban vigilante made the transition from western town to city street in the pages of the dime novels and pulp magazines. The most famous urban vigilante hero before World War II is perhaps Street and Smith's pulp magazine avenger, "The Shadow." Author Walter Gibson wrote many of The Shadow's 325 adventures (which first began publication in 1931), and this .45 automatic toting, grimly cloaked figure of the night became the driving inspiration for numerous other urban vigilante lawmen during the Great Depression, characters like "The Spider," "Captain Satan," and "The Phantom Detective," among numerous others. Basically, the urban vigilante "catered to the societal desire for simplified solutions to complex situations" (Hoppenstand 123), and they were immensely successful in accomplishing this cathartic function, as aptly demonstrated by their overwhelming presence on American newsstands of the 1930s. The urban vigilante then made the jump to the mass market paperback book in 1969. In the novel *War Against the Mafia*, Don Pendleton introduced his vigilante hero, Mack Bolan—otherwise known as "The Executioner"—and, as was done with Street and Smith's Shadow series nearly 40 years earlier, a host of paperback vigilante heroes blasted their way into the reading habits of many Americans, bearing such descriptive appellations as "The Death Merchant" and "The Butcher" and "The Destroyer."

The cinematic urban vigilante, like his literary antecedent, also drew most of his inspiration from early Western movies. In Hollywood's many popular film interpretations of the traditional Western story, it was soon learned that visual imagery could quickly and effectively provide essential background material without hindering the pace of the movie's narrative flow, action that was so crucial to a visually oriented adventure story. Objects like horses, clothing, the desert landscape, the Western town, and perhaps most importantly, the gun, provided the film audience with easy and certain reference to the good guy, the bad guy, and the plot. In his earliest guise, the urban vigilante hero evolved from the hard-boiled detective formula, from movies like *The Maltese Falcon* (1941)) and *The Big Sleep* (1946). Recently, the urban vigilante has been made popular in a number of action/adventure films featuring highly identifiable and charismatic male actors, such as Clint Eastwood, Charles Bronson, Chuck Norris, Steven Seagal, and Jean-Claude Van Damme. The movies showcasing these actors tend to highlight violence as entertainment, and also tend to be strongly masculine in their point-of-view. The urban vigilante discovered his greatest popularity in two movie series, the "Dirty Harry" films starring Clint Eastwood, and the "Death Wish" movies starring Charles Bronson. These two series have also defined the two major divisions, or categories, of the urban vigilante film. Paul Kersey in *Death Wish* has typified the traditional vigilante protagonist, an "average" character who has been terribly violated by city crime and who discovers the courage and skill within himself to fight back, while Harry Callahan in *Dirty Harry* best illustrates the cop vigilante, a policeman who should otherwise be bound by the regulations of his occupation and by the laws of society in general but who often takes the law into his own hands to combat more effectively the forces of crime. From these two motion picture series, a host of imitations, both good and bad, have assaulted the moviegoer and video junkie alike.

As with their print medium counterparts, the motion picture urban vigilante exploits several basic, powerful thematic devices that help to facilitate action, such things as myth-narrative structures, formulaic rituals, race and gender oriented stereotypes, and perhaps most importantly, icons. *The Popular Culture Reader* provides a social-psychological definition of what constitutes an icon:

Popular icons are objects that suggest emotional and/or intellectual meanings beyond their physical appearance or use. These are the three-dimensional "things" of our culture, and…they include the images of those things which have been created and disseminated in two-dimensional pictures…Icons are artifacts which are symbolic—they communicate ideas, beliefs and values; icons always *mean* something…Popular icons are all around, and every part of the environment which has been shaped or built by human forces is therefore a reflection of human values. Streets, buildings, signs, and all the other human-made objects are representative of our ideals, fears and aspirations. (Geist and Nachbar 97-98)

In the urban vigilante film, icons appear everywhere. They encompass such things as the city street setting, frequently detailing the crime-ridden, run-down condition of the city, yet some icons also suggest in an obvious way that if crime were eliminated, then the city would become a fine place in which to live. Icons also are emblematic of the movie's stereotypical characters. For example, note the three drug-crazed freaks' appearance as they rob and terrorize Paul Kersey's wife and daughter, a disgusting mien reflecting disgusting criminals. But the most important icon in the urban vigilante film is, undeniably, the gun. Equally important is the way in which the vigilante protagonist arms himself with his iconic gun to do battle with crime, an arming ritual if you will.

From the beginnings of our nation to the present day, America has had a love affair with guns and with what guns mean to us symbolically as part of our cultural identity. Naturally, during the early colonial period, the musket came in quite handy when attempting to prevent starvation, but the gun for early Americans meant much more than a tool for hunting (though that tool often meant the difference between life and death). It had political significance as well. Our nation's leaders, when designing the Bill of Rights, adopted as one of its amendments the right to bear arms. This was done in an attempt to prevent the types of repressive governments found in Europe at the time, the rationale being that if the population was well armed, then a totalitarian regime would have a much more difficult time establishing itself. The gun has remained for Americans through the years an object of reverence, and recently, an object of scorn. It has helped to define the nature of that most significant of American stereotypes: the rugged individualist. From Daniel Boone to John Wayne, a number of celebrated American heroes, both factual and fictional, have blazed their way through our history and our entertainment with their trusty guns. Our Western frontier was tamed by the Colt peacemaker, and as a variety of our traditional Western stories have shown us in images of print and film, civilization was achieved and protected by the most violent acts, specifically, by killing Indians and outlaws.

The gun has also been adopted as the weapon of choice by those urban cowboys, the city cop and the private dick. And yet, in many of our contemporary crime motion pictures, the gun has equally been portrayed as an object of evil, as the weapon of choice of the evil, nasty criminal. Guns in the urban crime film no longer are used just to protect law and order; they are also used to disrupt it. And as our mean city streets became meaner, the urban crime film took an interesting turn in the early 1970s. It became less concerned with law, and more concerned with order, order bought and paid for in the most ferocious manner possible. This new breed of crime movie, the urban vigilante film, was ultra-violent, first showing its viewers rape, murder, and general mayhem perpetrated by the lowest of criminal scum on the most vulnerable members of our society: women, children, and the elderly. Then, after our film's protagonist had had enough of this carnage, he (or she; in several urban vigilante films, the vigilante figure is a woman) becomes a self-appointed executioner, and with weapon in hand thus creates no small measure of his or her own carnage, but carnage that functions like a surgeon cutting a cancer from a sick body in order to make that body healthier. A specific examination of two of the most important urban vigilante films, *Dirty Harry* and *Death Wish*, will reveal just how important the gun as icon is to these movies specifically, and to the genre as a whole.

Dirty Harry, directed by Don Siegel, actually began the trend in the modern crime picture towards featuring an urban vigilante hero. It established several of the important motifs to be found in the genre, including the conflict between the vigilante hero and the established law enforcement bureaucracy, the portrayal of the crook as a psychopathic maniac possessing no redeeming moral or social value whatsoever, the potential for harm caused by these psychopathic criminals against those stereotyped vulnerable members of society (such as women and children), the hero's reliance on violence to solve the complex legal problem about what to do with crooks when caught, and most significantly, the thematic reliance on the hero's gun to kill the offending criminals in order to make society safe. Even though it features a cop as a hero, and not a true vigilante protagonist per se, *Dirty Harry* became the most influential film of the genre, setting the style and tone for the subsequent cinematic category for years to come, and influencing such popular movies as the "Death Wish" series, the "Lethal Weapon" series, and its own sequels.

Dirty Harry begins with Inspector Harry Callahan (Clint Eastwood) of the San Francisco police force on the trail of a serial killer, a rooftop sniper who calls himself Scorpio (Andrew Robinson). Scorpio is demanding from the city of San Francisco the sum of $100,000, or else he will *"enjoy* killing one person every day" until the money is paid (the emphasis on the work "enjoy" is mine; it underscores Scorpio's degenerate love of killing). Callahan is reluctantly teamed with an Hispanic rookie cop, nicknamed Chico Gonzales (Reni Santoni), and together they continue their tracking of the Scorpio killer, at one point engaging in a nighttime cross-rooftop gun battle. Scorpio abducts a teenage girl, buries her with a limited amount of air to breathe, and then raises his extortion demand to $200,000. Callahan becomes the drop-off man for the money, and is led on a merry chase from phone booth to phone booth, so that Scorpio can be assured that Callahan is not being followed. What Scorpio doesn't know is that Callahan is "wired," and that Chico is backing him up. Scorpio finally meets Callahan underneath a towering cement cross. After disarming Callahan, Scorpio takes the bag full of money, and then proceeds to beat the Inspector. However, before Scorpio can kill Callahan, Chico arrives at the scene and engages Scorpio in a gunfight. Chico is wounded, but Callahan is able to plunge a switchblade knife into Scorpio's leg, causing the killer to flee. Chico is hospitalized, and Callahan continues his pursuit of Scorpio, eventually tracking him to Kezar Stadium, where Scorpio lives and works. Callahan tortures Scorpio in order to find the location of the buried teenage girl, but when the girl is exhumed near the Golden Gate Bridge, she is already dead. Scorpio is released from custody on legal technicalities, and Inspector Callahan is reprimanded by the District Attorney's office for his failure to follow standard police procedures. Undaunted, Callahan continues to follow the recently freed Scorpio. To get Callahan off his back, Scorpio hires someone to beat himself up, and then Scorpio claims police brutality, that Callahan attacked him. Soon after, Scorpio abducts a bus load of schoolchildren; he uses them as hostages to barter for his $200,000 and a plane in which to escape. Callahan tracks down the abducted bus, jumps on it as it passes beneath a bridge, and then causes Scorpio to abandon his plan by leaving the bus and escaping into a factory and quarry nearby. Callahan chases his antagonist one last time through the factory, but as he nears the killer, Scorpio grabs a boy fishing nearby in a quarry pond and holds a gun to the boy's head. Callahan still shoots and wounds Scorpio, and the boy escapes. As Scorpio reaches for his gun, Callahan executes the psychopath. His job done, and done counter to what the "system" expected of him, Harry Callahan throws his police badge into the pond during the final scene of the film.

Sexual and religious images dominate *Dirty Harry*. Sex and humor play a minor role in the movie when a running gag is established where Harry Callahan is caught several times playing the voyeur. But these are harmless antics, employed to lighten the tension of the search for Scorpio, and also to bait a little bit the otherwise somber character of Inspector Callahan. During the opening scene of the film—when Scorpio, the rooftop sniper, is targeting through his high-powered rifle scope a beautiful woman who is swimming in a rooftop pool below him—the camera frequently cuts between images of the woman and a visually elongated shot of Scorpio's rifle with silencer attached. The overt connection between violence and a helpless, beautiful woman is intended; it establishes for the viewer the notion that Scorpio is a rapist of the worst sort, an assassin who kills innocent victims with his phallic weapon. Dirty Harry, on the other hand, several times, as he attempts to thwart Scorpio's evil plans, is surrounded by religious symbols. During Callahan's first battle with Scorpio, for example—a gun duel across the city rooftops at night—Callahan is standing beneath a revolving neon sign that vertically spells out the phrase "Jesus Saves," and later, when Harry is delivering Scorpio's ransom, both cop and killer stand (and fight) beneath a huge concrete cross. Countered against the sexual perversity of the serial killer Scorpio is the righteousness of the Biblical avenger, Harry Callahan. Opposing Satan's angel of death and destruction is the Lord's own agent. The movie *Dirty Harry* ultimately serves as a dialectic confrontation between sin and salvation, and the specific thing that makes the difference, that tilts the battle against crime in the direction of the "good guys," is Callahan's gun (a .44 Magnum, "the most powerful handgun in the world"), and Callahan's deadly skills using that gun.

A brief scene near the beginning of *Dirty Harry* nicely emphasizes not only the relationship in the film between Harry Callahan and his .44 Magnum, but also highlights how the urban vigilante hero's very identity is qualified by his gun. Callahan is eating lunch at a restaurant, when an armed robbery occurs at a bank across the street. With people screaming and alarms ringing, Callahan casually walks across the street and yells at the robbers to halt (with his mouth full of food, no less). Of course, the bank robbers attempt to flee; Callahan shoots and kills those trying to escape in a car. He also wounds a shotgun-wielding robber and approaches the still dangerous criminal. The robber eyes his gun, which is within arm's length, and Harry Callahan says:

I know what you're thinking. Did he fire six shots, or only five? Well, to tell you the truth, in all of this excitement I've kinda lost track myself. But being that this is a .44 Magnum, the most powerful handgun in the world, and would blow your head clean off, you've got to ask yourself one question. Do I feel lucky? Well, do you punk?

The robber decides not to challenge either Callahan or his luck. However, as inspector Callahan begins to walk away, the robber asks Callahan if he was indeed out of ammunition by stating: "Hey? I gots to know." Callahan turns to face the prostrate robber, raises and aims his .44 Magnum at the robber, and clicks off an empty shot. The crook is nearly scared out of his wits while Callahan smiles at his deadly jest. Callahan, most emphatically, loves tormenting those who torment others. In addition, Callahan's weapon is the "most powerful handgun in the world," and aside from the obvious sexual reference to the protagonist's masculine potency, it more correctly is a statement about the vigilante hero's crime fighting efficacy. The robber has a gun, but Callahan's is more powerful. The robber is skilled in the art of violence, but Callahan can be even better at being violent. This scene shows how the typical urban vigilante film narrative is basically a one-upmanship ritual: the crook kills someone, and the urban vigilante hero returns the deed, only more so (i.e. more criminals are killed than victims); and if the crook responds with even more violence, then the vigilante protagonist simply brings a bigger gun to the fray and wins the day for justice and order. Callahan repeats this specific one-upmanship ritual with the Scorpio killer at the conclusion of *Dirty Harry*, but whereas the bank robber has backed down earlier, Scorpio tests Callahan's resolve by going for his weapon, and consequently gets blown away by the cop vigilante hero for his gamble.

When Harry Callahan kills with his gun, it's as if he were a frontiersman killing a wild, dangerous animal so that his isolated family can sleep safer at night. Typically, in the urban vigilante film, crooks are portrayed as raving maniacs, with no sense of moral decency. They have no personality, no background, no human-ness. They kill indiscriminately, terribly. They are usually viewed terrorizing women or children, which thus reinforces exactly how vile they truly are. After all, Scorpio himself ferociously shoots both women and children during his killing sprees, and later kidnaps a bus full of children, no doubt in order to engage in additional, perverse violent acts. In fact, the crooks in the urban vigilante film are worse than animals, since animals kill for survival—these crooks kill because they like it. When Harry Callahan finally executes Scorpio, it's a jubilant moment because order has triumphed over chaos. Yet, ironically, order triumphs over violence in these movies with violence. The urban vigilante hero defeats his antagonist because he is a better killer. The vigilante's gun is the means for a cathartic purging—at one level a purging of society of its criminal cancer, and at another level a purging of emotions for the film's viewers, who have been trained, during the course of the movie's narrative, to believe that the crooks deserve to die (and die horribly).

Death Wish was strongly influenced thematically by the earlier released *Dirty Harry*. It recounts the story of New York City architect (Charles Bronson) Paul Kersey's transformation from a passive victim of violent crime to a gun-toting urban vigilante. The film begins with Kersey's wife, Joanna (Hope Lange), and daughter, Carol Toby (Kathleen Tolan), being violently attacked and robbed in the Kersey apartment by three young, brutal assailants. Joanna dies as a result of her severe beating, while daughter Carol sinks deeper each day into mental illness because she can't deal emotionally with her rape. Carol ultimately has to be committed to a sanitarium, and she finally becomes catatonic. In order to escape the scene of the tragedy, Paul Kersey decides to travel west to Tucson, Arizona on a business venture. His job entails the ironing out of the particulars of the Jainchill Realty's multi-million dollar housing development proposal. In Tucson, Kersey makes the acquaintance of Aimes Jainchill (Stuart Margolin), the boss of Jainchill Reality, and he gives Kersey a tour of "Old Tucson, the famous movie location and studio," where they witness a staged performance of a "Wild West" bank robbery by actors and stunt men. During this performance, Kersey deliberates about the value of Western style justice. Later, Jainchill invites Kersey to his "gun club," where Kersey ably demonstrates his proficiency shooting handguns. Kersey finally works out a compromise between his company and Jainchill Realty, and prepares to return to New York. Before Kersey leaves Tucson, however, Jainchill slips a mysterious present into Kersey's traveling bag. When Kersey returns to his apartment and unpacks, he opens Jainchill's present, only to discover a pearl-handled (or ivory-handled) .32 caliber revolver. With such a timely present, Paul Kersey takes to the city streets like a Western lawman. He seeks to kill criminals who attempt to mug him. He is attacked several times by vicious criminals, whom he promptly shoots and kills for their efforts. The New York City Police, led by Inspector Frank Ochoa (Vincent Gardenia), first attempt to identify the vigilante killer, and then when they learn that their vigilante is Paul Kersey, they seek to quietly warn him off, to get him to stop his activities, or better yet, to leave town. The police don't want to arrest Kersey, or bring him to trial, because the D.A.'s office is well aware that Kersey's activities actually have made the streets safer, that crime has significantly dropped. Inspector Ochoa eventually catches a wounded Kersey in the act of killing crooks and convinces him to leave town. Paul Kersey, at Inspector Ochoa's request, decides to transfer in his job to Chicago. At the Chicago airport, he witnesses a gang of wild hooligans knock a woman and her packages to the ground. As he bends down to help the woman, he points his finger like a gun at the cavorting youths and acts as if he is shooting at them. The implication in this scene is that Paul Kersey's days as a vigilante killer are far from over.

Despite its rather straightforward plot, *Death Wish*, directed by Michael Winner, is a film of complex stunning visual, and conceptual, contrasts. Hawaii, where Paul Kersey is vacationing with his wife Joanna as the movie begins, is enchanting, beautiful, fantasy-like, and is quickly counterpoised with a grim, dirty, cold New York City when the Kerseys return home from their trip. Serenity and tranquility literally surround the Kerseys as they frolic on the beach in the brief opening moments of the film. During the evening when the Kerseys are at a luau, they are serenaded by enchanting native songs. It's made obvious in the briefest of visual images that no other two people could be more in love than Paul and his wife. As they return home—during the opening credits of the film—a city gripped in the skeletal hands of winter awaits them. Ugly, polluted shades of dirty orange hang in the city sky. In Hawaii, they enjoyed privacy on an exotic beach, even deliberating whether to make love on the beach or not. In New York City, the Kerseys are stuck in city traffic when they take the cab home. Hawaii reveals the Kerseys to be alive and vital; New York shows them to be passive, almost zombie-like (e.g. note the vacant expression of their faces as they sit in the traffic-snarled cab at the beginning of the film, waiting to get home). Throughout the remainder of *Death Wish*, the setting of the film gives the viewer the powerful impression of death and dying—such moments as Joanna's funeral, Paul stalking the near lifeless city streets hunting for his next victim, and the sanitarium where the mentally disturbed Carol is confined.

In addition to these important contrasts established in the film's setting, a contrast in character and ideology is also advanced during the film's narrative. Near the beginning of *Death Wish*, Paul Kersey is jokingly described by his friend at work as being a "bleeding heart liberal." Kersey does not deny this appellation, but soon after the murder of his wife and the violent rape of his daughter, Kersey abandons his earlier so-called liberal attitude in favor of something much more violent, much more reactionary. Before the personal tragedy, Kersey is passive, a mere watcher of crime. After the tragedy, he becomes active in his dislike of crime.

Jainchill's Tucson "gun club" suggests not only Jainchill's own reactionary attitude about the importance of gun ownership to the community, but also the vigilante hero's general philosophical stance about how to make the city streets safe from criminals. Early in this scene, Aimes Jainchill states:

This is gun country. You can't even own a gun in New York City. Out here, I hardly know a man who doesn't own one. And I tell you something; unlike your city we can walk our streets and through our parks at night and feel safe. Muggers operating out here, they just plain get their asses blown off.

Jainchill then asks what war Kersey was in, and Kersey discloses that he was a "C.O." in a medical unit during the Korean War—a conscientious objector,

Kersey corrects Jainchill, not a commanding officer. Kersey subsequently proceeds to demonstrate his great skill with a handgun by shooting a target dead center to the amazement of a flabbergasted Jainchill. This seeming paradox of a conscientious objector knowing how to use a gun effectively illustrates the duality of Kersey's personality, a conflict between peace and violence, life and death. Kersey's desire for revenge ultimately consumes the passive, peace-loving side of his personality, and this love for revenge translates into a violent preservation of order, a lawless attack against those who would prey on the weak and helpless. Kersey tells Jainchill at that gun club that even though Kersey's father trained Paul in the handling of guns, after his father was killed in a hunting accident, Kersey's mother convinced him to avoid guns. But Kersey announces to Jainchill that he loved his father, and thus proclaims that his masculine, aggressive, gun-loving side has triumphed over his feminine, passive side.

After Paul Kersey is introduced to the "Code of the West" philosophy as illustrated at the Wild West performance at the Old Tucson movie set, a code fraught with a pro-vigilante stance, and when he returns from the moral West to the corrupt East, Aimes Jainchill clandestinely tucks a wrapped present into Kersey's luggage. Kersey's trip back home is metaphoric, as well as physical. This present will not only define Kersey's transformation from liberal pacifist to right-wing vigilante killer, it will also come to symbolize his re-birth. As mentioned eariler, Jainchill's gift to Kersey is a .32 caliber pistol. And despite Jainchill's pedestrian discussion about a gun being nothing more than a "tool," in Kersey's hand the gun becomes something more than a mere tool; it becomes the vehicle by which Paul Kersey enacts his epiphanous retribution against that class of people who have wronged him: criminals. His retribution is a symbolic act, since he never actually confronts the three specific assailants who attacked his family.

The new Paul Kersey is sexually connected to his gun. It defines both his evolving male identity, and his function as mythic, national hero. The gun embodies Kersey's masculine side of his personality. It reflects, on a larger level, a patriarchal, *Old Testament* "an eye for an eye" style of justice. In the urban vigilante film, when a gun is used to attack society—to terrorize those who are weak and helpless—then this is generally understood by the viewer to be a subversive use of the weapon, a use that undermines the mythic function and redemptive potential of the weapon. Subsequently, when Paul Kersey—as vigilante hero—uses his "special" gun to kill criminals, literally to make the city streets safe from evil desperados (like the town marshals of the frontier west), then he is assigning to the gun a function that it was originally meant to have in our society, an instrument by which the family can be fed and protected, a utensil for the establishment and defense of our nation, and a device that is ultimately emblematic of the American frontier itself, where civilization triumphs over savagery (in the sense that John Cawelti outlines the concept in his study, *The Six-Gun Mystique*, 1984), and where a decent, moral individual nobly guards those all-important symbols of civilization (i.e. the town itself, women, and children). Paul Kersey, and many other traditional urban vigilante heroes in popular crime movies, cognitively reinforce for us the notion that the gun is not inherently a bad thing. It is made bad by bad people, good by good people (thus returning us back again to Aimes Jainchill's original definition of a gun as a tool). Kersey shows us that the gun is an essential tool, an archetypal tool for progress like fire or the wheel, a tool that distinguishes the human killer from the animal counterpart, perhaps the *only* effective tool left to us. The urban vigilante film insists on the effective enforcement of order and justice. Indeed, in *Death Wish*, Paul Kersey and his gun are the only things that ultimately resolve the many anarchistic conflicts. Kersey's gun, like gunfighter Candy Dan's 1890 revolver (the weapon Kersey asks Jainchill if he can shoot in the gun club scene), is special, unique, one-of-a-kind, and representative of frontier justice, or more exactly, American justice—a justice embodying purity, simplicity, and individual heroism.

The arming ritual—a ritual by which the vigilante hero prepares himself to kill—that is common to many urban vigilante films begins in *Death Wish* before Paul Kersey receives his .32 caliber pistol from Aimes Jainchill. Immediately prior to when Kersey leaves on his trip to Tucson, he buys $20.00 worth of quarters from the local bank. He places these quarters in a sock and tests his "weapon," a home-made blackjack. One evening shortly thereafter, Kersey is walking down a dark city street. He is startled when a man lights a match in the shadows behind him, and as he tentatively continues his walk, he is suddenly attacked by a knife-wielding robber. In stereotypical fashion, the crook demands money from his victim, but as Paul Kersey swings around to face his assailant, he whips his sock blackjack out of his pocket and viciously strikes the thug. Like a beaten dog, Kersey's attacker turns and runs away from the scene. When Kersey arrives at his apartment, he is visibly shaken. Yet is he shaken from his close brush with violence, or by his effective dispatching of a criminal? The viewer soon learns that the latter more accurately reflects Kersey's actual feelings when he gleefully swings his weapon about, striking his furniture until the sock breaks open. Paul Kersey, it seems, enjoys the taste of violence. He likes being in control of a life or death situation, and he is excited by his aggressive stance towards crime, his attack on criminals.

After Paul Kersey returns home from his trip to Tucson, and after he discovers and opens Jainchill's timely gift, he takes a stroll through a deserted waterfront park, ostensibly to locate trouble, or encourage trouble to locate him. Kersey gets his wish, his literal "death wish," when a mugger attacks him at gunpoint. Kersey draws his own gun (as in a traditional Western gunfight), shooting and mortally wounding his assailant. The phrase "death wish" thus has two meanings: one that suggests that an unhappy Paul Kersey wants to die because of his tragic past, and the other that suggests that a retributive Paul Kersey "wishes" criminals to die. When Kersey returns to his apartment, he becomes sick, and vomits in the bathroom. Instead of wounding his attacker, as he had done earlier with his home-made blackjack, this time he has *killed* another person. The viewer supposes that this act of violence, the ultimate act of violence, has disturbed Kersey, but he quickly learns to tolerate death as he continues on his nighttime hunting trips in the city. Perhaps the new Kersey, the vigilante killer, is expelling the last vestiges of his old, liberal, pacifist self. And as the film progresses, Paul Kersey accepts his violent nature. He obviously looks more and more forward to each new confrontation with New York's criminal element. Kersey conditions himself to accept violence to the point where he, himself, becomes violence incarnate. He is as cold and deadly as the fancy gun he carries. He has trained himself to use a lethal weapon, to become a lethal weapon.

And this trait is a common element in a number of urban vigilante films: the idea that the vigilante hero and his gun are one. They function together, effectively, the gun and the hero. They both are representations of larger social issues reflecting the triumph of moral justice over senseless injustice, order over anarchy. Urban vigilante films like *Dirty Harry* and *Death Wish* detail the suppression of destructive forces by an even greater destructive force—the iconic gun—that, in the process, paradoxically creates peace out of violence. Urban vigilante films generally present an ultra right-wing political stance, and connect themselves to such concepts as religious salvation, as best seen in *Dirty Harry*, and the frontier ethic, as demonstrated in *Death Wish*. Uniting both sub-categories of the urban vigilante films (both the vigilante cop movie and the traditional vigilante hero movie) the gun—as a common, powerful thematic element—functions as a metaphoric example of rugged individualism, and also of a national mindset that has held the gun to be an essential part of American culture since the founding of this country. The gun, as it's portrayed in these films, is a special tool wielded by special people, heroes who are fed up with the ineffectual bureaucracy of "the system," and who are also fed up with criminal's animalistic preying on the weak in society. The urban vigilante hero simplifies the way in which justice is distributed, and the object that enables the hero to combat crime, to make the city safe, to defend women and children (those people who are symbolic of civilization and our future) against senseless evil is the gun. Certainly, it's plain to see upon an examination of the two prototypical examples of the genre—*Dirty Harry* and *Death Wish*—why the urban vigilante film draws such an emotional response from its audience, and so long as there exists a perception in our society that our legal system favors the criminal over the victim, then the urban vigilante film will continue to remain a popular cinematic form.

Works Cited

Geist, Chistopher D., and Jack Nachbar, eds. *The Popular Culture Reader*. 3rd ed. Bowling Green, OH: Bowling Green State University Popular Press, 1983.

Hoppenstand, Gary. *In Search of the Paper Tiger: A Sociological Perspective of Myth, Formula and the Mystery Genre in the Entertainment Print Mass Medium*. Bowling Green, OH: Bowling Green State University Popular Press, 1987.

Selected Filmography

Year	Film	Director
Traditional Vigilante (and Related) Films:		
1967	*Born Losers*	T.C. Frank
1970	*Joe*	John G. Avildsen
1971	*Billy Jack*	T.C. Frank
1971	*Dirty Harry*	Don Siegel
1973	*Magnum Force*	Ted Post
1974	*Trial of Billy Jack*	Frank Laughlin
1976	*The Enforcer*	James Fargo
1977	*Billy Jack Goes to Washington*	Tom Laughlin
1982	*Forced Vengeance*	James Fargo
1982	*Silent Rage*	Michael Miller
1983	*Sudden Impact*	Clint Eastwood
1984	*Angel*	Robert Vincent O'Neil
1985	*Avenging Angel*	Robert Vincent O'Neil
1985	*The Devastator*	Cirio H. Santiago
1985	*Sudden Death*	Sig Shore
1986	*Band of the Hand*	Paul Michael Glaser
1986	*Bullies*	Paul Lynch
1987	*Man on Fire*	Elie Chouraqui
1987	*Nowhere to Hide*	Mario Azzopardi
1988	*Angel III: The Final Chapter*	Tom DeSimone
1988	*The Dead Pool*	Buddy Van Horn
1989	*Blind Fury*	Phillip Noyce
1989	*Kickboxer*	Mark DiSalle
1989	*Road House*	Rowdy Herrington
1991	*The Perfect Weapon*	Mark DiSalle
Vigilante Cop (and Related) Films:		
1973	*Walking Tall*	Phil Karlson
1974	*Death Wish*	Michael Winner
1975	*Walking Tall: Part 2*	Earl Bellamy

1977	*Walking Tall: The Final Chapter*	Jack Starrett
1981	*An Eye for an Eye*	Steve Carver
1982	*Death Wish II*	Michael Winner
1982	*48 Hrs.*	Walter Hill
1984	*Beverly Hills Cop*	Martin Brest
1985	*Code of Silence*	Andy Davis
1985	*Death Wish 3*	Michael Winner
1986	*Cobra*	George P. Cosmatos
1987	*Beverly Hills Cop II*	Tony Scott
1987	*Death Wish 4: The Crackdown*	J. Lee Thompson
1987	*Extreme Prejudice*	Walter Hill
1987	*Lethal Weapon*	Richard Donner
1988	*Above the Law*	Andrew Davis
1988	*Action Jackson*	Craig R. Baxley
1988	*Die Hard*	John McTiernan
1989	*Lethal Weapon 2*	Richard Donner
1989	*One Man Force*	Dale Trevillion
1989	*Tango & Cash*	Andrei Konchalovsky
1990	*Another 48 Hrs.*	Walter Hill
1990	*Die Hard 2: Die Harder*	Renny Harlin
1990	*Hard to Kill*	Bruce Malmuth

Superweapons from the Past

John H. Lenihan

From Susan Sontag's "Imagination of Disaster" to recent cultural studies such as Spencer Weart's *Nuclear Fear* and H. Bruce Franklin's *War Stars: The Superweapon and the American Imagination*, considerable attention has been focused on the importance of science fiction for projecting American fantasies and fears regarding atomic power. Futurist reflections of current anxieties regarding technologically-advanced warfare predate the birth of the atomic age, but those anxieties were understandably intensified in the wake of Hiroshima and particularly after 1949 when the Soviet Union's acquisition of "the bomb" made the prospect of nuclear devastation frighteningly real. At the same time, American policy makers sought to calm public fears of the atom and to emphasize the defense needs for a nuclear arsenal in the face of growing Cold-War tensions. Some science-fiction films of the fifties captured this ambivalence between dread and defense by on the one hand conjuring a deadly threat that was the result of nuclear testing or radiation experiments and on the other hand affirming the need for some form of retaliatory response.

If Cold-War preoccupations with instruments of destruction were most emphatically voiced in scenarios set in the near or distant future, they also emerged in films set in the near or distant past. Costume-adventure formulas, whether ancient, medieval, or 19th-century West in setting, seem at first glance unlikely vehicles for registering present concerns about the future implications of advanced weaponry. Thus reviewers occasionally remarked about how distant a particular costume saga seemed from present-day realities. Compared with 12th-century England as depicted in MGM's *Ivanhoe* (1952), wrote one reviewer, "the twentieth century, with its hydrogen bomb and cold war, is a lazily swinging hammock on a peaceful summer day" (*Hamburger* 55). Another reviewer predicted that the same film would inspire a cycle of films about the days of chivalry "when men fought with lances, arrows, axes, swords and maces instead of with machine guns, long-range artillery and atomic bombs."[1] What is implied in such remarks is the film's escapist appeal for a modern audience confronted with the deadly banality of nuclear peril.

Filmmakers were obviously not averse to engaging their audiences with nostalgic visions of yesteryear. But neither were they averse to fashioning a particular story in ways that might trigger audience identification with their own times. From about 1949 through the mid-1950s, film scenarios involving

164

renaissance-Italian cannons, frontier-American Gatling guns, Arabian Nights "Greek fire" and other antique forms of advanced weaponry spoke directly to contemporary concerns about national security and/or the perilous implications of "the bomb" for the future of civilization.

In 1949, a year when the Alger Hiss case and the Soviets' testing of an atomic bomb brought home the urgency of national security regarding nuclear armaments, both *The Prince of Foxes* and *Bride of Vengeance* incorporated into their respective tales of 16th-century Italy pointed references regarding the indispensability of a revolutionary new cannon as a deterrent to aggression. Both films portray Cesare Borgia as a totalitarian aggressor who conspires to undermine the duchy of Ferrara as part of his campaign to conquer all of Italy. Meanwhile, Alfonso, who rules Ferrara, is hurriedly developing a new cannon (with 15 tubes allowing rapid fire—*Prince of Foxes*) with which to defend his people. "Who builds this first may well own the world," Alfonso explains in *The Prince of Foxes*, anxious that he rather than the tyrant-aggressor Borgia be the exclusive possessor of such a powerful weapon. While the plot of *Prince of Foxes* moves on to other considerations, *Bride of Vengeance* remains focused on Alfonso's race against time to complete his secret weapon (carefully guarding the project against would-be spies) before Borgia'a army can strike.

An earlier script (January, 1948) for *Bride of Vengeance* contained a timely note of foreboding that was dropped for the final film. Screenwriter Michael Hogan chose in that earlier script to conclude the film with the following exchange between Alfonso (called Alonzo in this draft) and Leonardo da Vinci:

Alonzo—This weapon, Leonardo, is so terrible I doubt that men will fight again for simple fear of it.

Leonardo—No fear of weapons will keep men from fighting—only reason. This gun will seem puny and childish compared to the terrors man will invent. Eh, Alonzo; there shall come out of the earth that which will stun men by its report, and its breath will kill, and it shall devastate cities and countries.[2]

Hogan thus attributes to Leonardo da Vinci the same anxiety about the destructive potential of superweapons that atomic scientists were voicing in the wake of Hiroshima. In dropping this concluding dialogue, *Bride of Vengeance* becomes instead an apologia for developing the ultimate weapon as a necessary response to aggression. In the same way, according to historian Paul Boyer, "in the context of the Cold War, the Russian bomb, and repeated assertions of Soviet aggressiveness and perfidy, bigger American bombs seemed to many the only hope.... The dread destroyer of 1945 had become the shield of the Republic by 1950" (Boyer 339, 349).

Like *Bride of Vengeance*, *The Prince of Foxes* emphasizes the need for preparedness, to include (in one sequence early in the film) exclusive possession of a superweapon with which to deter aggressors. Samuel Shellenbarger, upon whose popular novel Twentieth Century-Fox based its production of *The Prince of Foxes*, predicted that the historical novel (and film) will continue to be in great demand "as long as we live in a turbulent age with the threat of the atomic bomb hanging over us." In periods of great peril, people "turn to other centuries. Since no one knows any security today, there is this urge to flee to those times when there was at least a sense of tranquility between wars."³ Yet, interestingly, the past which the film version of Shellenbarger's novel defined for its audiences embodied perils regarding national security comparable to those that plagued the atomic age in which the film was released. It seems no coincidence that Twentieth Century-Fox assigned the project of adapting Shellenbarger's *The Prince of Foxes* to Milton Krims whose recent script for *The Iron Curtain* (1947) was Fox's initial entry into the postwar spree of anti-communist melodramas. In both films Krims's protagonist is employed in espionage activity by an aggressor power (Borgia's Italy, Stalin's Russia) and in both films he comes to recognize the evil designs of his leaders and defects to the other side.

Tyrone Power who played the spy to Orson Welles's Borgia in *The Prince of Foxes* was again cast opposite Orson Welles in Fox's *The Black Rose* (1950). As a Saxon nobleman who leaves Norman-controlled England to seek his fortune in China, Power falls in with a ruthless general (Welles) who is on the march to conquer all of China for the great Kubla Khan. In a situation practically identical to that of *The Prince of Foxes*, Welles sends Power on a mission to infiltrate a Chinese court that possesses the "iron tube that shoots fire." Pondering the implications of what Welles can do with this powerful weapon, not only against China but eventually his native England, Power's patriotic feelings come to the fore (even a Norman King is preferable to an Asiatic conqueror) and he absconds to England with the iron tube.

Likewise, in Fox's *The Egyptian* (1954), a young physician (Edmund Purdom) exiled from his native country (Egypt) discovers in the course of his wanderings that the Hittites are about to employ a revolutionary new weapon (a sword of black metal that can cut "through our Egyptian copper like a knife through straw") to invade his homeland. "I think this new metal of the Hittites may change the history of the world," Purdom observes. He accordingly escapes from the Hittite camp and returns to Egypt bearing the enemy's new secret weapon. As in *The Black Rose*, an earth-shaking superweapon becomes a plot device with which to highlight the urgency of loyalty and consensus in the context of saving a center of civilization from enemy aggression. So too was loyalty to country deemed vital in the early fifties if America was to save the West from barbarians to the east capable of unleashing atomic annihilation.

After all, so it was believed, it had been the disloyalty of those like Alger Hiss and the Rosenbergs that accounted for America's inability to keep its own secret weapon out of the hands of its Cold-War adversary.

An even deadlier secret weapon from centuries past, "Greek fire," was the centerpiece for what plot there was in *Son of Sinbad* (1955). Howard Hughes produced this Arabian Nights tale with his customary relish for half-naked women and suggestive sexual banter—so much so that the film earned the Catholic Legion of Decency's severest rating of "Condemned." For the most part a comical burlesque with cheap exotic sets and costumes, *Son of Sinbad* nevertheless kept a straight face in portraying espionage efforts on the part of the Mongol conqueror Tamarlane to steal the secret formula of Greek fire from the Caliph of Baghdad. Early in the film, the inventor of Greek fire impresses upon the Caliph the need for security precautions "in order that the secret not fall into the hands of the enemy of mankind." In the climactic battle to stop Tamarlane's aggression, Sinbad and the "daughters of the 40 thieves" hurl debris and arrows soaked with Greek fire and thereby decimate the Mongol horde with mushroom-shaped explosions.

While iron tubes and Greek fire endangered past civilizations in Europe and Asia, advanced weaponry proved similarly ominous in the American West in films of the early fifties. Westerns adopted much the same premise regarding the urgency of securing new weapons from irresponsible use. In a news story to publicize the release of its latest Randolph Scott Western, *Colt .45* (1950), Warner Brothers highlighted the theme of keeping a new weapon "out of the hands of the wrong element—Indians and bandits in the Colt days, Russians and the Iron Curtain now."[4] *Springfield Rifle* (1952), essentially an espionage thriller that pits a Union intelligence officer (Gary Cooper) against a Confederate spy ring, makes clear the importance that the newly-developed rapid loader will have in determining the outcome of the Civil War. Rod Cameron in *Cavalry Scout* (1951) works undercover to stop the smuggling of Gatling guns to hostile Indians, while, in *Siege at Red River* (1954), Confederate spy Van Johnson assists Unionists to prevent warring Indians from acquiring a Gatling gun by which they could annihilate Northerner and Southerner alike.

The producer of *Siege at Red River*, Leonard Goldstein on more than one occasion argued that entertainment should be the principle function of motion pictures: "People go to the movies to be entertained, not to be educated or propagandized....it seems to me that audiences are being taken advantage of when propaganda and education is thrown at them from the screen."[5] Yet Goldstein engaged in a bit of propaganda-throwing of his own in productions such as *Arctic Manhunt* (1949) which involved communist spies or *I Was a Shoplifter* (1950) which was a lurid but timely crime expose. He also contributed to the trend of more sympathetic treatments of the Indian in such films as *Tomahawk* (1951) and *Battle at Apache Pass* (1952).

By the time Goldstein approached Darryl Zanuck at Twentieth Century-Fox in late 1952 with a drafted screenplay for "Gattling Gun" (the basis for *Siege at Red River*), he had established an enviable track record of successful films which he considered principally entertainment albeit not to the exclusion of topical themes. In a memorandum to Zanuck in October, 1952, Goldstein emphasized the contemporary relevance of his story about "America's first machine gun" and the possibility of "this earliest of wholesale murder weapons" falling into enemy hands. "Here, after all," Goldstein added, "is the secret weapon, terrifying and unbelievable—the atom bomb of a century ago. This fact we are pointing up and dramatizing." In terms that would have applied with minor variations to Zanuck's own *The Prince of Foxes* and *The Black Rose* or Howard Hughes's *Son of Sinbad* as well as the script he was trying to sell at present, Goldstein explained that early in the film "we briefly dramatize the incredible fire power of the new weapon, learn that it is stolen, realize that it may get into the hands of the enemy." The story will be constructed like "a modern day *spy hunt*—the same hide-and-seek, the same tension. Only it is played in our Western locale." Three days later, Zanuck responded approvingly, encouraging Goldstein to play up the mystery and "the spy story angle."[6]

Present-day concerns about weapons security were rendered more explicit in some B Westerns aimed at juvenile audiences. By virtue of having modern settings for his Republic Westerns (not uncommon for series-Western stars), Roy Rogers could address the issue of atomic espionage without recourse to metaphorical Gatling guns. As early as 1947, Roy helps Dale Evans in *Under Nevada Skies* recover a stolen crest that contains a map showing the location of a "pitchblend" deposit, for which, the villain confesses to Roy, "certain foreign countries would give everything they own.""Pitchblend! Isn't that what uranium comes from?" asks Roy. "Yes," the villain replies, "uranium, the atom bomb, power over life and death." Three years later in *Bells of Coronado* (1950) Roy and Dale again thwart a plot to steal uranium for shipment to a foreign power. A trailer for *Spoilers of the Plains* (1951) promised audiences the thrill of seeing "Roy and Trigger don asbestos suits to fight an oil fire,...a fire started by our enemies...men who are after our country's newest secret weapon."[7]

The foreign enemy in these films goes unnamed, but audiences would have had little difficulty in filling in the blank. While not, strictly speaking, period films, the Republic-Rogers Westerns nonetheless employed much of the imagery and material conventions (cowboy attire, wide-open spaces, horses, six-guns) associated with the cinematic 19th-century West. Such iconographic hybrids serve to illustrate just how tenuous was the distinction between Hollywood's past and present scenarios regarding superweapons and related security issues.

On occasion adventure films set in the past (usually the 19th century) did specify Russia as the principal menace. Thus, Russian agents conspire to undermine British rule in India in *Kim* (1950) or to take over Spanish California in *California Conquest* (1952). The Crimean War is the backdrop for Russian espionage in *Charge of the Lancers* (1954), a technicolor B film which in its opening narration calls the audience's attention to "a war destined to create the pattern for future world wars" and a war involving Czarist Russia's "planned conquest of Turkey...and domination of many lands." Most of the film deals with British efforts to prevent "the Russkies" from stealing a new breech-loading cannon. After demonstrating the cannon's unparalleled fire power, a British army major cautions his officers: "Above all, what you see here today must be kept secret. I'm sure there's no need to tell you that this information in the hands of the Russians could turn the tide of war against us."

By emphasizing national preparedness in the face of imminent aggression or subversion, costume-adventure films (to include Westerns) seldom entertained the notion raised by scientists and others in the wake of Hiroshima that the mere existence of the ultimate weapon spelled unforeseen consequences of mass destruction. Two costume films that did raise this question, however, were among the more popular of family entertainments produced in the early fifties. The fanciful, comic buccaneer tale, *The Crimson Pirate*, concludes with Burt Lancaster defeating the forces of tyranny by employing a veritable arsenal of advanced weaponry (mobile flame thrower, balloon, Gatling gun, nitroglycerin explosives). But earlier in the film, the inventor-scientist responsible for this arsenal expresses doubts about developing an "explosive that moves mountains." "Anyway, I'm not really sure I want to discover it. If you can remove a mountain, how do I know it won't remove an island," the scientist cautions Lancaster. "In science," Lancaster replies, "one knows nothing unless one experiments." This exchange expresses the dilemma voiced a few months after Hiroshima by Rockefeller Foundation president Raymond B. Fosdick: "What do we do—curb our science or cling to the pursuit of truth and run the risk of having our society torn to pieces" (Boyer 269).

If *The Crimson Pirate* resolved the dilemma it raised in favor of defense considerations, as had the Truman administration at the time the film was made, Walt Disney's *20,000 Leagues Under the Sea* (1954) left the audience to draw its own conclusions. No science-fiction or nuclear melodrama of the 1950s approached the commercial success of this blockbuster adaptation of the Jules Verne novel. Yet, it is a film virtually overlooked in film studies of the Cold-War years, owing perhaps to its having been a Disney costumer, marketed for family consumption and therefore presumably devoid of presentist social messages. Interestingly, the film's contemporary relevance did not escape the notice of some film critics, one of whom took note of the climactic "explosion of what appears to be an atomic energy plant to rival Los Almos" (*Crowther* 7). In light of this film being the product of a corporation whose stock and trade was providing wholesome, happy fantasies for America's baby-boomers, it is significant that its depiction of nuclear destructiveness was not altogether consistent with the mentality commonly ascribed to a decade that had presumably "learned to love the bomb."

Published in 1870, Jules Verne set his novel in the 19th-century present. Lacking was the sense of potential nuclear disaster that would characterize science fiction decades later, to include the Disney adaptation of Verne's classic. The novel was in large part an environmental odyssey, euphoric about the prospects of discovering the wonders of nature beneath the sea and, at one point, cautionary about the wanton destruction of sea life (specifically, whales). Captain Nemo is both the menacing Gothic figure out to avenge a mysteriously tragic past and a scientific idealist committed to unlocking the secrets of nature. It is the latter quality that Verne emphasizes at the end of the novel when the French scientist, Arronox, expresses hope that Nemo has escaped the "Maelstrom" to continue contemplating the wonders of the sea ("his adopted country"): "May the judge disappear, and the philosopher continue the peaceful exploration of the sea! If his destiny be strange, it is also sublime" (Verne 288). In the best latter-day Hollywood tradition, Verne had left the way open for a sequel, which he delivered with *Mysterious Island* (also adapted to the screen).

Director Richard Fleischer and writer Earl Felton took considerable liberty with Verne's novel by introducing the timely issue of nuclear energy. Verne had offered little explanation of the source of power that propelled Nemo's submarine, except that Nemo was able to use sodium extracted from coal. In so far as the Nautilus was used for destructive as well as scientific purposes, Verne was positing a dilemma of his own time as well as the future. The world stood to benefit or suffer according to how the dynamo was put to use. In Verne's novel, electricity itself, as opposed to the submarine that destroys simply by ramming its targets, seems to have no inherent destructive power comparable to atomic energy. By substituting for Verne's electricity an unnamed energy source that bears all the characteristics of atomic power, Fleischer and Felton brought to Verne's classic an element of nuclear foreboding, climaxed by a mushroom-shaped explosion that obliterates Nemo's island hideaway.

Early in the film, Arronox (Paul Lucas) is beside himself in amazement over the dynamic power propelling the Nautilus. Such energy could "revolutionize the world," he exclaims. Nemo replies, "Or destroy it!" Verne had originally fashioned this exchange by having Nemo cynically comment upon the slowness by which modern man has progressed beyond the ancients: "It required many ages to find out the mechanical power of steam. Who knows if in another hundred years, we may not see a second Nautilus. Progress is slow, M. Arronox." Arronox agrees that the Nautilus "is at least a century before its time, perhaps an era. What a misfortune that the secret of such an invention should die with its inventor" (Verne 158). Nemo offers no reply, nor does Verne register the kind of skepticism advanced in the film version about the world's responsible use of Nemo's energy source.

The film introduces a sequence not in the novel when Nemo again expresses skepticism about the future. He shows Arronox the prison-island of Rorapandi where he had once been sentenced and where prisoners are still being brutally forced to mine nitrates and phosphates for the manufacture of ammunition. The product of this slave labor, Nemo adds, will make the world die a little more.

In the film, Nemo eventually considers negotiating an exchange of his secrets with the outside world, although he remains skeptical as to whether his energy source will be used to build or destroy. But shortly thereafter, he is pursued by a fleet of warships and proceeds to detonate his island-hideaway (Vulcania). Realizing that the world is not yet ready for his secret energy source, Nemo nevertheless confides to Arronox; "But there is hope for the future. When the world is ready for a new and better life, all this well someday come to pass, in god's good time." Nemo goes to his watery grave in the Nautilus while Arronox and his two companions escape. At first angry that Ned (Kirk Douglas) did not bother to salvage Nemo's journal, Arronox reconsiders, "Perhaps you did mankind a service, Ned." The film concludes with a mushroom-shaped explosion followed by Nemo's ghostly voice repeating his last words to Arronox: "When the world is ready for a new and better life, all this will come to pass, in God's good time." It is doubtful, given the tension-filled international climate at the time of the film's release in 1954, that audiences felt totally reassured that the age they lived was in "God's good time." Perhaps Ned had done mankind a service after all.

Jules Verne was also the literary source for Michael Todd's opulent production of *Around the World in 80 Days* (1956). Although this three-hour-long opus was played tongue in cheek and as a display case for an impressive array of state-of-the-art visual effects, Todd chose to precede the story with a homiletic prelude quite at odds with the jaunty tenor of what follows. Instead of immediately lavishing the audience with Victorian-era splendor embellished in the much-publicized wide screen innovation of Todd AO, the film opens onto a normal screen frame of journalist Edward R. Murrow seated at a desk in a modern suit and holding a cigarette. As though he was beginning his weekly "See It Now" television program, Murrow reports on how Jules Verne's "fantastic fiction" has become fact, to include "flying machines, submarines, television, rockets." The screen widens onto a shot of a rocket blasting its way to the stratosphere. The music score turns eerie as Murrow soberly explains that in this power of destruction there is hope: "Man has devised a method of destroying most of humanity, or of lifting it up to high plateaus of prosperity and progress never dreamed of by the boldest dreamer." The journey Verne dreamed of making in eighty days can now be done "in less than half that time," but speed requires wisdom and purpose: "The end of this journey, whether to the high horizons of hope or to the depths of destruction, will be determined by the collective wisdom of the people who live on this shrinking planet."

Murrow's preachments about the future of civilization hanging in the balance had little to do with the comic adventures of Phineas Fogg in Todd's *Around the World in 80 Days*. The film raises no question about the world's being able to accommodate advanced weapons of destruction, as was the case with *20,000 Leagues Under the Sea* and as would continue to be the case with science-fiction films for the remainder of the decade. Meanwhile the message of securing superweapons for the sake of deterring aggression seemed to run its course by the latter half of the fifties. Olden cannons, Greek fire, and Gatling guns had been appropriate material conventions for what were for the most part costumed espionage yarns, produced during those years when anti-communist sentiment ran strongest and atomic spy revelations captured the headlines. Such scenarios lost their currency following the decline of McCarthyism and the subsequent promises of big power summitry—to include constraints on nuclear testing. America remained steadfast in its policy of containing Soviet expansionism, but with a greater openness to communicate differences, in hopes that, at the very least, a nuclear confrontation could be avoided.

The alternatives to deescalating big power tensions in a nuclear age seemed unthinkable, as envisioned in doomsday fare ranging from *On the Beach* (1959) to *Dr. Strangelove* (1964). *The Story of Mankind* (1957) was a rare attempt to combine historical pageantry with a nuclear doomsday warning. Producer-director Irwin Allen concocted this ludicrous polemic about a heavenly tribunal reviewing the history of the earth to determine whether to allow earthlings to destroy themselves with the super H-bomb. As historical characters glide in and out of stock footage from earlier Warners costume epics, Ronald Coleman and Vincent Price debate the worthiness of the human race for some form of heavenly salvation from nuclear annihilation. Predictably, the film ends with the head of the heavenly tribunal delaying judgement to allow humankind to set its house in order. Looking directly at the camera, the tribunal head (in a cautionary tone much like Edward R. Murrow's at the beginning of *Around the World* or James Mason's/Nemo's haunting off-screen voice at the end of *20,000 Leagues Under the Sea*) warns the film audience, "The choice is up to you."

Notes

[1]*Los Angeles Herald and Express*, 10 October 1952, no page, clippings file, "Ivanhoe," Margaret Herrick Library, Academy of Motion Picture Arts and Sciences, Beverly Hills, California (hereafter Academy Library).

[2]Revised script by Michael Hogan, "Bride of Vengeance," 19 January 1948, p. 155, Paramount Collection, Academy Library.

[3]*Los Angeles Examiner*, 16 November 1949, no page, clippings file, "Prince of Foxes," Academy Library.

[4]Production file, "Colt .45," Warner Brothers Collection, Special Collections, Doheny Library, University of Southern California, Los Angeles.

[5]*Showman's Trade Review*, 20 August 1949, no page, Scrapbook, Leonard Goldstein Collection, Academy Library.

[6]Binder on *Siege at Red River*, Leonard Goldstein Collection, Academy Library.

[7]Cutting Continuity of Trailer for *Spoilers of the Plains*, Special Collections, Doheny Library, University of Southern California, Los Angeles.

Works Cited

Boyer, Paul. *By the Bomb's Early Light: American Thought and Culture at the Dawn of the Atomic Age*. NY: Pantheon, 1985.

Crowther, Bosley. "The Screen in Review: '20,000 Leagues' in 128 Fantastic Minutes." *New York Times*, 24 December 1954, p. 7.

Franklin, H. Bruce. *War Stars: The Superweapon and the American Imagination*. NY: Oxford UP, 1988.

Hamburger, Philip. "The Current Cinema: The Bad Old Days." *New Yorker*, 9 August 1952, p. 55.

Sontag, Susan. "The Imagination of Disaster." Chap. in *Against Interpretation and Other Essays*. NY: Farrar, Straus & Giroux, 1966.

Verne, Jules. *20,000 Leagues Under the Sea*. Trans. H. Firth. NY: E.P. Dutton, 1953.

Weart, Spencer R. *Nuclear Fear: A History of Images*. Cambridge, MA: Harvard UP, 1988.

Filmography

The following lists only costume films (including Westerns) addressed in the text that deal thematically with advanced weapons.

Year	Film	Director
1947	*Under Nevada Skies*	Frank McDonald
1949	*Bride of Vengeance*	Mitchell Leisen
1949	*Prince of Foxes*	Henry King
1950	*The Black Rose*	Henry Hathaway
1950	*Bells of Coronado*	William Witney
1950	*Colt .45*	Edwin Marin
1951	*Cavalry Scout*	Leslie Selander
1951	*Spoilers of the Plains*	William Witney
1952	*The Crimson Pirate*	Robert Siodmak
1952	*Springfield Rifle*	Andre de Toth
1954	*Charge of the Lancers*	William Castle
1954	*The Egyptian*	Michael Curtiz
1954	*Siege at Red River*	Rudolph Mate
1954	*20,000 Leagues Under the Sea*	Richard Fleischer
1955	*Son of Sinbad*	Ted Tetzlaff
1956	*Around the World in 80 Days*	Michael Anderson
1957	*The Story of Mankind*	Irwin Allen

The Object Realm of the Vietnam War Film

Steve Lipkin

One of the advertising logos for the Darryl F. Zanuck/Ken Annakin epic *The Longest Day* (1962) showed a helmet perched atop an M1 carbine, bayonet affixed and thrust into the ground. The logo, as an image, reduced the epic sweep of the film to its barest essentials. These key objects, the readily identifiable American helmet and the gun, evoked in one brief, efficient stroke much of the visual feeling of the Hollywood World War II combat film.

To whatever extent we might associate a type of film with certain identifying characteristics, the war film remains recognizable for us not only because of its action (the waging of combat, usually within the larger context of a political conflict), but also because key objects make major contributions to its iconography. Weapons, uniforms, vehicles (when I think of *The Longest Day* I think first of gliders, and then of Red Buttons dangling from the top of a bell tower by his entangled parachute rigging)—all these form some of the most accessible threads of the war film's visual fabric.

Beyond situating the film's generic identity, the logo/image from *The Longest Day* also evokes absence, loss (the empty helmet; the gun stuck downward into the ground), death in combat and sacrifice for the greater good. Given their place within the context of the World War II combat film, the loss and sacrifice this image suggests become warranted by our knowledge of the Allied victory in the war.

By the same token, objects also help establish the visual identity of the Vietnam war film. As close relatives of the World War II combat film, Hollywood films centered on depicting combat in Vietnam and its immediate consequences foreground an equally identifiable array of uniforms, weaponry, vehicles, and other paraphernalia. Just as objects in the traditional war film contribute to and operate within ideological parameters (the depiction of the political history of the war, Fascist aggression, eventual Allied Victory, the Holocaust, etc.), so too objects within the Vietnam war film must be viewed within larger contexts. These include the politics of the period, the "meaning" of American commitment in the war, the war's fragmentation of American society, the repercussions of the withdrawal of American forces from the field of combat, and the eventual occupation of Vietnam by the National Liberation Front. In sum, objects in the Vietnam war film function within filmic treatments of a "lost" war.

175

A consideration of objects in the Vietnam war film leads quickly to the question of coherence: how do readily identifiable objects help these films help make sense of the war itself? The very legibility of objects in the Vietnam war film contributes to the larger effort in these films to provide, through the "lens" of the film, a clearer moral perspective on the war than the war itself allowed. This purposeful legibility relates the Vietnam war film to not only the traditional World War II combat film, but also to melodrama.

As melodrama, Vietnam war films articulate their subject in moral terms. The films view the war more as a set of moral problems, rather than as the expression of international political conflicts. While some of the major Vietnam war films, including *Coming Home* (1978), *Platoon* (1986), and *Born on the Fourth of July* (1990) can also stand clearly as melodramas, others that explore unique stylistic ground, most notably *The Deer Hunter* (1978), *Apocalypse Now* (1978) and *Full Metal Jacket* (1989), arguably feature similar melodramatic characteristics. The melodramatic view of the war may be both the most accessible and perhaps most acceptable mode of fictionalizing the Vietnam War on film.

Objects function in Vietnam war films to help convey the essentially melodramatic nature of the films' depiction of the war. After examining briefly how the Vietnam war film relates to defining characteristics of the traditional war film, it will be possible to see how weapons, props, and medical paraphernalia make their contributions to creating a moral perspective toward the war.

Kathryn Kane identifies three defining conventions of the traditional war film genre: the war itself is the manifestation of a clear political conflict; combat between uniformed forces occurs on foreign soil; and the "group" of American soldiers featured in the film provides a melting pot of ethnic types, acting as a microcosm of a democratic American society (5). Kane posits the clear conventionality of traditional war film iconography and thematics: "The films are highly conventional...the war is seen to provide an opportunity to rediscover and evaluate certain qualities that are considered to define America. The films by and large confine themselves to examining these few qualities" (5).

The straightforward "American" qualities Kane describes as conventions of the World War II combat film become in Vietnam war films a part of the larger problem of questioning ideology. Lloyd B. Lewis has argued that any understanding of narratives about the war in Vietnam stems from comprehending "the ways in which meaning was compromised and subverted *in* Vietnam" (19). Closure within the narrative becomes problematic if the war is "lost," or worse, continued in the guise of conflict transferred to another country (Cambodia) or to another level of conflict (MIA's).

Deprived of the ideological certainty characteristic of the traditional war film setting, the fragmented worlds imaged in Vietnam war films become coherent through the narratives' dependence upon melodramatic structures. Robert B. Heilman in *Tragedy and Melodrama: Versions of Experience* suggests that war stories and melodrama come in close proximity in their graphic depiction of the clash for control of a chaotic universe between forces of good and evil (105-8). In *The Melodramatic Imagination* Peter Brooks argues that without a clear source of moral system and order, the size as well as the source of evil in a universe where "the traditional imperatives of truth and ethics have been violently thrown into question" becomes unclear; in such a "desacralized" world drama becomes melodrama "which takes as its concern and *raison d'être* the location, expression, and imposition of basic ethical and psychic truths" (5). A basic premise here will be that the world view of melodrama helps to impose moral coherence upon the meaning of combat in the "desacralized" world of Vietnam war films.

Whatever affect these films generate attains coherence to the extent that it is inscribed within a moral system. The object realm of the Vietnam war film contributes directly to the visual excess of these films, excess that is characteristic of melodrama generally. As melodramas, the visual texture of Vietnam war films is integral to their "musical" punctuation of emotional/moral contrasts, and so is instrumental in creating (and conveying) their ideology.

Peter Brooks argues that melodrama makes real, accessible, and "legible" the signification of good and evil: "While its social implications may be variously revolutionary or conservative, it is in all cases radically democratic, striving to make its representations clear and legible to everyone. We may legitimately claim that melodrama becomes the principal mode for uncovering, demonstrating, and making operative the essential moral universe in a post-sacred era" (xi).

The action film will center on the outward, external direction of physical action. The "passion" film views the significant movement of external forces inward. Thomas Elsaesser argues that "melodrama, at its most accomplished, seems capable of reproducing more directly than other genres the patterns of domination and exploitation existing in a given society, especially the relation between psychology, morality and class-consciousness, by emphasizing so clearly an emotional dynamic whose social correlative is a network of external forces directed oppressingly inward, and with which the characters themselves unwittingly collude to become their agents" (14). The films examined here also foreground as internal experiences characters' mental and emotional changes, as well as the moral and ethical dilemmas that confront them. In the fashion of melodrama, Vietnam war films display on center stage the constraining social structures of the worlds of their characters.

Visual environments, costumes, and the props attendant to both will help identify in the Vietnam war film this "correlation" between external, social forces, and their emotional, psychological and ideological impact on the films' characters. The visible features of the worlds of these films clarify the progressive movement into the sensibilities of central characters in order to emphasize their emotional and moral development. As in melodrama generally, the gateway to the moral is through the emotional, so that through characters' internal experiences the films clearly delineate good from evil.

The iconography of weapons marks clearly the Vietnam war film as a sub-genre of the war film in general. M-16 automatic rifles, M-60 machine guns, M-79 grenade launchers, the Browning Automatic Rifle (BAR) and the UH-1 "Huey" helicopter, for example, help define visually the distinctive look of the Vietnam war film. Images of this hardware distinguish the waging of the war in Vietnam from other wars recreated on film. Distinct from the function of weapons in the traditional war film, however, the vast destructive power of weapons in the Vietnam war context underlines systematically the futility of war.

The use of a weapon, much like the use of any tool, extends the reach of the human hand, allowing a larger "reach" of the tool-user's will to effect change. The only Vietnam war films that most clearly show the effective use of weapons without profound damage to or destruction of the central American characters using them are the Rambo fantasies (*First Blood* 1982 and *Rambo* 1985), films that by self-proclamation endeavor to rewrite history ("Do we get to win this time?").

In the progression of films that show combat in the Vietnam war from *Apocalypse Now* and *The Deer Hunter* through *Platoon*, the exercise of weaponry by American troops becomes more explicitly self-destructive. *Apocalypse Now* concludes in what is to be the cataclysmic napalming of the renegade American Colonel Kurtz's (Marlon Brando's) stronghold, however, as the swirls of flame echo the churning fan blades of the opening of the film, the film's final images show the destruction of a jungle landscape, devoid of any sign of human life or habitation. The firefights in *Platoon* are comparably "apocalyptic" as they develop from Chris (Charlie Sheen) firing blindly at shadowy figures that seemingly melt into the jungle in his first night ambush (afterward they find no VC bodies), to the vast destruction of the landscape at the film's conclusion. These scenes suggest how these films depict the massive destruction of the enemy as an armed, uniformed opposition. Battle scenes where weapons are brought to bear on the enemy tend to be dark and/or opaque, building upon slow motion, reverberating visual and aural distancing more than clarity and direct, proximate display of the consequences of the weapons of war. The uniformed enemy these weapons are used to destroy is often barely-glimpsed, or even absent altogether.

The moments in these films that do display the awesome effectiveness of weaponry in eliminating human beings tend to show the destruction of civilians, or American soldiers (deliberately or accidentally) destroying each other. Apparently unarmed Vietnamese civilians fall victim to the relentless possibility that they might be VC. We see this, for example, when the Vietnamese boat family is ripped apart by the patrol boat crew's heavy caliber machine guns in *Apocalypse Now*, so that only their puppy survives, or when Sergeant Barnes (Tom Berenger) blows the top of the head off an old woman villager in *Platoon*.

Aside from their sheer visceral brutality, these scenes are hauntingly uncertain. As in the case of the disappearing enemy of *Platoon*'s firefights, it is simply never clear if this really is the enemy. The human beings we see most effectively damaged by weapons remain the helpless, exploited victims of larger social forces; as such, they mark the films' melodramatic articulations.

With no obvious enemy there to destroy, the "right" or "proper" exercise of weapons in warfare becomes highly vulnerable to the verdict of reasonable doubt. When American weapons destroy American characters in American films, the very objects that would traditionally allow the proper waging of war demonstrate instead its immoral futility. Ironically, these scenes foreground weapon/objects as strongly as the proper, more effective use of the weapons of war does in the traditional war film.

The following examples suggest how the display of weapons in Vietnam war films tends to foreground self-destruction. In *The Deer Hunter*, revolvers assume a paramount importance because of one of the film's main metaphors, the comparison of waging the war in Vietnam to playing Russian roulette. The initial Russian roulette scene emphasizes through close-up cross-cutting the chambers of the revolver, the number of shells Michael (Robert DeNiro) wants inserted into the revolver, and the bloodthirsty excitement of the prisoners' NVA captors. The revolver is equally prominent in the penultimate Russian roulette scene, in which Nick (Christopher Walken) comes to his inevitable fate as a professional player in the Saigon Russian roulette "league." (The film also suggests, in one of its hunting scenes, that the revolver that Steven [John Cazales] fires futilely at a weakly escaping deer is thereby a sign of impotence, especially compared to Michael's masterful use just before of a hunting rifle.)

Less metaphoric and more direct is Barnes's shooting of Elias (Willem Defoe) in *Platoon*. In this second instance of the "wrong" use of weapons, the M-16 each man carries chest high as he runs, particularly, of course, the one Barnes jerks to his eye to shoot the smiling Elias, is foregrounded in the scene as prominently as the skilled movement of both men through the wooded terrain of the battlefield.

The prominence of fragging in Vietnam war films heavily underscores the morally problematic nature of the war. The deliberate murder of one American soldier by another would be morally objectionable even under circumstances stretching the bounds of what might constitute "proper" and "improper" action in battle. *Casualties of War*, for example, suggests that Erickson (Michael J. Fox) has betrayed his platoon, at least in their view, and has earned a death sentence accordingly. The grenade that rolls into Erickson's view at the latrine thus "sets off" action on his difficult decision to bring charges against his platoon. Here the attempted destruction of one American by others, along with the successful prosecution Erickson brings against his fellow soldiers crystallizes the film's moral perspective on the self-destructive nature of the war.

A last example of how the displayed effects of weaponry illustrate the futility of the war comes from *Born on the Fourth of July*. Before Kovic (Tom Cruise) is shot in the back, he inadvertently fires on Wilson, another American GI, thinking Wilson is one of the attacking NVA. Wilson's death by Kovic's friendly fire proves to be almost as deep and destructive a wound to Kovic as the one that cripples him. As with the close-ups of the revolvers in *Deer Hunter* or of the grenade lobbed into Erickson's latrine in *Casualties*, the slow motion footage of Wilson getting shot, and then Kovic becoming wounded emphasizes not only the immediate consequences, but also the moral functions of weapons as exercised in these films.

These images of weaponry act to contradict the conventions of the traditional war film, and illustrate instead the kind of moral direction characteristic of melodrama. External environments, costumes, and their associated props provide a similarly melodramatic sense of social system. They allow us to see relationships morally inscribed within such systems.

Contrasting bunker scenes in *Platoon* demonstrate how features of the visual environment can function both socially and morally. Visible features of the prefilmic world reflect here the "codes" of the platoon's social structure. Chris Taylor finds himself in a society rife with father figures. This platoon's paternalism, however, creates a constraining, destructive social system. *Platoon* provides the central combat unit with not one, but two sergeant/father figures, in addition to the obligatory combat-bitten Colonel and the upper-class, indecisive Lieutenant. Taylor's closing comment about how Barnes and Elias have both been fathers to him during his passage in the platoon only reinforces what has resulted from the platoon's excess of father figures. All tensions in the group have derived from the split. Barnes and Elias act as fundamentally different models, and provide radically opposed view points on how the war should be fought.

As the platoon becomes the battlefield, the film figures the war in increasingly moral, and ultimately in spiritual terms. Which of these sides in this house that is divided against itself will be the "right" side, for Chris Taylor, and by extension, for us? Clearly the quasi-political division of the platoon into lifestyle "camps" reflects the larger American society of the late 1960s, the division of American public opinion over the waging of the war, and the self-destructiveness America incurred in its involvement in Vietnam. *Platoon* imposes coherence upon the war by drawing the arena of action within the ranks of the platoon itself. The "right" or "wrong" thing to do or think stems from the father-like images of the sergeants in conflict with each other, thus setting their house in conflict with itself.

The clearly-divided groups in *Platoon* provide one of the best examples of how a film's visual environment and its attendant props foreground characters socially and morally. The base camp scenes after the first night ambush mark off the contrasts resulting from the way the platoon has polarized around its two leaders: in one bunker, the "heads" are getting high; Elias indoctrinates the now "resurrected" Chris by turning a gun barrel into a bong. "Go Ask Alice" in the soundtrack segues into "I'm Just an Okie from Muskogie" as we see the contrasting action in the "red neck" bunker, where Bunny, O'Neil and Barnes are drinking Budweiser and playing poker. Their lieutenant enters and tries to talk to the men, can't do it very well, and leaves. In the course of the scene, Bunny (Kevin Dillon) takes a bite out of his beer can.

On the one hand, a weapon, an instrument of violence, becomes "defused" as it is turned into an instrument of pleasure, and allows group acceptance of an outsider. On the other hand, a beer can, drained of whatever pleasure it can offer, becomes part of a show of the potential to wreak destructive violence, and accompanies the alienation of an individual not completely within the group. The "sides" subsequently square off in proportion to the intensity of the conflict between Elias and Barnes over the "right" way the war should be fought, and the "right" way the GI's should behave. Each faction adheres to "proper" codes of belief and action—Barnes and the "red necks" adopt an "any gook is a dead gook" and "every man for himself" approach to waging the war which leads from biting the sides out of beer cans and crass anti-Semitism to rape, the murder of villagers, and fragging. The "heads" line up behind Elias's "smart," "cool" approach to handling the war. Caught in the middle momentarily, Taylor develops an allegiance toward Elias, who helps him, but Taylor also shares the rage and frustration the Barnes-like prosecution of the war allows him to vent when he shoots at the feet of a boy in the village.

Costuming also situates characters in Vietnam war films socially and morally. By definition, the military "family" has imposed rank order and its attendant rules, policies and structures on what would be otherwise a more random pattern of relationships. As opposed to the clear-cut dualism of the social world of *Platoon*, *Full Metal Jacket* shows the close proximity of military order to hellish chaos.

One of the central images of *Full Metal Jacket* becomes that of Joker's helmet. Joker's costuming, like his name, marks only one of the ironies that form the film. Joker's helmet has lettered on it his name, a peace symbol, and the legend "Born to Kill."

The chaotic world of *Full Metal Jacket* takes a grunt's-eye view of the war. The film develops an increasingly arbitrary sense of events and fatalities. To end the first half of the film, its heaviest military presence, Sergeant Hartmann, is brought down by one of his own trainees (an incompetent nicknamed "Gomer Pyle," no less). Ending the film's second half, the culminating vision of Hue during the Tet Offensive shows a literal hell, even worse than boot camp, where buildings burn and the wounded are repeatedly wounded as a means to entice more men to come out and be wounded in their own turn. The woman/sniper who decimates the group Joker has attached himself to begs at the film's end for her enemies to shoot her. As Joker stands there, considering this last request, hearing in his mind lines his buddies have spoken throughout the film about what actions mean (or don't mean), we see with equal clarity his face, and the mixture of messages inscribed on his helmet. The last sequence of the film is a fitting end to all of this ironic nihilism: from a low angle silhouetted against the red background of the buildings of Hue ablaze, American troops march en masse to "Who's the Leader of the Gang," the theme from the Mickey Mouse Club.

Visual environments and their attendant props in these films delineate visually social structures and values. Some settings also reinforce the marginality of social order and individual existence within worlds riddled so pervasively by uncertainty. For example, through all the chaos of the battlefield, the helicopter in these films (both as an environment and itself as a weapon) provides a reference point for order. Along with providing a shelter, a temporary sense of place and social unity, the helicopter allows the transition for the troops it carries from a protected social group to more vulnerable surrounds (usually the jungle) and then back again. The helicoptered retreats from the battlefield in a film like *Platoon*, for example, afford relief from the open threat of battle. The possibility of retreat and relief in this film is two-sided: at the film's conclusion, the camera tracks along Chris's point of view through the remains of the American force, onto the helicopter, and away from all that has changed him. His life, if not his identity, is intact. Earlier, however, the same possibility of helicoptered retreat (also shot to emulate point of view) becomes agony as it removes Chris from the battle, preventing him from helping Elias, as Chris believes he sees that good man gunned down in his futile run across open paddies for the departing helicopters.

The UH-1 helicopter shot from the front, with its protruding nose and eye-like windshield partitions, also projects an image of an insectile beast of prey. Perhaps the best examples of the ambivalent possibilities of the helicopter as an object within the Vietnam war on film, both as tentative shelter and as an instrument of aggression are in *Apocalypse Now*. *Apocalypse* opens with the remembered throbs of helicopter motors, memory which sets up Willard's (Martin Sheen's) breakdown. Later, those sounds replaced by "The Ride of the Valkyrie" accompany some of the most effective, clearly purposeful (if not markedly irrational) combat in any Vietnam war film, the clearing of the beach so that Kilgore's (Robert Duvall's) boys can "surf the point."

The patrol boat as an object/environment in the same film offers a similar sense of unreliable shelter. Like helicopters, the patrol boat provides illusory protection, since attacks on both underline their vulnerability. The patrol boat allows a sense of order, continuity and sheltering space amidst the film's irrational settings, actions and events. The boat is strong enough to be dropped onto the Mekong River from a helicopter, and reliable enough to get Willard to his destination deep within the unknown, forbidden Cambodian territory. It can't protect its own chief (Albert Hall), however, from the Montagnard spear that suddenly pierces his chest without warning, nor can it protect the life of Chef (Frederic Forrest), its last surviving crew member, who makes it as far as Kurtz's stronghold with Willard only to be decapitated at what is apparently Kurtz's whim. Like the helicopter, the boat is a tentative bulwark both physically and socially against the chaos of the war.

As melodramas, Vietnam war films imbue with moral weight the visible effects of the war on visual environments and on figures. Nowhere is this more explicit than in the effects of the war on the human body. Medical paraphernalia constitute a special sub-group of props, since they mark the (wrongful) damage to the human body not only on the battlefield, but also into the continuity of life after the battle is over. Perhaps the most prominent of all such objects is the wheelchair, which acts as the moral center for actions and events in *Coming Home* and *Born on the Fourth of July*. In both cases the wheelchair provides a visual pivot, turning the thrust of each film into melodramatic articulation. (To a lesser degree, as it contrasts with his wedding, which opens the film, the later image of the wheelchair-bound Stan [John Savage] in *The Deer Hunter* marks the effects of the war explicitly as loss, impotence and distortion in the social pattern that holds together the film's characters.) In the case of *Coming Home*, the wheelchair actually brings the main characters together, providing the platform for their moral dilemma. Their love affair must confront the moral conflict that results from their adultery. *Coming Home* is as explicitly a melodrama as it is a "wounded veteran" film in the mode of *The Best Years of Our Lives* (1946).

Both *Coming Home* and *Born on the Fourth of July* rely on one of the most traditional of all melodramatic images, the cripple, to orient their moral universes. In discussing cripples and those deformed, Peter Brooks in *The Melodramatic Imagination* says that: "[These] correspond...to a repeated use of extreme physical conditions: as well as mutes, there are blind men, paralytics, invalids, of various sorts whose very physical presence evokes the extremism and hyperbole of ethical conflict and manichaestic struggle" (56). The body serves a graphic moral statement. The wounded body in Vietnam war films generally serve to drive home points about the war as destructive and therefore "wrong." In *Platoon* the most evil character, Barnes, is the most explicitly disfigured by his wounds.

Ron Kovic, the hero in *Born on the Fourth of July*, changes from whole to severely wounded, both physically and emotionally. The recuperation of his spirit lags behind his physical adjustment to his damaged body, however, the overall structure of the film takes us into and through both movements. We witness his physical experience, and so we come to understand the series of spiritual transformations that Kovic undergoes. The film's movement into the interior world of Ron Kovic serves to instruct us in the profound transformation in his position toward the morality of the war. *Born on the Fourth of July* goes beyond *Platoon* and *Casualties of War*, however, in depicting the main character as reaching the end to his search for completion. By the film's conclusion, he appears to have found a place outside of himself, where, most important, he has become articulate. After the search for a means to complete his body, the Kovic character apparently completes his soul by becoming a spokesman for the anti-war movement. By finding his voice, by finding a means to express his anguish and rage, he fulfills his need to express what is wrong about the war. Thus through the central character the film can end with a fully articulated moral condemnation.

Born on the Fourth of July *shares with* Platoon *a systematic sense of the* main character placed within social and familial relationships, although here these are more literal. Along with the physical and emotional development of the Kovic character, the film is built on a narrative movement within, then away from, and then back to family, a movement qualified by objects, particularly Kovic's wheelchair, prominent within the films *mise en scène*. Clearly, the film's central image of the main character as a wheelchair-bound paraplegic is a metaphor for the devastation wrought on the country as a whole by the war. Here, as the combat unit did in *Platoon*, "family" bears a metonymic relationship to "country." The failure of the Kovic family to cope with what Ron has become suggests a comparable failure of the larger society as well, the society that, for example, endorses the inadequately equipped and staffed veterans hospital in which Kovic attempts to begin his recovery. Here, as at the Kovic home, appearance is everything. the adaptation of the Kovic home to accommodate Ron's wheelchair can't prepare the family in essence for what their son has become. The mother who nurtures—apparently ideologically as much as physically—becomes the most aggressive in her lashing out at her son's transformation. Confinement in a wheelchair is the last in a line of her son's failures to become what his family has encouraged him to be: a wrestler in high school, then an appropriately, patriotically motivated grunt in Vietnam.

The wheelchair also figures prominently in Kovic's ultimate turnaround. Kovic and his new-found, paraplegic cohort Charlie (Willem Defoe) circle each other in their wheelchairs on a roadside in the middle of the Mexican desert. They circle closer, faster, till they grab each other and spit in each other's face. They rip at each other. The fight leaves them both sprawled helpless on the desert floor, their chairs abandoned back up on the road.

The chair, along with the physical damage it signals work in part as a scab, shielding a deeper spiritual wound underneath. The cover has to be stripped away so that full healing can begin. Kovic and Charlie fight about authenticity. As the fight escalates, the chairs as vehicles allow them to reach a state of honesty. The last layer in the veneer of pretense must be brutally stripped away. Charlie confronts Kovic about killing babies, about whether he ever really put his soul into the war. Kovic is full of shit, Charlie says, he never fought the war. He taunts Kovic to "come clean," to talk about what he's hiding.

He does. Admission finally arrests Kovic's descent into failure. What he must admit to, what he must confront, is his own role in the damage the war has wrought on families. Just as Erickson, in *Casualties* must go to the extreme of pressing charges in a court-martial in order to be heard, no one really seems to hear what Kovic has to say about his unit's mistaken violation of a Vietnamese family until he commits an act demanding the extreme courage of personal confrontation. He visits the Wilsons and tells them about his group's murder of the Vietnamese family in the same moment he must tell them that he is responsible for the accidental death of their son. The significance of what he is doing is not lost on him (nor us) as he must look squarely at Wilson's mother, father, wife and infant son, and tell this family about the other, and then about the family member he has deprived them of.

That he must shed his own family in order to find a new place in society with a more adequate, nurturing, surrogate family begins at this moment of admission of the destruction he has inadvertently wrought on other families. It is clearly meant to be understood as an ironic process.

Along with the wheelchair that signals Kovic's new and drastic difference from his family, other related objects mark the irony of his dilemma. Kovic suffers a horribly broken femur at the moment he appears, despite the odds, to be learning to walk successfully on crutches. He dreams in the hospital of being once again whole and clean, only to wake up with unkempt hair and beard, apparently after laying in his own vomit for hours. Kovic takes on with new eyes what had once been his own viewpoint as a child. He now becomes the wounded war veteran in the Fourth of July parade who cringes involuntarily at the sound of firecrackers. He sees a child much like he once was at the film's opening, watching the Fourth of July parade on his father's shoulders; now, instead of waving a flag as Kovic did, the child pretends to shoot at him as he rides in the parade. In the first shot we see of him in the dress uniform he wears to the parade, we see Kovic emptying his colostomy bag in the toilet. Kovic and other veterans against the war are assaulted outside the Republican National Convention at the precise moment, in the editing of the sequence, at any rate, that Richard Nixon is addressing the convention about "honoring" Vietnam veterans.

That Kovic finds his voice, and therefore regains on some terms his wholeness overshadows the irony through which we see the process unfold. These priorities help explain the strength, melodramatically, of the film's argument against the immorality of the war.

For all their widely varied differences in tone and form, Vietnam war films share the burden of clarifying for their audiences the meaning of that war. They differ from the traditional war film not iconographically, so much as in their systematic and necessary placement of the significance of their icons in moral contexts. These films situate the weapons, the visual environments, and the attendant props and costumes of the Vietnam war within a melodramatic narrative world, where the politically and ideologically uncertain meaning of the war itself can become, at least in filmic terms, viewed in the more legible form of issues of right and wrong. Objects in the Vietnam war film, often put to the ironic use of showing the futility of the "effective" waging of war—the rifles, handguns, grenades, helicopters, latrines, barracks, helmets, uniforms and wheelchairs—help mark this path in the worlds of their films to a sense of clarity we could never hope to find within the war itself.

Works Cited

Brooks, Peter. *The Melodramatic Imagination*. New Haven: Yale UP, 1974.

Elsaesser, Thomas. "Tales of Sound and Fury." *Monogram* 4 (1972) .

Heilman, Robert B. *Tragedy and Melodrama: Versions of Experience*. Seattle: U of Washington P, 1968.

Kane, Kathryn. *Visions of War: Hollywood Combat Films of World War II*. Ann Arbor: UMI Research P, 1982.

Lewis, Lloyd B. *The Tainted War: Culture and Identity in Vietnam War Narratives*. Westport, CT: The Greenwood P, 1985.

Filmography

Year	Film	Director
1968	*The Green Berets*	John Wayne and Ray Kellogg
1977	*The Boys in Company C*	Sidney J. Furie
1977	*Heroes*	Jeremy Kagan
1977	*Rolling Thunder*	John Flynn
1978	*Coming Home*	Hal Ashby
1978	*The Deer Hunter*	Michael Cimino
1978	*Dog Soldiers*	Karel Reisz
1978	*Go Tell the Spartans*	Ted Post
1979	*Apocalypse Now*	Francis Ford Coppola
1982	*First Blood*	Ted Kotcheff
1985	*Rambo*	George Cosmatos
1986	*Platoon*	Oliver Stone
1989	*Casualties of War*	Brian DePalma
1989	*Full Metal Jacket*	Stanley Kubrick
1990	*Born on the Fourth of July*	Oliver Stone

Reel Wheels:
The Role of Wheelchairs in American Movies

Martin F. Norden

Wheelchairs and their users have found their way into dozens of Hollywood films over the decades, and it might be tempting to conclude that the reason moviemakers have included such vehicles is to replicate their main purpose in society: to allow people with permanent or temporary ambulatory disabilities a greater degree of mobility and independence. As we shall see, however, the appearance of such devices in films is hardly that simple. Unlike other elements of the material world that often dissolve into movie backgrounds (cars, furniture, buildings, etc.), wheelchairs draw immediate attention to themselves and virtually never appear in movies by accident. Their strong presence is usually in service to an able-bodied agenda questionable at best, divisive and hurtful at worst. Moviemakers have ascribed a wide range of qualities and functions to wheelchairs over the years, including humor, evil, helplessness, confinement, deception, heroism and dehumanization, and the point of this essay is to examine such representations in typical American films. Wheelchairs play relatively incidental roles under the best of circumstances, in which the filmmakers make us aware of their presence and issues related to them but do not underscore their prominence at every turn. Under the worst, they become so conspicuous that we have difficulty looking beyond them to the persons using them. Unfortunately, moviemakers have gravitated far more often toward the latter extreme than the former, a tendency that stretches back to the earliest days of the medium.

Filmmakers initially used wheelchairs as a means of gaining laughs in slapstick comedies. One of the first directors to do so was D.W. Griffith's predecessor as the Biograph company's primary director, Wallace "Old Man" McCutcheon. With the assistance of a then-obscure cinematographer named G.W. "Billy" Bitzer, McCutcheon fast became a specialist at orchestrating pandemonium before his camera. Among the things he learned while developing his comedies of pursuit were the reasonably close matching of action among the shots, in-depth compositions that often showed pursuers and pursued in the same frame, and occasional shots that highlighted comic bits of business involving individual pursuers. The latter was well-illustrated in McCutcheon's *The Lost Child* (1904), about a stranger chased by townspeople

187

who erroneously believe him guilty of kidnapping a child; the unfortunate had among his pursuers an elderly wheelchair-using man who nimbly dodges all sorts of obstacles that come his way.[1]

Other filmmakers saw similar potential in wheelchairs. Harry and Herbert Miles, one-time Biograph exhibitors remembered in the film history books for establishing the world's first film exchange in 1902, were also responsible for something called *The Invalid's Adventure* (1907). No doubt influenced by the McCutcheon film noted above, the film shows what can happen when a wheelchair-using man "seized with a mad desire to do a little exploiting on his own account," to cite a description in *Moving Picture World*, a trade journal of the time. He escapes from his attendant, and a wild chase ensues "with any number of ludicrous and highly amusing accidents en route, in each of which the invalid manages to retain his equilibrium." He eventually falls into a stream and almost drowns before local townspeople rescue him.[2]

Similar mayhem occurred in *Cured*, a short comedy directed by Frank Powell, written by Eleanor Hicks, and photographed by Percy Higginson for Biograph in 1911. In this film, a man with gout uses a wheelchair occasionally to get about town, and one day he makes the mistake of leaving his chair behind to get a drink. Lee "Doc" Doherty, Biograph's chief publicist who provided descriptions of the company's films for its catalog and trade-paper advertisements, characterized the ensuing action this way:

He has hardly departed when Happy Jack enters and decides to take a ride. This proves to be a most exciting trip, bumping into objects and human beings, down a long flight of stairs to the very edge of the wharf facing the sea. Here he finds the owner hobbling close behind him, so he vamps. The invalid finds this point a most attractive one at which to sit and enjoy the cool breezes of the sea, and here he sits. Shortly after those into whom Happy Jack in his peregrinations has run, approach stealthily and thinking the man in the chair is Jack pounce upon him and overboard he goes.[3]

The actor who played Happy Jack, Mack Sennett, found himself particularly enamored of this type of comedy and left Biograph the following year to form his own company dedicated to movie mayhem, the famous Keystone studio. Not surprisingly, Sennett and Keystone kept alive the comic use of wheelchairs, most notably in *His New Profession* (1914), a one-reeler written and directed by a young Sennett protege named Charles Chaplin. In this film, laden with what critic Uno Asplund has characterized as "disagreeably sadistic humour," (57), a man hires a vagabond (played by Chaplin himself) to push the wheelchair of his crotchety old uncle through a park, a job which the Chaplin character quickly comes to regret. After several misadventures with his increasingly quarrelsome charge (including the repeated aggravation of the uncle's leg, a routine that Chaplin reprised in his 1917 Mutual film, *The Cure*, the tramp finally pushes the uncle in his wheelchair over an embankment. To add insult to injury, police arrive and arrest the latter character for disturbing the peace.

Despite the continuing popularity of physical comedy, the "disagreeably sadistic humour" of *His New Profession* and the earlier one-reelers was showing signs of weakening. A number of moviemakers had begun expanding the length and complexity of their works during this time, and, perhaps under the spell of high-mindedness exerted by the international film d'art movement (which relied heavily on masterworks of the stage and printed page for source material), they finally recognized the tastelessness of placing wheelchair users and other disabled people at the center of slapstick comedies. The unsettling image of people careening wildly in wheelchairs for the benefit of ableist audiences looking for laughs fell off sharply and, except for sporadic reappearances in the following decades, thankfully remains dormant.

Early silent-era feature films that presented wheelchairs tended to treat the devices and their users in a relatively incidental way. In 1912, the newly formed Famous Players Film Co. recruited J. Searle Dawley, a writer-director who created about 300 films during his tenure with the Edison and Rex companies. One of the first movies he wrote and directed for this fledgling company was *Chelsea 7750* (1913), a four-reel crime mystery that followed the activities of a sleuth named Kirby (Henry E. Dixey, then one of Famous Players' "famous players") who happened to use a wheelchair. The villain of the piece, the head of a counterfeiting ring named Grimble (House Peters), abducts the detective's daughter Kate (Laura Sawyer) in retaliation for Kirby's role in his son's imprisonment years before. En route to a happy ending, the wheelchair-using sleuth used his considerable mental agility not only to save himself—at one point, he eludes Grimble's thugs by setting fire to his own apartment in the hope that firemen will rescue him, which they do—but also to save his daughter. Another representative feature of the time was *Bonnie, Bonnie Lassie* (1919), directed and co-written by a one-time underling of D.W. Griffith named Tod Browning. It's about a young Scots woman named Alisa Graeme who visits and enchants her grandfather's well-to-do American friend, Jeremiah Wishart. The latter character, a paternalistic fellow who tries several times to marry Alisa off to one of his nephews, happens to use a wheelchair.

We may view these films' incidental use of wheelchairs as a generally positive development, but nevertheless the filmmakers held an ambivalent regard for such vehicles and what they may represent. Believing the success of *Chelsea 7750* was due primarily to audience interest in Kirby's able-bodied daughter, Dawley followed up with a four-reel sequel about a month later called *An Hour Before Dawn* (1913). This new film changed the focus of the story line begun in *Chelsea 7750* by concentrating on Kate in her new profession as a detective following her father's semi-retirement. Though the film helped spark an interest in risk-taking young women (the Kate Kirby movies soon began sharing screen time with such serialized films as *The Perils of Pauline* and *The Exploits of Elaine*), it also had the unfortunate effect of shoving its wheelchair-using character into a background role and eventual oblivion.[4]

Tod Browning expressed his conflicting views in ways both subtle and obvious. In the case of *Bonnie, Bonnie Lassie*, Browning diminished the role of its wheelchair user just as Dawley had done in *An Hour Before Dawn*; indeed, the working title of *Bonnie, Bonnie Lassie* was *Auld Jeremiah*, based on a short story of the same name, but Browning changed it to reflect his repositioning of the main characters. In addition, the film gave little clue as to its creator's eventual obsession with physically disabled people who, Ahab-like, relentlessly pursue some able-bodied person with the intent of wreaking revenge for some actual or imagined transgression. In one of these films, *West of Zanzibar* (1928), Browning's frequent collaborator Lon Chaney played a professional magician who becomes paralyzed from the waist down and uses a wheelchair after his wife's lover, a cad named Crane (Lionel Barrymore), pushes him off a balcony. His desire to seek revenge on the lover is only heightened later after he finds his wife dead alongside a little girl. Thinking Crane is the girl's father, the magician (now called "Dead Legs" in the film) devises a most sinister, and certainly contrived, form of revenge: he abducts her, raises her to young adulthood, and then plans to have the young woman murdered while Crane watches. The plan backfires after Dead Legs learns that the young woman is his own daughter, however, and he dies after saving her from his hired killers. The unsavory Dead Legs uses a wheelchair throughout much of this convoluted scenario, and the vehicle quickly becomes associated with his maniacal qualities.

Despite Browning's attempts to connect the demonic with wheelchair users and others with disabilities, the succeeding decade saw few imitations. Several filmmakers returned to the idea of linking wheelchairs with humor, albeit humor far removed from the slapstick of the earlier, silent-era films. In 1935, for example, Paramount's Mitchell Leisen directed *Hands Across the Table*, a romantic comedy that focuses on a couple of Depression-era gold diggers—a manicurist named Reggi Allen (Carole Lombard) and a dashing but impoverished fellow named Theodore Drew III (Fred MacMurray)—who fall in love amid a series of comic misrepresentations and misunderstandings while pursuing separate quests to seek out well-heeled mates. Drew's rival for the young woman's affections is Allen Macklyn (Ralph Bellamy), a wealthy ex-aviator who uses a wheelchair after having sustained injuries in an airplane crash several years before. Among the comedy's questionable messages (most notably, that disabled people should sacrifice their happiness and "nobly" withdraw from romantic relationships with able-bodied people) was the inappropriate design of its disabled character's chair. As movie analyst Lauri Klobas has noted, "a lavish art-deco wheelchair was designed to mesh with the set. The result was a huge monstrosity of a chair that further disabled Macklyn" (117).

Humor was also an ingredient in *Block-Heads* (1938), a Metro-Goldwyn-Mayer vehicle for the comedic talents of Stan Laurel and Oliver Hardy. In this film, Laurel played a World War I soldier unaware that the conflict has been over for twenty years. He finally comes home a hero and stays at a national soldiers' home. His long-lost friend (Hardy) learns where he's staying and discovers him in a wheelchair on the home's grounds, his leg apparently lost as a result of combat. He's full of sympathy and remorse until he learns what the audience had observed minutes before: that his friend had merely folded his leg under himself before sitting down in an unused wheelchair.

The latter part of the 1930s also witnesses a return to the more incidental use of wheelchairs courtesy of MGM's "Dr. Kildare" movie series. Commencing with *Young Dr. Kildare* in 1938 and lasting until 1947's *Dark Delusion*, the 15-film series co-starred Lionel Barrymore, one of Hollywood's very few actors who used a wheelchair off-screen. Barrymore, who had acted in dozens of movies prior to the Kildare series (including Tod Browning's *West of Zanzibar*, noted above), started using a wheelchair in 1937 following an accident that aggravated his ever-worsening arthritis. He played roles of considerable variety and depth in more than three dozen films after that decision but remains best remembered for his portrayal of that cantankerous diagnostician of the Dr. Kildare films, Dr. Leonard Gillespie.

The Kildare series was hardly perfect in its rendering of Gillespie and his use of the chair. It rarely showed the doctor's life outside the hospital and the accessibility and prejudicial problems he might thus encounter, for example, and the filmmakers occasionally had the other characters acknowledge his use of a wheelchair with varying degrees of insensitivity. In *The Secret of Dr. Kildare* (1939), for instance, a hospital administrator refers to Gillespie as "an inspiration to the whole medical profession" but in the same breath notes that "his legs are hopelessly crippled," while in that same year's *Calling Dr. Kildare*, the title character devalues other people with disabilities by praising Gillespie as "the greatest diagnostician in the world today. Why, if anyone else couldn't walk, they—they'd fold up and quit. He's pushed his way right up the top in a wheelchair." The filmmakers kept such slams to a minimum, however, and generally handled Gillespie's use of a wheelchair in a low-key, unobtrusive way.

As the Kildare series began winding down, the Hollywood movie industry started developing different types of wheelchair-using characters. Historians have often characterized the years immediately following World War II as a time when the concerns of society's victims took center stage, and, for good or ill, Hollywood filmmakers perceived wheelchair users to be very much a part of that trend. Perhaps the most infamous of the resulting movies was Henry Hathaway's *Kill of Death* (1947), a *film noir* which contains a sequence involving a psychotic killer named Tommy Udo (Richard Widmark) and a wheelchair-using mother of a "squealer" he's been assigned to find. The final images of the sequence remain as shocking as they were back in 1947; after binding the woman to her chair with a lamp cord, Udo wheels her out of her apartment and shoves her down a long flight of stairs. A less graphic, more extended example, *Key Largo* (1948), co-starred the wheelchair-using Lionel Barrymore as a hotel owner on one of the Florida keys who along with his daughter-in-law (Lauren Bacall) and his late son's commanding officer (Humphrey Bogart) are held captive by gangsters during a hurricane.

The most conspicuous member of the post-WWII "helpless victim" trend was also one of the comparatively rare films that depicted a person using a wheelchair as a result of a temporary injury: Alfred Hitchcock's *Rear Window* (1954), in which a professional photographer named L.B. Jeffries (James Stewart) uses a wheelchair after breaking a leg while snapping away at an auto race. The filmmakers restricted his activities to his Greenwich Village apartment while he recuperates and, to pass the time, he begins to watch his neighbors in apartments across the courtyard. He later finds himself in a precarious situation when a man whom he thinks has murdered his wife in an apartment across the way comes over and threatens him.

Hitchcock clearly saw the wheelchair as an instrument of confinement leading to helplessness. In his celebrated interview with Francois Truffaut, he called the Jeffries character "an immobilized man" and referred to the main character in the Cornell Woolrich short story on which he and screenwriter John Michael Hayes based *Rear Window* as "an invalid who was confined to his room." Truffaut suggested a second Hitchcock agenda with his important observation, which Hitchcock did not dispute, that Jeffries "is exactly in the position of a spectator looking at a movie." In other words, filmgoers are similar to Jeffries in that they are temporarily "immobilized," sit in the dark before a window-like rectangle, and watch intimate events unfold. Hitchcock took this idea one step further by using Jeffries' voyeurism to indict the passive quality of the film-going experience, a quality which by implication extends to the wheelchair-using experience. Indeed, the director noted with a certain glee that, when the killer actually enters Jeffries' apartment and menaces him, the wheelchair-using man "deserves what's happening to him!" (Truffaut 213-219).

Kiss of Death, *Key Largo*, and *Rear Window* are similar in that they show characters at the mercy of some criminal able-bodied force after they have adjusted to life in a wheelchair. During this same period, filmmakers also experimented with victimization of a different sort: people whose dreams are shattered as a result of a disabling accident. It reflected, and continues to reflect, one of the most deeply entrenched mainstream beliefs about people with physical disabilities. As suggested by sociologist Nancy Weinberg, "The general public tends to believe that people with disabilities have suffered a terrible tragedy and are forever bitter about their misfortune," a view often at odds with the way disabled people themselves feel about their disabilities and adapt to them (141). Nevertheless, mainstream society's definition of disabled people as hard-luck individuals who must heroically undergo a long personal struggle (as opposed to the more modern view that they are minority-group members subject to alternating rounds of bigotry, paternalism, and indifference) served as the philosophic basis for numerous films that depicted wheelchair use during this time.

Disabled soldiers returning from overseas were very much among the disadvantaged social subgroups that caught the country's attention after the war, and their appeal, box-office and otherwise, prompted Hollywood filmmakers to initiate this specific wave of films. Wheelchairs took on a prominent role in one disabled-vet film in particular: *The Men* (1950), written by Carl Foreman and directed by Fred Zinnemann. In this film, Bud Wilchek (Marlon Brando, in his film debut) is paralyzed from the waist down as a result of a bullet to the spine and spends a considerable amount of time in a wheelchair as a part of his recuperative process. He has a difficult time containing his smoldering intensity, but the film, which faces wheelchair issues squarely, shows him gradually accepting his new life as a post-rehabilitative person and husband. Though Wilchek is the main focus of the movie, he is by no means the only wheelchair-user; numerous other vets with disabilities help this *primus inter pares* with his adjustment, and in general the film does a good job of showing "the men" pursuing a variety of strategies that go beyond coping with life in a wheelchair. Director Zinnemann added a strong degree of authenticity to *The Men* by shooting much of it in a V.A. hospital and recruiting 45 veterans who actually used wheelchairs to act in the film.

Despite the power and relative sensitivity of *The Men* and other disabled-vet films, Hollywood's interest in the topic began waning during the early 1950s. Believing audiences were tiring of such fare, moviemakers developed the idea of examining the lives of world-class performers in such fields as politics, sports, and the arts who had been "felled" by disabilities only to triumph over them. (They tended to avoid such heavyweights in the field of medicine, perhaps believing that MGM had exhausted that possibility with the world-renowned diagnostician Dr. Gillespie of its "Dr. Kildare" film series that concluded in 1947.) As they did in the disabled-vet films, wheelchairs came to symbolize the terrible price that these characters had paid and often the object to be overcome; more often than not, the films ended by showing the person "conquering" the wheelchair by walking, however haltingly and temporarily. The filmmakers were clearly treating the vehicles as objects of confinement, things from which to be liberated.

One of the earliest of such films, *With a Song in My Heart* (1952), demonstrated Hollywood's de-emphasis of wheelchair-using veterans in favor of civilian "superstars" who use the vehicles. It begins at an award ceremony in New York honoring Jane Froman (Susan Hayward), and we learn through flashbacks that her career as a singer in nightclubs, stage musicals, movies and on radio had been disrupted after a plane crash en route to a USO tour in London that left her with a leg almost severed below the knee. We see numerous wheelchair-using vets in the film after Froman has dealt with her personal struggles and gallantly resumed her USO tour, but they distinctly play background roles. They are simply her fans, and she has no qualms about performing before them as a disabled person (she appears on crutches in front of the vets at one point). When singing before the general able-bodied public, however, she often hides her heavily encased leg under a long, flowing gown.

Interrupted Melody (1955) covered similar territory by following the story of Marjorie Lawrence King (Eleanor Parker), a globe-trotting opera singer who contracts polio at the height of her career. Her doctor husband (Glenn Ford) persuades her that life remains worth living, but she's convinced her career is over. One day, an old friend of her husband, an Army doctor, asks her to sing for some of the "boys" at the local V.A. hospital, but she states flatly that she does not sing in public anymore. When the doctor queries, "But if your voice is okay, why not?," she responds by referring to her wheelchair: "Well, you see, I—I'm in this thing all the time." The doctor's scene-concluding response drips with poignancy: "So are a lot of the boys." Needless to say, she does perform in the hospital (she sings "Over the Rainbow" while wheeling through a ward full of disabled vets, many of whom also use wheelchairs), and she finds it such an uplifting experience that she does eventually resume her operatic career. It's interesting to note, however, that when she again reaches the professional stage she abandons the chair and sings while propping herself up against the scenery. The message, identical to the one in *With a Song in My Heart*, is clear: it is acceptable to be seen performing in the chair while among one's "own kind" (i.e., other wheelchair users, family, close friends, rehab professionals) but not in front of general able-bodied audiences.

Sunrise at Campobello (1960), directed by Vincent Donehue, examined a three-year period in the life of Franklin Delano Roosevelt that commenced with the onset of his paralysis and ended triumphantly with his appearance before the 1924 Democratic national convention. Stung by accusations that he had created propaganda on behalf of that year's Democratic national ticket, writer-producer Dore Schary tried to downplay the political significance of its wheelchair-using character by suggesting that *Campobello* was "a very simple, contained story about a man struck down by a crippling disease, and the effect it had upon his immediate family. He was a man who happened to be a political figure.... It could have been about any man" (II:9). Like the other films of this trend, *Campobello* ends with its disabled main character returning to a former glory whole concomitantly avoiding the use of the wheelchair, or, to put it bluntly, trying to "pass" for an able-bodied person. Schary saw FDR's lonely walk to the convention podium to nominate Al Smith for President as the film's climax: "At that moment, the entire convention broke loose. This was the moment that was to affect the entire world because this was the moment at which Roosevelt returned to politics" (Schumach 24). Yet for Schary, the thing that defined the "moment" was not the speech itself (indeed, the movie ends before FDR gives it) but Roosevelt's emergence from his wheelchair to walk those ten long steps. Though FDR conducted much of his eventual presidency from a wheelchair, Schary found it necessary to conclude *Sunrise at Campobello* with the implication that he had to liberate himself from the vehicle in order to resume his career.[5]

The trend took an unusual turn in 1964 with the appearance of Stanley Kubrick's *Dr. Strangelove or: How I Learned to Stop Worrying and Love the Bomb*. This dark satire on cold-war relations features Peter Sellers in three roles: a British colonel, an American President, and a German advisor to the President. The third of this trio, the film's title character, also happens to use a wheelchair. Unlike the disabled characters in the films already discussed, Dr. Strangelove uses a wheelchair at the time the film introduces him. Like his peers, however, he is an extraordinary person (an expert on international political affairs, in his case) and does rise out of his chair near the film's end. "Mein Führer, I can walk!" he exclaims to the President, albeit mere nanoseconds before a montage of atomic bomb blasts concludes the film.

Paralleling the growth of movies featuring recently disabled people of international renown was a trend involving the idea of able-bodied characters using wheelchairs to disguise the fact that they are indeed able-bodied. Films such as *House of Wax* (1953), *The Man with the Golden Arm* (1955), and *The List of Adrian Messenger* (1963)—a Victorian-era horror film, a drug addiction drama, and a murder mystery, respectively—each had among their characters an able-bodied person who bamboozles fellow characters and audiences alike into believing that he or she is incapable of leaving the chair. (In the case of *The Man with the Golden Arm*, this person is played by Eleanor Parker, the same actress who played the wheelchair-using opera star Marjorie Lawrence King in *Interrupted Melody* that same year.) That people who use wheelchairs do indeed get out of them from time to time is a point that seems to have eluded the filmmakers responsible for these works.

Deception of a different sort involving a wheelchair occurs in *What Ever Happened to Baby Jane?* (1962). In this famous shocker about two middle-aged show-biz sisters, we and just about everyone in the film are led to believe that Baby Jane Hudson (Bette Davis) accidentally hit her sister Blanche (Joan Crawford) with a car while in a drunken stupor, forcing the latter character to use a wheelchair the rest of her life. We learn much later in the film that the circumstances surrounding Blanche's disabling accident were far different from the generally believed version of them; it was Blanche, humiliated by her sister at a party only moments before, who tried to run down Baby Jane. Blanche missed her target, however, and struck a stone gate instead, the force of which snapped her spine. She was still able to gain revenge on her sister by keeping her awash in endless waves of guilt, but her scheme comes back to haunt her when Baby Jane learns the truth 25 years later and torments the wheelchair user with unbelievably macabre acts.

Helplessness, confinement, and surprise were thus the dominant and highly questionable characteristics that filmmakers bestowed on wheelchairs for decades following World War II. Even in the case of the civilian "superstar" films, which presumably were meant to be inspirational, wheelchair users in the audience could not help but perceive the films' implicit message: if you don't stage a dramatic comeback (including a mandatory, climactic attempt to get up out of the chair and walk), you are a failure. These images did not change in any substantial way until the mid-1970s, after filmmakers had had the chance to absorb the political ramifications born of the late 1960s and early 1970s. People with physical disabilities were among the socially disadvantaged subgroups that had stepped up their activism during this time, and their actions led Congress to pass important pieces of legislation, including the Architectural Barriers Act of 1968 and the Rehabilitation Act of 1973. In addition, a number of private and public groups established Independent Living centers dedicated to helping wheelchair users and others reclaim control over their lives. Vietnam veterans disabled by the war were conspicuous players in these actions, as historians Leonard Quart and Albert Auster have argued: "The nation's concern over the returning [wounded vets] stimulated and focused attention on the world of the disabled" (25). This concern resulted in, among other things, the creation of films that started giving a more realistic and sympathetic treatment of wheelchair users and other disabled people.

The Other Side of the Mountain (1975) and *The Other Side of the Mountain, Part 2* (1978) vividly illustrate Hollywood's changing attitudes. In detailing the life of Olympic hopeful Jill Kinmont (Marilyn Hassett) before and after the skiing accident that left her paralyzed from the shoulders down, the movies follow the civilian superstar pattern established in the early 1950s. (*Other Side 2* even begins with Jill about to accept the city of Los Angeles' Woman of the Year award for her work as an educator, reminiscent of Jane Froman's Courageous Performer of the Year ceremony that starts *With a Song in My Heart*.) Yet some significant differences are apparent beneath their old-fashioned trappings. In particular, the *Other Side* films do not try to have their disabled character return to her former greatness or "pass" for an able-bodied person at their conclusion, and they do show her encountering prejudice related to her use of a wheelchair (a boyfriend in *Other Side 1* backs out of their relationship, for example, while a school administrator tells her he won't allow her to study for a teaching certificate). For all of their notorious tear-jerking qualities, the *Other Side* films exhibit a better understanding of the wheelchair experience than do their post-WWII counterparts.

As the realities of the Vietnam war continued to hit home through the 1970s, filmmakers followed the lead of their peers of the World War II era and began focusing their attention on the plight of returning disabled veterans. Among the first films to deal with wheelchair-using Vietnam vets were *Coming Home* and *The Deer Hunter* (both 1978) as well as the misbegotten *Modern Problems* (1981).

Coming Home remains one of the finest Hollywood attempts to deal with the experiences of wheelchair users. It focuses on Luke Martin (Jon Voight), a tempestuous Vietnam vet paralyzed from the waist down, and his relationship with Sally Hyde (Jane Fonda), a bored military wife and V.A. hospital volunteer. Some audiences and critics found Luke's transformation from a volatile cynic to an impassioned antiwar crusader to be unrealistically quick, but nevertheless *Coming Home* contains numerous scenes of insight and power.

Coming Home differs from many previous wheelchair-user films in that, near the end of the film, Luke's wheelchair has become relatively incidental to the film's story. He still encounters problems related to his use of the vehicle— late in the film, for instance, he is blocked in a grocery store by a frumpy woman who acts as if he does not exist—but the strength of his convictions de-emphasizes its prominence while simultaneously investing it with a special quality. As Luke shackles himself to the gates of a Marine Corps recruiting depot in a symbolic effort to prevent others from going to Vietnam and later gives an emotional speech to high school students about the wrongness of the war, his ever-present chair becomes an emblem of heroism in its low-key way.

Coming Home has several attributes that give its depiction of wheelchair use a ring of truth. Voight, an able-bodied actor, lived in the paraplegic ward of the V.A. hospital in Downey, Calif., during the making of the movie and while there spent five weeks learning to play wheelchair basketball. In addition, *Coming Home* featured the use of actual wheelchair-using vets in supporting roles, as *The Men* had done a generation before. The film introduces them in the first scene of the movie as they play pool and talk about Nam in a V.A. hospital rec room. We later see them engaged in activities ranging from basketball to frisbee throwing to football. Concerned about the way he photographed them, the cinematographer for *Coming Home*, Haskell Wexler, devised a special camera dolly that placed the camera at the same height as the men in wheelchairs. He was thus able to film them in a straightaway fashion, thereby avoiding high camera angles and the sense of powerlessness they often ascribe to their subjects. (Keller 21).[6]

The Deer Hunter also depicted a wheelchair-using Vietnam vet: Stevie (John Savage), a young man who lost both legs and an arm after falling from a helicopter. A key moment in the films occurs when his hometown pal Mike

(Robert DeNiro) visits him in the V.A. hospital and Stevie declares that he does not want to go home. What ensues is a power struggle with the wheelchair as its object: Mike tries to push the chair while Stevie tries to anchor himself to his surroundings and shove Mike away. Mike wins the clash of wills by the sheer strength of able-bodied force, and as Mike wheels him down a hospital corridor, Stevie says, "I'm sorry. You do as your heart tells you, man." During that moment he is, in the words of Quart and Auster, "nothing but a helpless, dependent victim" (30), but he does manage to re-integrate himself quietly into his circle of friends by film's end, his chair becoming inconspicuous in the process.

A wheelchair is also present in *Modern Problems*, but, unlike Stevie's in *The Deer Hunter*, it largely avoids the connotation of victimization. Its occupant is Brian Stills (Brian Doyle-Murray), a Vietnam vet who owns his own publishing company. Unfortunately, his story, particularly his postwar adjustments and burgeoning romance, take a back seat to the film's inane main narrative concerning his friend, Max Fiedler (Chevy Chase), an air traffic controller who develops psycho-kinetic powers after a truck splashes him with nuclear waste. Brian exhibits only a hint of victimization, and it occurs after he and Max have played one-on-one basketball, Brian from his chair; they enter the former's den filled with high school basketball mementos, and Brian notes with a touch of bitterness that Vietnam ended any Olympic hopes for him. The filmmakers otherwise treated his use of a wheelchair in a refreshingly positive and incidental way.

A movie project that fell through in 1978 but finally made it to the screen in 1989, *Born on the Fourth of July*, told the poignant story of Ron Kovic, a one-time gung ho soldier who returns from Vietnam paralyzed from the chest down. Initially supportive of the war, the wheelchair-using Kovic gradually turns against it and like Luke Martin of *Coming Home* becomes an impassioned anti-war protestor. The film certainly makes us aware of problems he faces as a wheelchair user (for instance, a security guard at the 1972 Republican National Convention dumps the activist out of his wheelchair, an act that fails to diminish its user's resolve), but Tom cruise, the actor who portrayed Kovic and who worked with a wheelchair off and on for a year in preparation for the role, was quick to point out that the movie was more than a personal, coming-to-terms kind of story: "The film isn't about a man in a wheelchair. [It's about] the country, what it went through, was, became. You know, an invalid....It was a crippling time for this country, and you had to get beyond this man and a chair."

The Vietnam vet portrayals led the way for a renewed moviemaker interest in incidental treatments of other, non-veteran wheelchair users. As Quart and Auster have argued, these films "began to evoke a more consistently honest and realistic portrayal of the disabled from Hollywood" (25). Movies as otherwise disparate as *Nine to Five* (1980) and *Marie* (1985), for example, presented wheelchair-using secondary characters engaged in day-to-day activities with little if any comment. The trend reached a peak of sorts with the 1985 fantasy-horror film *Stephen King's Silver Bullet*. Using one of horrormeister King's celebrated small-town settings as its backdrop, *Silver Bullet* tells the tale of Marty Coslaw (Corey Haim), an appealing 11-year-old who tools around town in the film's "title object"; a motorized wheelchair dubbed the Silver Bullet. The film generally presents Marty as a high-spirited fellow who seldom allows his disability to interfere with life (indeed, his attitude toward disability-related issues seems limited to those times when his wheelchair is about to run out of gas), but his lifestyle as a disabled person quickly takes a back seat to a more pressing concern: the discovery that a werewolf is running amuck in the community. After Marty has gone on the offensive, the werewolf in human form comes close to running Marty down with his car. Riding in a newly souped-up vehicle made by his uncle that's more hot rod than wheelchair, however, the youngster manages to elude the murderous semi-human en route to a predictable ending.

The incidental treatment of people with physical disabilities gave rise to a new stereotype tied to the growth of high technology during the 1970s and 1980s: wheelchair-using people who are highly adept at using computers and other sophisticated electronic equipment. *The Anderson Tapes* (1972) and *Three Days of the Condor* (1975) were among the first films to feature such depictions. In the case of the former film, a sharp-witted boy uses a roomful of communications gear to notify the police of burglars in his parents' townhouse, while the latter film presents a CIA officer known simply as "the Major" who adroitly manipulates a communications console. Both characters use wheelchairs. The trend continued well into the 1980s, with increasingly prevalent computers replacing communications equipment as the technology of choice to be manipulated by the wheelchair-using technological gurus in such movies as *Starman* (1984), *Power* (1986), *The Imagemaker* (1986) and *No Way Out* (1987). As I noted in a previous *Beyond the Stars* essay,

Though each film certainly works as an affirmation of its disabled character's high level of intelligence, it unfortunately seldom if ever shows the character outside of his electronic lair. The films' common-denominator image—a wheelchair-using man who, at the request of some able-bodied superior, expertly manipulates the computers and associated paraphernalia surrounding him—leaves the impression that the character is all brain and no body, and that high technology coupled with high loyalty to an able-bodied boss are the only meaningful things in his life. (Norden 231)

In addition, it is arguable that the wheelchairs in such depictions act as a dehumanizing factor, in the sense that they begin to mesh figuratively with the other prominent forms of technology present. The impression often left by these films is that the person is eminently suited to operating the high-tech equipment because, by virtue of his use of a wheelchair, he appears to be part machine himself.

In looking back on the history of wheelchairs in American popular movies, it would be a mistake to assume that the films' generally positive progression (and I do emphasize the word "generally") has precluded filmmaker slippage back to the more negative depictions. Indeed, I would be the first to argue that the older filmmakers held no monopoly on damaging imagery. Most notably, the spirit that motivated moviemakers to use wheelchairs as vehicles for slapstick comedy during the earliest days of the cinema reappeared decades later. In the dreadful *Fire Sale* (1977), for example, a mentally and physically impaired World War II veteran played by Sid Caesar escapes from a V.A. hospital and, in classic slapstick fashion, goes careening down a highway in his motorized wheelchair while pursued by a motorcycle cop. The concluding image of the more recent *The Naked Gun: From the Files of Police Squad!* (1988)—a spectacularly inept police lieutenant named Frank Drebin (Leslie Nielsen) slapping his wheelchair-using associate (O.J. Simpson) on the back, blithely unaware that this action sends the latter skittering down a stadium stairway before being catapulted out of his chair and onto the field—seemed merely the point of departure for even more wheelchair sight-gags in *The Naked Gun 2 1/2: The Smell of Fear* (1991).

The linkage of wheelchairs and morally questionable behavior has also resurfaced from time to time. Lionel Barrymore essayed the role of the miserly, opportunistic banker Henry Potter in Frank Capra's 1946 *It's a Wonderful Life* (though, to be fair, his wheelchair is virtually invisible in the film). In *Frogs* (1972), Ray Milland played a thoroughly unpleasant wheelchair-using patriarch of a wealthy Southern family who has been systematically fouling the environment in the name of corporate greed and who gets his comeuppance at the hands (or, more appropriately, the webbed feet) of hundreds of mutant amphibians. In Arthur Penn's *Dead of Winter* (1987), a wheelchair-using man abducts a young actress for some nefarious scheme and holds her captive in his gloomy mansion.

Finally, there have been films that dwell on the issue of wheelchairs as modes of confinement, victimization, and helplessness. Some of their references are brief, such as the short scene in *The Hidden* (1987) that shows a wheelchair-using man mowed down by a speeding car. Others are lengthy and take up virtually the entire film, as in *Eye of the Cat* (1969), about a young man and woman (Michael Sarrazin, Gayle Hunnicutt) who plan to murder his cat-loving, wheelchair-using aunt (Eleanor Parker, perhaps the queen of actresses who performed in the vehicle), and *Whose Life Is It, Anyway?* (1981), about a sculptor played by Richard Dreyfuss who becomes so embittered after an auto accident leaves him paralyzed from the neck down that he loses his will to live.

In addition to these regressive depictions, moviemakers new and old have been guilty of various sins of omission or indifference. For all of their interest in wheelchairs, they have seldom addressed the major issues that wheelchair users encounter all too often in real life: restricted access, prejudice, the infringement of civil rights. As Lauri Klobas has observed, moviemakers have further demonstrated their insensitivity by often placing their characters in chairs ill-suited to their needs:

A "hospital chair" is a standard-sized chair with straight arms. Many studios have such chairs in their prop department and sock actors into them without regard to their individual stature. These huge chairs often hinder and further limit a character. Different chairs of different weights, back support and size are the ones seen in the real community. Their selection is determined by several factors, such as appropriate size, what the user's general level of daily activity is, and more commonly these days, aesthetic concerns. Studio prop chairs, besides being inappropriate for the characters seen using them, are extensions of the "hospital" and "patient" designations of people with limitations. (114-115)

The key to achieving more accurate depictions of wheelchair use is to include a greater number of performers who use wheelchairs in daily life and thus know the real concerns. It will be a struggle, however, since the Hollywood power structure has traditionally resisted recruiting such actors. In comments on a made-for-TV movie in which she appeared called *Skyward* (1980), Bette Davis illustrated the conflict between the old and the more enlightened ways of regarding such performers:

Skyward was about a fourteen-year-old girl, a paraplegic, who dreams of escaping from her wheelchair and, by learning to fly, she does. A real paraplegic, Suzy Gilstrap, played the part. I totally disapproved of this kind of realism. I thought the film would be better served by giving this opportunity, a super acting part, to an actress who could act as if she were paralyzed. I also felt it was cruel, if not exploitative, to expose Suzy to a new world which, from a talent standpoint, it was obvious she could never be a part of. My director and producer [Ron Howard and Anson Williams, respectively] totally disagreed with me. They were enraptured at the idea of casting a person who was actually handicapped as the paraplegic. (76)

By way of conclusion, I can only express my hope that other filmmakers who plan to represent wheelchairs and their users will likewise become so enraptured.

Notes

¹The film is described briefly in Joyce E. Jesionowski, *Thinking in Pictures: Dramatic Structure in D.W. Griffith's Biograph Films* (Berkeley: University of California Press, 1987), 15, 61.

²*Moving Picture World* lists *The Invalid's Adventure* as a "Miles Brothers" film, but it's not clear if the brothers produced the film themselves or merely secured the rights to it from an unnamed production company. See *Moving Picture World* 28 Sept. 1907, 473.

³Cited in *Biograph Bulletins, 1908-1912*, ed. Eileen Bowser (NY: Octagon Books, 1973), 285. Credits for this film may be found in Cooper C. Graham, Steven Higgins, Elaine Mancini, and Joao Luiz Vieira, *D.W. Griffith and the Biograph Company* (Metuchen, NJ: Scarecrow Press, 1985), 107-108.

⁴Discussions of *Bonnie, Bonnie Lassie, Chelsea 7750* and *An Hour Before Dawn* may be found in *The American Film Institute Catalog of Motion Pictures Produced in the United States: Feature Films 1911-1920*, ed. Patricia King Hanson (Berkeley: University of California Press, 1988), 88, 136, 425.

⁵For a more detailed discussion of this film within its political context, see Martin F. Norden, "*Sunrise at Campobello* and 1960 Presidential Politics," *Film & History* 16 (Feb. 1986), 2-8.

⁶See also John Eastman, *Retakes: Behind the Scenes of 500 Classic Movies* (NY: Ballantine Books, 1989), 66-67.

Works Cited

Asplund, Uno. *Chaplin's Films: A Filmography*. Trans. Paul Britten Austin. Newton Abbott, U.K.: David & Charles Ltd., 1973.

Cruise, Tom. Interview. *The Today Show*. NBC-TV 19 Dec. 1989.

Davis, Bette, with Michael Herskowitz. *This 'n That*. NY: Berkeley Books, 1988.

Keller, David. "Making *Coming Home*: An Interview with Haskell Wexler." *Filmmakers Newsletter* 11 (March 1978).

Klobas, Lauri E. *Disability Drama in Television and Film*. Jefferson, NC: McFarland & Co., 1988.

Moving Picture World. 28 Sept. 1907.

Norden, Martin F. "Victims, Villains, Saints, and Heroes: Movie Portrayals of People with Physical Disabilities." *Beyond The Stars: Stock Characters in American Popular Film*. Eds. Paul Loukides and Linda K. Fuller. Bowling Green: Bowling State University Popular Press, 1990.

Quart, Leonard, and Albert Auster. "The Wounded Vet in Postwar Film." *Social Policy* 13 (Fall 1982).

Schary, Dore. "Road to 'Campobello'." *New York Times* 25 Sept. 1960.

Schumach, Murray. "Democrats 'See' 1924 Convention." *New York Times* 21 Apr. 1960.

Truffaut, Francois, in collaboration with Helen G. Scott. *Hitchcock*. NY: Simon and Schuster, 1984.

Weinberg, Nancy. "Another Perspective: Attitudes of People with Disabilities," *Attitudes Toward Persons with Disabilities*. Ed. Harold E. Yuker. NY: Springer Publishing Co., 1988.

Filmography

Year	Film	Director
1904	*The Lost Child*	Wallace McCutcheon
1907	*The Invalid's Adventure*	Harry and Herbert Miles (?)
1911	*Cured*	Frank Powell
1913	*Chelsea 7750*	J. Searle Dawley
1913	*An Hour Before Dawn*	J. Searle Dawley
1914	*His New Profession*	Charles Chaplin
1919	*Bonnie, Bonnie Lassie*	Tod Browning
1928	*West of Zanzibar*	Tod Browning
1935	*Hands Across the Table*	Mitchell Leisen
1938	*Block-Heads*	John G. Blystone
1938	*Young Dr. Kildare*	Harold Bucquet
1939	*Calling Dr. Kildare*	Harold Bucquet
1939	*The Secret of Dr. Kildare*	Harold Bucquet
1946	*It's a Wonderful Life*	Frank Capra
1947	*Dark Delusion*	Willis Goldbeck
1947	*Kiss of Death*	Henry Hathaway
1948	*Key Largo*	John Huston
1950	*The Men*	Fred Zinnemann
1952	*With a Song in My Heart*	Walter Lang
1953	*House of Wax*	Andre de Toth
1954	*Rear Window*	Alfred Hitchcock
1955	*Interrupted Melody*	Curtis Bernhardt
1955	*The Man with the Golden Arm*	Otto Preminger
1960	*Sunrise at Campobello*	Vincent Donehue
1962	*What Ever Happened to Baby Jane?*	Robert Aldrich
1963	*The List of Adrian Messenger*	John Huston
1964	*Dr. Strangelove or: How I Learned to Stop Worrying and Love the Bomb*	Stanley Kubrick
1969	*Eye of the Cat*	David Lowell Rich
1972	*The Anderson Tapes*	Sidney Lumet
1972	*Frogs*	George McCowan
1975	*The Other Side of the Mountain*	Larry Peerce
1975	*Three Days of the Condor*	Sydney Pollack
1977	*Fire Sale*	Alan Arkin
1978	*Coming Home*	Hal Ashby
1978	*The Deer Hunter*	Michael Cimino
1978	*The Other Side of the Mountain, Part 2*	Larry Peerce
1980	*Nine to Five*	Colin Higgins
1980	*Skyward*	Ron Howard
1981	*Modern Problems*	Ken Shapiro
1981	*Whose Life Is It Anyway?*	John Badham
1984	*Starman*	John Carpenter
1985	*Marie*	Roger Donaldson

1985	*Stephen King's Silver Bullet*	Dan Attias
1986	*The Imagemaker*	Hal Wiener
1986	*Power*	Sidney Lumet
1987	*Dead of Winter*	Arthur Penn
1987	*The Hidden*	Jack Sholden
1987	*No Way Out*	Roger Donaldson
1988	*The Naked Gun: From the Files of Police Squad!*	David Zucker
1989	*Born on the Fourth of July*	Oliver Stone
1991	*The Naked Gun 2 1/2: The Smell of Fear*	David Zucker

Old and New Technologies

Digital Delusions:
Intelligent Computers in Science Fiction Film
Susanna Hornig

Science fiction serves a unique niche in a technocratic culture, exploring the future relationship between technology and society under conditions of rapid change in both areas. Like all popular culture forms, science fiction films both reflect and reinforce prevailing belief systems. But science fiction's subject matter is an unwritten future, and popular beliefs about the character of this future—evil or benign, free or controlled, technologically driven or socially determined—therefore have a special potential for becoming self-fulfilling prophecies.

Perhaps no other developments symbolize America's stormy romance with science and technology as well as developments in artificial intelligence. Here, fears of technology marching out of control, of machines controlling man, reach their apex. Here, too, visions of technological potential rapidly outstrip the boundaries of contemporary scientific knowledge. Intelligent computers in science fiction film have personalities, gender and free will; they act independently and in their own interests; they often trample on human values.

Intelligent technologies, as seen in these portrayals, seem to have an unbounded potential for good or for evil. Their capacity for evil comes into play most often when they "outgrow" their dependence on the human beings who create them. Their capacity for good—a less common theme that appears to emerge more often in more recent films—is most apparent when they work in close concert with a flesh-and-blood counterpart. Thus the image of unbridled, ill-conceived technology that turns against man is counterbalanced with a softer image, more congruent with an earlier American mythology in which technology was to be a tool for creating more benevolent human social conditions. The conflict represented here between technology-for-good and technology-for-evil is a central theme in contemporary American culture, as well as the subject of scholarly debate.

Does society drive technology, or does technology drive society? In these films, technologies emerge as independent (and sometimes evil) instruments only as a result of human miscalculation. But once unleashed, they can indeed behave as though they had minds of their own. This message reflects popular fears that unchecked technological growth can have ominous consequences. It may also reflect a deeper fear of the loss of free will and of power over the material world. If human scientific and technological progress is associated with the conquering of the natural world by artificial means, a belief that seems to be embedded in Western culture, a corollary is suggested. Technology can erode, as well as enhance, self-determination, especially when misused.

The late 1960s and very early 1970s saw a proliferation of films that dealt explicitly with the implications of computer-based intelligence for society. These films set the stage for later treatments, and their message was uniformly one of warning. This message becomes softer, however, in later years.

In the 1970 film *Colossus: The Forbin Project*, well-intentioned people turn too much control over to a computer, which quickly learns to act independently, increases its own computational speed, takes over its USSR counterpart, and proceeds to conquer the world (for its own interpretation of humankind's best interests) by threatening to detonate the missiles it controls. Opening scenes juxtapose radiation warnings with glimpses of a gigantic computer complex that, we later learn, has been given "responsibility" for the entire U.S. military defense system. (The radiation derives not from the computer itself, as it turns out, but from a defensive belt around it.) The rapidity with which the world of computer science is underscored for today's viewer by the physical size of the installation and the slightly dated computerese with which the film is sprinkled: "Dump the terminal buffer," "background programs," "overload."

In a press conference, the computer's jubilant creator (Forbin) announces that although Colossus "can absorb and process more knowledge than is remotely possible for the greatest genius that ever lived," it has "no emotions" and is incapable of creative thought. These "achievements," of course, become the world's undoing, as the computer takes its mission of paving the way for the emergence of the human millenium all too literally. At first Colossus communicates only on a large overhead screen; later it designs a primitive male voice for itself in which it announces monotonically that "freedom is an illusion." Colossus has information, intelligence and power; it lacks compassion and a recognition that freedom (or at least the appearance of freedom) is necessary to human happiness. The film is an allegory not only about the perils of runaway artificial intelligence, but also about the use of totalitarian means to achieve humanistic ends.

Dark Star (1972), set in the middle of the twenty-first century, conveys a similar message softened by post-sixties surrealism. The crew of the scoutship "Dark Star," whose mission is to blow up unstable planets, have been in space for 20 years, and their reality is beginning to slip. The computerized control system of the ship incorporates both male and female elements; the main ship control system is female, but the bombs themselves are independently intelligent and male. When Bomb Number Twenty insists on leaving the bomb bay on its own initiative, the main computer warns the crew. "Normally I wouldn't bother you boys," she says, but the ship's defenses are faulty. Only as a result of her insistence does Number Twenty petulantly agree to return.

Eventually Doolittle, one of the crew, enters the ships' cryogenic freezer to consult with their former captain, who is now deceased. The dead captain advises Doolittle to "talk to the bomb" and "teach it phenomenology." Number Twenty's artificial brain is not particularly smart, and Doolittle is able to confuse it temporarily by persuading it that it doesn't really know whether it exists or not, or what the world is like, since all the data it has available are subject to error. In the end, however, the bomb decides that Doolittle himself represents "false data" and must be ignored. Once again, humans are "done in" as a result of their inability to control the actions of an artificial intelligence clearly more limited than their own.

Another film from this period, George Lucas' *THX-1138* (1969), is a futuristic fantasy about a mechanized, computerized, industrialized society in which artificial intelligence takes a different and yet more menacing form. With human love outlawed, roommates are selected by computer match; pervasive computer systems monitor and evaluate every human move, including the consumption of tranquilizing medication; and therapy takes the form of computer-generated expressions of sympathy dispensed in confessional-like booths. Law and order are maintained by (not particularly brainy) robot police. Women's heads are shaved, and men and women alike wear identical plain white clothes.

THX-1138 himself (the film's primary character, identified by serial number) unwinds at the end of a taxing day by watching television footage of a police beating that goes rhythmically on and on. But when he starts cheating on his medication, he begins to see his society for what it really is. He is eventually successful in escaping the controlled "city" (in the course of attempting the escape he meets up with an escaped hologram who is much more human than any of the film's "real" people), but how he will survive in independence remains unclear.

This group of earlier films is thus unanimous in its warning message, seeing increasing mechanization and computerization as threats to human values and human freedom. In later films, however, we begin to see less unqualified fear of technology and more of an explicit realization that the potential for good and evil of technological alternatives is rooted in how human beings choose to use them. And lighter treatments of artificial intelligence themes and of technology generally suggest a sort of truce has been established between "us" and the machines. Arthur C. Clarke's *2001* and *2010* illustrate this transition.

Clarke, who first imagined the geosynchronous satellite, brought us his early statement on the artificial intelligence theme in *2001: A Space Odyssey* (1968). The film opens on a group of hairy primates competing with other animals for food. Following the appearance of a mysterious black monolith (which apparently symbolizes the arrival, perhaps from elsewhere in the universe, of intelligence), one of the primates discovers that bones can be used to smash other bones, other animals, and its own primate enemies. It throws the bone into the air in triumph; down comes a cylindrical space vehicle, and the film cuts to a shot of a circular space station in orbit. Thus the stage is set for a portrayal of the tool as an instrument for evil as well as good, including the ultimate tool that is a key character in the story that follows: the HAL 9000 computer, who always speaks softly and reasonably in a warm male voice.

HAL, the "latest result in machine intelligence…which can reproduce, though some experts still prefer to use the term 'mimic,' most of the activities of the human brain," is a "sixth member" of the crew of the spaceship "Discovery," traveling to Jupiter where (unknown to the human crew) another black monolith awaits. HAL himself, in a pre-departure news interview, states that he is "foolproof and incapable of error." His personality is far more developed than that of other film computers of this era; he declares confidently that his dependence on humans bothers him "not in the slightest bit." Of course the humans in his ship turn out to be far more dependent on him than he is on them. HAL engineers the deaths of all of the human crew except Bowman, who finally manages to disconnect HAL despite the computer's insistence that "I feel much better now. I really do." *2001*'s HAL is manipulative as well as smart, and his mistakes appear to be his own, not those of his programmers.

But in Clarke's later continuation of this chronicle in *2010: The Year We Make Contact* (1984), this message is substantially transformed as HAL's earlier malfunctions are attributed unambiguously to human error. HAL knew the original purpose of the *2001* mission, we learn, but was prevented by a misguided White House directive from revealing this information to the crew. The instruction to lie was contrary to his other programming; the results were therefore uncertain. HAL's voice and personality are also revealed as remarkably similar to that of his human creator Floyd, whom we meet for the first time in *2010*; thus this film's HAL is more clearly a reflection of human intent than an independent entity.

In a joint operation with the USSR, the crew of *2010*'s follow-up mission manage to reconnect HAL, despite Floyd's uncertainty as to whether HAL is "homocidal, suicidal, neurotic, psychotic, or just plain broken." HAL eventually receives a mysterious message from *2001*'s Bowman that the new mission must leave within two days or face extreme danger. Both the USSR and U.S. crews decide to comply, but they can only do so by leaving the Discovery—and HAL—behind. Floyd decides to be candid with HAL about this plan and, given the truth, HAL cooperates for the sake of the mission—although he asks plaintively at the end, "Will I dream?" Carried out without deviousness, human will triumphs over technological "will."

In other more recent treatments, too, what is human generally wins. *War Games* (1983) picks up on the war theme treated earlier in *Colossus* as a teenage hacker accidentally triggers the thermonuclear "game" on a U.S. Defense Department computer. Like *Dark Star*'s Doolittle, *War Games*' teenage hero tries to outfox the machine, but his strategy is to teach it rather than confuse it. He teaches the computer to play tic-tac-toe, and the computer "learns" that some games have no winners. More sophisticated, perhaps, than even the Hal 9000, if less personable, *War Games*' less literal-minded computer is able to carry the analogy over to thermonuclear war, discovers it is also an unwinnable game, and halts it—in the nick of time, of course.

The commercial spaceship in *Alien* (1979), like the ship in *2001* and *2010*, is also directed by a computer presence ("Mother"). But Mother's power is circumscribed in comparison to the power of Hal; she is treated as a personality by the crew but she is clearly their tool, not their controller, and is used in familiar ways: to analyze data, to decode messages, to calculate probabilities. When she is asked to calculate the crew's chances against the alien that has crept aboard, however, she returns only that she is "unable to compute" and that "available data [are] insufficient." *Alien* also features an android science officer whose covert mission is to bring back the creature at any expense, a task given higher priority by the corporate interests that put the android on board than saving the crew's lives. Here again an artificial intelligence (the android, with Mother's compliance) behaves in an evil way because it is in the service of evil human interests.

Cyborgs (man-machine hybrids), like androids (human-like robots), are special cases of artificial intelligence and deserve at least passing mention here. Cyborgs may sometimes be more threatening than computers that live in square cases because they can "pass" as human beings, as do the androids in *Android, Westworld, Futureworld* and other variations on this theme, as well as because they generally straddle the boundary between the biological and the mechanical. (An exception is *Cyborg*'s cyborg, a cybernetic "good guy," who remains intractably human, a woman with a silicon-enhanced memory.) But most androids seem to have more in common with industrial robots than Babbage machines; their limited intelligence and computer-like literal-mindedness seems to curtail their threat to human beings. Cyborgs are more complex.

In *Robocop* (1987) smart technology is enlisted not to conquer space but to control urban crime. An injured policeman is reconstructed into a cybernetic being (part human, part robot) by a private company given control of law enforcement in Detroit. The new creature's human memory (and values) are supposedly erased in the process, and the robot's programming successfully prevents it from taking direct action against members of the firm, which turns out to be infested with bad guys. But in the end the human triumphs; Robocop remembers he is Murphy and blows the whistle on the chief bad guy, who is destroyed the moment the company president fires him and Robocop's "Directive 4" protecting him becomes inoperative. Murphy's integration with his robotic half seems to hold promise that the human can triumph over the technological.

Machines putting down a human rebellion in the Los Angeles of A.D. 2028 send a cybernetic assassin back in time to destroy the mother of the rebellion's future leader in *The Terminator* (1984). The humans respond by sending back one of their own. Although, as in *Robocop*, the plot revolves around a cyborg, this battle is not between the two halves of a cybernetic creation but between something hardly human, programmed by machines, and a very human opponent. Yet the conflict between humanity and technology echoes that in *Robocop*. The humans in this chapter win, although the long-term outcome is reserved for the sequel.

In the children's film *The Flight of the Navigator* (1986), a damaged spaceship stops on earth to recruit the human navigator it requires to operate at its full potential. The film's "bad guys" are the U.S. military interests who attempt to hold both the ship and the boy hero captive, but the ship itself—a personable creature—is entirely innocuous. It is also dependent on human control, although this circumstance is a result of accidental damage.

A similar theme arises in *The Last Starfighter* (1984), a technological Horatio Alger tale in which a poor teenager living in a trailer park is selected on the basis of his video game prowess to direct a last desperate battle against an evil army about to take over the universe. The war technology in this film, like *The Flight of the Navigator's* ship, requires human direction: only an exceptionally skilled individual human being (since the alien starfighters have all been destroyed) can save the day for the forces of good. The starfighter is temporarily replaced on earth by an android who later sacrifices himself to prevent the hostile aliens' realizing the real hero is off in space preparing to do battle, but only a biological being can be a starfighter.

In the latest chapter of the "Star Trek" film series, *Star Trek V: The Final Frontier* (1989), technology provides the comic relief but it is humanity, again, that wins the day. The new starship "Enterprise" is still being tested when its crew is recalled from leave on an emergency basis. The competent, compliant female computer familiar to viewers of the television series has been replaced by a system that sends false warning signals and refuses to make entries to the captain's log; the ship also sports elevators that don't stop at the right floors and a malfunctioning transporter. (Chief Engineer Scotty never stops griping about these, of course.) But despite the attention to technology's failings and to contemporary computer fashion in the design of the new control room, the walls of which are covered with the latest in large-screen graphics and hypertext, technology neither wins nor loses the battles of *The Final Frontier*. Future technological progress moves along on the same sort of bumpy track we see in the real world of today; humans succeed despite technology's failings.

Robots like *Star Wars'* (1977) R2-D2 and C-3PO are another form of machine intelligence, although they are neither disembodied macrointelligences nor hybrid creations but simply clever mechanical inventions. However, they are no more than harmless minor characters despite their possessing intellect and personality—not to mention enormous appeal. Certainly they are not threats.

Neither is *Short Circuit*'s (1986) Robot Number Five, which acquires human-like emotions, the ability to laugh at jokes, and an awareness of the meaning of death (or "disassembly") after being zapped by a stray bolt of lighting. In a humorous ironic twist on the theme of war technology gone awry, Number Five is a military robot that develops a sense of morality along with his sense of humor. The military is anxious to reclaim and "repair" him; the reemergence of positive human ideals in this "malfunctioning" creation—who escapes the attempted recapture—reflects faith in the endurance of those ideals.

Not just actions but appearance belie the interpretation of these more sympathetic mechanical characters as anything but benevolent. Unlike the disembodied computers we have seen controlling spaceships, defense systems, or a future society, robots, cyborgs and androids have a physical body—usually a very human-like physical body. While androids by definition mimic the appearance of human beings, robots and cyborgs are represented by parodies of human form. The Terminator and Robocop are quintessentially powerful and menacing—the former as played by bodybuilder Arnold Schwarzenegger, the latter through its appearance in larger-than-life metallic form. R2-D2, C-3PO and Robot Number Five, on the other hand, are both physically smaller and indisputably cute. They invite identification as pets, mascots or children. Robot Number Five's large and curious eyes are reminiscent of the eye-bearing extension on the ship control computer in *The Flight of the Navigator*, which bobs around the cockpit engagingly as its curiosity and its teasing interchanges with the film's child-hero dictate; compare Colossus' various communication and data-gathering extensions, which are both ubiquitous and inhumanly stiff.

In *Blade Runner* (1982) we meet the humanized robot in yet another form: that of androids that cannot be distinguished from people without special testing and that have been exploited as slave labor by corporate interests. Because of the fear that these creatures might eventually develop human emotions, which is perceived as a threat, they are manufactured with a built-in four-year lifespan. Some are provided with ersatz memories of childhood, so that they don't even know they are not human. This film plays on the division between the biological and the mechanical; the "blade runner" (slang for "replicant" killer) sent to hunt down a group of the rebellious robots comments that the rebellious robots only want the same answers we all seek—a sense of past and future. The theme is still the persistence of humanistic concerns, whether embedded in man or machine.

Despite the emergence of benign robotic characters, and even of the idea that technological creations might be unfairly exploited by society, the films discussed here generally caution against granting technology itself too much power. Even "good" technologies are portrayed as powerful, somewhat mysterious entities certain to loom large in our future. Thus while on one level these films, especially the earlier ones, warn us against a future in which technology is uncontrolled, on another they "prop up" an ideology in which technological change is both inevitable and inevitably linked to social development—the ideology of post-industrial society. Although more recent messages are optimistic, older themes warning against the power of unrestrained technology recur, and both older and newer treatments tend to revolve around the same theme of conflict—not over technology's development, but over its control and the interests it serves.

This unresolved conflict between the desire for control and fear that in pursuing it we will lose our way represents two halves of the same coin. Both aspects are rooted in a belief—reflected in almost all science fiction—that technological development is in effect foreordained, and at the same time suggest a sense of alienation from its goals. Although more recent films suggest a reemergence of faith in the power of human values (good) over base technology (evil), a major crisis of contemporary democracy emerges from this theme. The forces that in fact shape technological development (technocratic decision-making and the influence of capitalistic interests) are largely invisible to society at large, to whom end results (both technological and social) may appear as alien faits accomplis. Perhaps the trend in more recent film treatments toward a more humanized technological future—reflected in both sympathetic machine characters and technological systems firmly under the control of human beings—suggests a degree of accommodation between social and technological change. New technology may still be seen as integral to our fantasies of the future, but it is no longer seen as the controlling force.

If science and technology are envisioned as independent forces that march on unconstrained by human control, whether for benevolent or malevolent ends, we lose the opportunity to shape the direction of the march. Technology is ours to do with as we please; its deployment will continue to reflect the distribution of power within society. The older vision of science and technology as not only threatening but self-driven might have blinded us to the significance of the choices we face with respect to its use. Technology is not harmless but carries awesome potential for escalating war, degrading the environment, and (perhaps) eroding human values—as well as an enormous potential for good—and we cannot escape responsibility for the decisions we face with respect to its use. The continual reemergence of these themes in film reflects our ongoing struggle to come to grips with this issue.

Filmography

Year	Film	Director
1968	*2001: A Space Odyssey*	Stanley Kubrick
1969	*THX-1138*	George Lucas
1970	*Colossus: The Forbin Project*	Joseph Sargent
1972	*Dark Star*	John Carpenter
1973	*Westworld*	Michael Crichton
1976	*Futureworld*	Richard T. Heffron
1977	*Star Wars*	George Lucas
1979	*Alien*	Ridley Scott
1982	*Android*	Aaron Lipstadt
1982	*Blade Runner*	Ridley Scott
1983	*War Games*	John Badham
1984	*The Last Starfighter*	Nick Castle
1984	*The Terminator*	James Cameron
1984	*2010: The Year We Make Contact*	Peter Hyams
1986	*The Flight of the Navigator*	Randal Kleiser
1986	*Short Circuit*	John Badham
1987	*Robocop*	Paul Verhoeven
1989	*Cyborg*	Albert Pyun
1989	*Star Trek V: The Final Frontier*	William Shatner

Renegade Robots and Hard-Wired Heroes:
Technology and Morality
in Contemporary Science Fiction Films
Donald G. Lloyd

Consciously or not, science fiction films are most often judged by their futuristic sets, pyrotechnic weapons, and ultratech machines. Indeed, it is the presentation of an advanced material world rather than the presentation of an advanced human society that is the most recognizable characteristic of the genre. The best science fiction films, however, have always shown more than just superficial fascination with technological gadgets and advancements, using the material creations of science to comment on aspects of human nature. For instance, the futuristic sets of Fritz Lang's classic, *Metropolis* (1926), would have lost their power if the idea they conveyed, that the machines of society devour the men who work them, did not have a lasting power of its own. Similarly, the monolithic robot, Gort, of *The Day the Earth Stood Still* (1951), would lose much of his enigmatic presence if he did not on some level also represent the alien Klaatu's all-too-human compassion.

Contemporary science fiction films, spurred in part by a tremendous sophistication in special effects technology, continue to explore the ways in which our advanced material world complicates and aggravates age-old questions of human nature and identity. Any contemporary anxiety of identity is complicated by the growing feeling that technology has supplanted the individual, that machines and not people are in control, and that that which we have created will destroy us.

The 1984 movie *Terminator* captured this anxiety precisely in its central image, that of a fiery explosion from which emerges a glittering robot burned clean of the remnants of human flesh that once clothed it. This robot has returned from the not-too-distant future to kill Sarah Connor, the mother of unborn John Conner—JC, humankind's only hope in an upcoming holocaust—so that the future rule of cognizant computers goes unchallenged. And, while the movie's symbolism is, perhaps, heavy-handed, *Terminator*'s phoenix image brilliantly conveys the unsettling idea that technology can be reborn free from the imprecise pollution of its human origin. The subject is all the more compelling because of our growing realization that society is now run by a computer-driven technology we are largely ignorant of.

216

Terminator is typical of many science fiction films set in the near or not-too-distant future in its handling of our hopes and fears about technology. Rather than address technological issues solely through thematic extrapolation, such films often use robots or other technological devices as symbolic representations of all we find good or evil about science and technology. Such a tactic is of course not new. We can look to Frankenstein's unnatural creation in Mary Shelley's classic as an early fictional attempt to embody anxieties over technology as an actual destructive and potentially malignant character.

As technology has pushed society towards the twenty-first century, robots (whether biological or mechanical) have taken on a growing technical sophistication while still retaining many of the basic elements of the Frankenstein myth. Janice Rushing and Thomas Frentz, in "The Frankenstein Myth in Contemporary Cinema," identify an important process illustrated by the myth, that of the "increasing mechanization of the human and humanization of the machine, a process moving toward an ultimate end in which the machine is god and the human is reduced either to slavery or obsolescence" (62). An obvious way this process is illustrated in *Terminator* is through the opposition of scenes in which the Terminator robot further refines its ability to pass for human (selecting in one scene an appropriately coarse reply to a hotel manager from the menu display superimposed over its visual field) with scenes in which Sarah Connor (Linda Hamilton) is drilled in the basic technical demolitions skills she will need to survive. The superiority of the machine is further established by contrasting the impressive physique of Schwarzenegger with the slight build of Reese (Michael Biehn), the future warrior who returns to aid Connor. Even with the destruction of the Terminator, the threat that it represents—that cognizant computers are superior to humans—is not eliminated, and Sarah Connor realizes she must leave behind the comfortable "human" world made possible by modern technology and discipline herself (i.e.—become machine-like) in order to prepare for the coming holocaust.

A movie with more than a few similarities to *Terminator* in plot and subject matter is Richard Stanley's *Hardware* (1990), which tells another story in which a young woman and her doomed lover attempt to flee and/or destroy a nearly indestructible killing machine, the Mark-13. The mechanization of the female protagonist, Jill (Stacey Travis), is already well underway at the movie's opening, which includes the presentation to Jill of the head and disassembled parts of what is supposedly a non-functioning robot by her boyfriend, Moses (Dylan McDermott). Jill uses the various parts in her work, the creation of huge metal sculptures, technological nightmares on biological themes, which she builds to the accompaniment of violent heavy-metal rock videos on her TV.

The humanization of the machine, which in *Terminator* is suggested by the living skin that covers the robot, is suggested in *Hardware* through the Mark-13's ability to rebuild itself utilizing almost any available materials and power source. That this progenitive process represents a parody of biological reproduction is suggested in part by the rebuilt Mark-13's appearance, a caricature of its original design reconstructed from Jill's tools and materials and garishly decorated with red, white, and blue patterns Jill had earlier painted on the robot's head. As an imitator of biological life, the Mark-13 also threatens Jill's role as a biological mother (Jill understands that the Mark-13 represents a perverse form of birth control).

What saves the protagonist in *Hardware* is essentially the same formula as in *Terminator*—human love, sacrifice and perseverance—and in both films the male warrior is sacrificed so the woman can live to continue the race. Jill's role as potential mother is emphasized through her association with water, especially in a love scene with Moses in the same shower that is later used to disable the Mark-13. After Mo's death, Jill uses a computer terminal in her apartment to interface with the robot's central processing unit and its memory chips, apparently gaining access to Mo's final words and revealing the weakness in the Mark-13's insulation. Jill successfully lures the robot into the shower where it is shorted out and destroyed. In effect, then, Moses returns from the dead to give Jill the final clue she needs to destroy the Mark-13 by bathing it in the waters of life.

While the religiously-oriented symbolism in both *Terminator* and *Hardware* effectively answers the physical threats posed by technology and simultaneously comments on humankind's ability and apparent wish to exterminate itself through the proliferation of technical armaments, the use of such symbolism suggests that technology (or at least a certain kind of technology) is good or evil in and of itself. Such cinematic strategies make inevitable movies like *Terminator II: Judgment Day*, a hundred-million-dollar sequel to the original in which Schwarzenegger returns as the good-guy underdog sent back to protect Sarah and her son. As a "good" Terminator robot, we might expect that the Schwarzenegger character will be used to suggest what constitutes "good" technology, but the movie never gets much deeper than the revelations that technology is good in good hands, bad in bad hands, and that there are some things we were probably better off not knowing.

In contrast to its reductionistic moral, *Terminator II* tries to take the mechanization of the human and the humanization of the machine to incredible extremes. The humanization of the Terminator is attempted by placing the stoic Schwarzenegger in the company of ten-year-old John (Edward Furlong) so that the machine can learn correct moral behavior—"You can't just go around killing people," an exasperated John tells a blank-faced Schwarzenegger—and enlarge his vocabulary with phrases such as "Hasta la vista, baby." Despite its own constant reminders that the Schwarzenegger robot is not of biological origin, the movie tries hard to make the viewer forget this very thing, so that the Terminator's sacrifice of itself to insure John's safety appears to be a moral and emotional victory for the "good" robot and humans.

Linda Hamilton also returns as a Sarah Connor whose eccentric commando behavior and doomsday philosophy have landed her in a mental institution. Although she has failed to achieve the mechanical discipline she believes she needs, her character is redeemed in the early part of the movie by her compassionate attempts to stop the technological developments leading to the Terminator robots, even though it means she mush commit acts of extreme violence she finds morally abhorrent. The real message of the story is in fact hers, although it is overpowered by the developing John Connor-Terminator relationship and the nonstop action of the second half. The movie culminates with Sarah Connor's failure to destroy the evil Terminator until the final intervention of the Schwarzenegger Terminator, a development which suggests that the human qualities of love, compassion and perseverance may not alone be enough to answer the dangers of technology.

These dangers are portrayed as potentially more destructive than those in the original; the evil Terminator Schwarzenegger faces is so incredibly advanced that it is no longer even recognizable as a machine. The first Terminator generated a lot of tension because the original robot almost (but not quite) passed for human. In the sequel, the evil Terminator's ability to mimic its victims and immediate environment is so perfect that it is indistinguishable from them. Not visually a machine at all, this Terminator's promethean abilities and quicksilver appearance create a technological leap far beyond the Schwarzenegger model. At one point, in an interesting reversal of the first movie's fiery phoenix image, the evil Terminator is first frozen and then shattered like brittle glass (an assault it presumably cannot recover from) and the good Terminator must watch in disbelief (or its mechanical equivalent) as its evil counterpart pools together like mercury and rises up unimpaired. Such a portrayal is an unavoidable reminder that to the majority of people in our society who have little or no understanding of our advanced technology such a creation might as well be magic.

Through their use of active robots to embody our nightmare visions of technology's dangers, *Hardware, Terminator* and *Terminator II* suggest that the greatest threat from technology arises from humanity's own, often conscious, misuse of that technology. But such a portrayal recognizes only the most obvious dangers and complications of technology. Norbert Weiner, a founding parent of cybernetics in the 40s and 50s, was quick to point out that in the oppositions of good and evil, order and chaos, we have less to fear from active dangers, than we do from passive dangers. Peter L. Abernathy characterizes this distinction in this way: "the principal threat to modern man...is not from an active force driving humanity toward chaos but from passive tendencies within ourselves and our society which leave the direction of our destiny to the inhuman, random 'logic' of technology and bureaucracy" (21).

This "inhuman, random logic" is recognized at least partially in science fiction films which use passive rather than active technological creations as their focal points. In *Darkman* and *Total Recall* we find two such creations/inventions, a liquid skin and a memory-implanter, representing technological and social advances that carry very real hidden dangers. These advancements illustrate ways in which technology complicates identity and function in the stories to upset the protagonists' understanding of themselves and their places in the world.

Sam Raimi's *Darkman* (1990), a cinematically visualized comic book, tells the story of research scientist Peyton Westlake (Liam Neeson) who is developing an artificial liquid skin for the victims of severe burns. Before he can perfect the skin, which breaks down under prolonged exposure to light, Peyton becomes the target of a violent attack by mobsters when his girlfriend, lawyer Julie Hastings (Frances McDormand), uncovers high-level corruption at Strack Industries and unknowingly leaves important evidence at his lab. After the attack and subsequent explosion of his riverfront lab, Peyton literally loses his identity, ending up as a John Doe in the burn ward in a local hospital. Thus begins a series of parallels, the first equating the disfigurement of the protagonist with the decay of the inner city riverfront setting, and the second equating his attempts to hide his burns under his artificial skin with the corrupt industrialist Strack's attempts to cover the ruins of the old city under a shining, modern skin of steel. These two equations are tied together by Julie and her love for Peyton and sexual attraction to Strack (with whom she seeks consolation, unsuspecting of Strack's role in Peyton's apparent death).

Peyton tries to effect his own resurrection and regain his former identity by completing the development of his liquid skin in an abandoned factory and with damaged equipment from his former lab. He sees the liquid skin as both the means of returning to his former identity, and of gaining revenge on Strack and his associates. But the medical technology which saved his life has changed him more than he realizes. In order to free him from the crippling pain of his burns, Peyton undergoes an operation that severs his sensory nerves where they enter the brain, an operation which, his doctor explains, has serious side effects:

When the body ceases to feel, when so much sensory input is lost, the mind grows hungry. Starved of its regular diet of input, it takes the only remaining stimulus it has—the emotions—and amplifies them, giving rise to alienation, loneliness—uncontrollable rage is not uncommon. Now surges of adrenaline flow unchecked through the body and brain giving him augmented strength.

Although the operation gives Peyton superhuman strength to fight Strack's mobsters while the liquid skin enables him to disguise himself from them, it is his trysts with Julie in his reconstructed face that teach Peyton just how much he has lost.

His final battle, this time for Julie, is against Strack on the scaffolding of one of his half-completed high-rises. Peyton eventually knocks Strack to his death, but not before Strack has made the equation between them complete— which one of us is really the freak, he asks Julie. Although, as the outcome suggests, Strack's moral decay is ultimately worse than Peyton's appearance, Peyton realizes things cannot be the same between Julie and himself. He tells her that he said to himself, "it's just a burn, skin deep, it doesn't matter. And if I covered it, hid behind a mask, you could love me for who I was inside."

Peyton's technological development of the liquid skin helps him recover his physical appearance, but there is no technology that can help reverse the moral decay he has suffered. In the same way, our technology can help us build shining, modern buildings, but it can do nothing to answer the social decay of our inner cities, and, as much as it diverts our attention from the real problems by seducing us with the appearance of a healthy society, it is decidedly dangerous. As with Peyton, our control over our appearance makes us paradoxically less sure of our identity.

Total Recall, the 1990 blockbuster starring Arnold Schwarzenegger, also relies on a change of identity similar to the Peyton/Darkman transformation, except that Schwarzenegger's sympathetic character "Quaid" begins life as the immoral "Hauser" (momentarily disregarding the evidence that most of the movie is really Quaid's psychotic dream). Supposedly, Hauser is a deep cover operative who undergoes a memory wipe, using the Rekall, Inc. memory-implanter, in order to infiltrate the rebel underground on Mars led by the psychic mutant, Quatto, who can read minds and thereby identify any ordinary plant. To effect his infiltration, Hauser is given the identity of Quaid, a not-overly-intelligent construction worker but one who is sympathetic to the morally just cause of the mutant rebels. Quaid seeks out the rebels, not realizing he is leading the suppressive government forces straight to Quatto. When he learns of his role in the exposure and killing of Quatto, Quaid successfully fights the memory restoration that would turn him back into Hauser and, after battling his way through the bad guys, turns on an ancient alien machine that releases Mars' stored oxygen atmosphere, freeing the rebels from their unjust dependence on corporate air.

An obvious implication of this plot is that Quaid *is* the true identity suppressed by the character of Hauser and thus is why he is able to retain this morally attractive identity. Although Rekall, Inc. uses technology to sell false memories of ego-inflating vacations for profit, good is ultimately served because the Rekall process returns Quaid to himself. Read at this level, technology is good because it can help us to discover our true selves. However, while Quaid wants to believe that visiting Rekall has removed a memory cap implanted by the suppressive government, there is ample evidence that the Rekall device has actually caused a "paranoid embolism" in Quaid's psyche. If this the case, then the only liberation the Rekall device brings is the liberation from the real world provided by insanity.

Such an escape is in keeping with Quaid's escapades throughout the movie, a fantasy in which the protagonist's physical skills more than compensate for his ignorance of the highly technological world he finds himself in. Unlike Westlake, Quaid is ignorant of even simple technological devices—excluding, of course, guns. In an early scene, Quaid charges through a subway weapon detector with a gun in his waistband. Later, he almost fails to make it past Mars customs when his animated disguise malfunctions. But his ineptitude is perhaps best characterized by his emotional exchange with a user-friendly "Johnny Cab." Quaid jumps in the mechanized cab in order to escape his pursuers, but, when the literal-minded cab fails to respond to his vague directive "Drive!" Quaid reacts with emotional and physical overkill, ripping the "driver" from the floor and accelerating down the street out of control. Despite its secret agent gadgets and technical wonders, then, *Total Recall* is really a chronicle of the dangers and frustrations of technology. What makes Quaid attractive is his physical prowess alone, his truly unbelievable ability to use violence to get himself out of the trouble his ignorance puts him in.

One of Quaid's fears, a fear presumably shared by much of the movie's audience, is that he will be one of the individuals denied access to the fruits of technology. This subtext is made explicit through the presentation of the subclass on Mars, descendants of the original Mars settlers who, because their living quarters are unshielded from the sun's ultraviolet rays, are often born with severe mutations. The startling appearances of the deformed workers becomes, as Fred Glass points out (in his *Film Quarterly* article, "Totally Recalling Arnold: Sex and Violence in the New Bad Future"),"a continuous reminder to the viewer of technological issues: control over the most important technologies on the planet, the air machines and [protective] domes, as well as a reminder of the real inhumanity of their oppressor, is part of the mutant make-up" (5). The movie displays, then, an aversion to and longing for technology, warning on the one hand of the frustrations of high-tech society while asserting the necessity of free access to advanced technology and its benefits.

While all the films examined so far require that the protagonist change psychologically in response to technological creations or developments, some recent science fiction films envision the interfacing of the human and machine on a microbiological level, so that the protagonist changes both psychologically *and* physically. Representative of this class of films is *Robocop* (1987), a westernesque tale of law and order in crime-ridden New Detroit in which a lone lawman is hardwired into a cybernetic carapace complete with its own quick-draw sidearm. Unlike the Dodge city of old, however, New Detroit is threatened not by lawless gunmen but by lawless corporations that buy and sell essential city services like stock commodities and manipulate the lawful and lawless forces in the city to their own ends.

Robocop's tale begins through the failure of Omni Consumer Products, OCP, to control its experimental technology, technology intended to abolish crime in New Detroit. The failure of the ED-209 police robot creates an opportunity for the testing of the Robocop program, which requires for its Central Processing Unit a biological system—a human brain. The human subject for this program is also provided by OCP, although in a less direct way. After Murphy, a good cop, is crucified by Boddicker's gang of outlaws (who work for Senior President Dick Jones of OCP), Murphy's body is picked up for use in the Robocop program.

While Murphy's death most obviously plays on our growing fear of escalating crime, Julie Codell (in her 1989 *Jump Cut* article, "Murphy's Law, Robocop's Body, and Capitalism's Work") points out that the violences against Murphy only begin with Boddicker's torture and killing. It continues through the technical gadgets used to revive him, the support systems that sustain him, and the cybernetics that finally reshape him: "His body endures violence from all quarters, even unwittingly from himself, since Murphy signed a release form when he became a cop" (13). This violent attention reduces Murphy to a commodity, something which has *value* only because technology has not yet advanced to the point that it can create a CPU as compact and as capable of advanced and subtle value decisions as the human brain.

Murphy's identity is erased by the mechano-medical transformation that creates Robocop, initially fulfilling *Terminator*'s dread that technology will devour us. What the procedure cannot erase are his physical reactions to and nightmares of his death—both functions of Murphy's memory. According to Codell, "Murphy's gun twirling," in particular, "becomes his signature, his emblem of human vulnerability....This gesture is the one memory not removed by the corporation, his last link to his family and his former body, the communicator of his identity and the sign of his humanness" (15). Were it not for these remaining memories, Murphy's mechanization would be quite literal and quite complete. Murphy's identity, however, is more subtle and tenacious than the corporation believes, and the remainder of the film details his quest to rehumanize the machine he has become.

Murphy's rebirth begins with violent nightmares sparked by his remaining memories that drive him out into the street to fulfill his programmed directives—to protect and to serve. His first confrontation as Robocop is with Emil (one of Boddicker's gang responsible for Murphy's death) who recognizes him and tries to kill him a second time by catching him in the fiery explosion of the gas station he is robbing. What Emil cannot know is that Robocop has also recognized him and has literally inscribed him in his memory as he begins to reconstruct his history. The scene that follows, with Robocop striding out of a wall of flames, is visually quite similar to the phoenix scene in *Terminator*, only here the machine is reborn with a human identity.

By reclaiming his identity as Murphy, Robocop also gains a new purpose, and he begins to systematically bring to justice those people responsible for his death. In his quest, he becomes a creature straddling two worlds. He is a cyborg and his effectiveness as a lawman is greatly increased by his cybernetic additions, especially his ability to link directly with police computers and thereby access their vast data stores. But Robocop is also part human—he cannot win his battle without help from his partner, Lewis. In one scene, Lewis must help Murphy to realign his visual targeting system, suggesting his reliance on her to remain a straight shooter.

In this role—half machine, half human—Robocop helps mediate anxieties we feel at our helplessness before unfeeling machines and impersonal corporations. According to Glass, such characters may operate as "cultural transitional objects":

[Science fiction] films provide viewers with an unconscious vehicle for dealing with the collective issues raised by the transition, under capitalist control, from a relatively stable national, mechanical/industrial society to a new and uncertain transnational information technology order.... The cyborg, part human and part computer, struggling to achieve a meaningful identity, in this context becomes a character with which a sizeable fraction of the audience can identify...(3)

We relate to Murphy/Robocop then because, even though he is part machine, he represents the very values we feel are most threatened by multinational capitalism, escalating drug crime and technology. Robocop's rebirth is largely believable because Murphy is able to retain his family values and integrate them with Robocop's cybernetic programming. As in *Total Recall*, technology is implicitly good because it provides individuals with the power necessary to correct social inequities; here, however, the threat that these technical advances will irreparably change us is made explicit.

While Murphy has rediscovered his identity, Robocop remains very much the property of the very corporate structure that will remake Detroit into "Delta City," the type of futuristic society that will breed Quaids, sans physique, in the millions. This is answered in *Robocop II*, which envisions the possibility of constructive individual action outside the corporate structure and yet inside of a social order. Central to *Robocop II* is the question of control: the police are controlled through money, both given and withheld; Robocop is controlled through OCP programming; and Cain, the evil drug lord rebuilt into a bigger, badder Robocop, is controlled through his addiction to drugs.

In the original *Robocop*, even with a hidden directive installed that makes it impossible for him to act directly against any executive of OCP, Murphy proves himself an incredibly efficient enforcer of the law. In the sequel, his initiative proves too threatening to Cain's and OCP's plans for Delta City, and he is debilitated by OCP's antagonistic programming after being ambushed and dismantled by Cain's gang. Stripped of his ability to function morally, Robo makes a radical decision and shorts himself out. Robo's second rebirth, out of the cleansing fire of electricity, proves to have removed all his OCP programming, even his prime directives—to protect and serve.

But being stripped of programming does nothing to diminish Robocop's purpose: his first statement upon regaining his feet is "Are we cops?" and he leads his fellow officers off strike to mobilize against OCP's Robo-Cain. This is significant because the officers now operate not as employees of the city or of OCP, but as servants of the public trust. In the final scene of the movie, Lewis bemoans the fact that the Head of OCP is getting off scot free. "Patience," Robo advises, "we're only human." It would seem that even though he no longer serves the letter of the law (formerly inscribed in his memory), he serves an ideal law based on human understanding.

In the complex metaphor which equates the literal mechanization of the human that initially threatens Murphy's identity with the dehumanization of individuals in the lower strata of a corporate structure, the emphasis of the second movie has largely shifted away from a fear of technology and corporations to a fear of what uncontrolled corporations will do with that technology. In order for *Robocop II* to resolve the mechanization of the human and humanization of the machine, the film must not only incorporate the desirable qualities of human and machine into a single entity, it must then free that entity from the restrictive value system of the powerful corporation that created him.

This attention to corporations' growing technical and governmental power is of course nothing new and is given much attention in *Blade Runner*, Ridley Scott's 1982 film version of the Philip K. Dick novel *Do Androids Dream of Electric Sheep*. In the movie, Tyrell corporation manufactures androids for use in dangerous and dehumanizing work in off-world colonies. As genetically constructed beings, these androids (replicants) represent a scientific advancement beyond the mechanically sophisticated robots of *Terminator* and even the computer-brain interface of *Robocop*. Scott, however (as reported in a 1982 *Film Comment* interview), made a conscious decision not to explore genetic engineering too deeply. Instead, he asked, "What if large combines in the next few decades became almost as powerful as the government?" (Kennedy 66). Such combines would move into areas of research formerly only open to the government (such as genetics) and gradually redirect research goals to create new lucrative markets. Scott further realized that from there "you can quite easily slip into breeding a second-class generation to do things which normally you or I wouldn't care to do, or psychologically couldn't stand to do. For instance, going into Space knowing you're not going to come back" (66).

Technology offers the corporation a way to literally reconceive humanity to turn a profit. In order to maintain control over its "second-class generation," Tyrell Corporation "programs" its Replicants, giving each a set of human memories to make them emotionally stable, and encoding a four-year life span into the genetic make-up so each will die before evolving emotions above and beyond the implanted identity.

The story centers around ex-cop Deckard's (Harrison Ford) attempts to identify and "retire" a group of advanced Replicants who have stolen an offworld shuttle and returned to Earth illegally in the hopes that they can learn how to extend their lives. The movie addresses what it means to be human by contrasting Deckard's cynical behavior with that of his biologically created quarry. As Michael Dempsey points out (in his 1983 *Film Quarterly* review): "Ford abets the movie's consideration of the human/machine dichotomy by setting himself up, film-noir style, as the first half of a parallel dichotomy—hero/villain—then blurring it out of existence" (36). We initially feel sympathy for Deckard because he is pressed into service against his will—"I'd had a belly-full of killing," he says—making him an appropriate counterpart to the violently dangerous Replicants, one of whom shoots Deckard's partner in the movie's opening. But what we come to realize is that Deckard is a passionless man with neither the energy nor courage to quit a business he finds morally reprehensible: his distaste for his job doesn't keep him from killing his first Nexus-6 by shooting her in the back. The Replicants, on the other hand, are driven to passionate violence by their love of life, by their unwillingness to give up. As cruel and manipulating as they sometimes are, these creatures are far more alive than any of the humans in the movie, especially Deckard. At the movie's end, when Batty actually saves Deckard's life because he knows he will himself not live, "the distinction between human and machine no longer has any real meaning" (Dempsey 38).

Technology in *Blade Runner*, as in the other films already discussed, comes to represent our ability to revisualize and replace our natural world with one of our own construction, as humans might be replaced by Replicants with no obvious difference. But as these traditional boundaries between human and machine are broken down, societal value systems governing human/machine interactions are lost and future relationships are open to be shaped by corporate values as well as human ones. It is in part our own fascination with a technology that reaches ever-closer approximations of life that represents yet another subtle danger to our own existence. As J.P. Telotte suggests, in "Human Artifice and the Science Fiction Film" (*Film Quarterly*, 1989):

when this abiding fascination with doubling becomes a dominant force in man's life, he clearly runs the risk of becoming little more than a copy of himself, potentially less human than the very images he has created in his likeness. Man's scientific advances, in sum, threaten to render him largely irrelevant, save as an empty pattern within which knowledge might be stored and through which it might extend its grasp, further increase its capacities, and expand the realm of artifice. (50)

The process of the mechanization of the human and humanization of the machine drives so many science fiction films because it simultaneously communicates our vast technical power over the natural world and our helplessness before the technological world we have created.

Taken together, these films, with their renegade robots and hard-wired heroes, provide cautionary parables for a technological age. What we come to in each is not just an awareness of how we have changed the world, but an awareness of how we have changed ourselves. Although we may feel secure in our humanness, the human/machine dichotomies in these films reveal how unsure and tenuous our identities may really be. Although we presumably use our technical ability for the good of society, our rational and humanistic impulses often seem subverted by a love of technical gadgetry. Through their revisioning and reconstruction of the physical worlds of their fictional frames, contemporary science fiction films hold a dark mirror up to our values and morality, suggesting that we might yet become the victims of our own curiosity and imagination.

Works Cited

Abernathy, Peter L. "Entropy in Pynchon's *The Crying of Lot 49*." *Critique* 14 (1972-73): 18-33.

Codell, Julie F. "Murphy's Law, Robocop's Body, and Capitalism's Work." *Jump Cut* 34 (1989): 12-19.

Dempsey, Michael. "Review of *Blade Runner*." *Film Quarterly* 36 (Winter 1983): 33-38.

Glass, Fred. "Totally Recalling Arnold: Sex and Violence in the New Bad Future." *Film Quarterly* 44 (Fall 1990): 2-13.

Kennedy, Harlan. "Ridley Scott Interviewed by Harlan Kennedy." *Film Comment* 18 (1982): 65- 68.

Rushing, Janice Hocker, and Thomas S. Frentz. "The Frankenstein Myth in Contemporary Cinema." *Critical Studies in Mass Communication* 6 (1989): 61-80.

Telotte, J.P. "Human Artifice and the Science Fiction Film." *Film Quarterly* 36 (1983): 44-51.

Filmography

Year	Film	Director
1926	*Metropolis*	Fritz Lang
1956	*Forbidden Planet*	Fred McLeod Wilcox
1968	*2001: A Space Odyssey*	Stanley Kubrick
1975	*Rollerball*	Norman Jewison
1976	*Futureworld*	Richard T. Heffron
1979	*Alien*	Ridley Scott
1980	*Altered States*	Ken Russell
1982	*Blade Runner*	Ridley Scott
1982	*Videodrome*	David Cronenberg
1984	*Adventures of Buckaroo Banzai: Across the 8th Dimension*	W.D. Richter
1984	*Runaway*	Michael Crichton
1984	*Terminator*	James Cameron
1984	*2010: The Year We Make Contact*	Peter Hyans
1986	*Aliens*	James Cameron
1986	*Fly*	David Cronenberg
1987	*Robocop*	Paul Verhoeven
1987	*Running Man*	Paul Michael Glasser
1989	*Moontrap*	Robert Dyke
1990	*Darkman*	Sam Raimi
1990	*Hardware*	Richard Stanley
1990	*Robocop II*	Irvin Kershner
1990	*Total Recall*	Paul Verhoeven
1991	*Circuitry Man*	Steven Lovy
1991	*Terminator II: Judgment Day*	James Cameron

The Other Kind of Movie Trailer: Mobile Homes in American Movies

Greg Metcalf

Mobile homes. Motor homes. Trailers. Caravans. RVs. Purists may make distinctions between the various types of mobile homes, but the defining characteristic which they all share is that they are a home that you can take with you. Given the importance of the American myth of the road, a vehicle that allows you to have your "home on the road" can become a powerful symbol.

The mobile home's symbolic force arises from its supposed resolution of contradictory aspects of the American Dream. While "mobile" offers freedom, escape, modernity, individuality and a temporary state, "home" suggests stability, tradition, family or community and permanence. The juxtaposition of these apparently incompatible sets of concepts in a single object has made the mobile home a cinematically useful oxymoron.

American film draws heavily on this inherent tension. In the pages that follow, the mobile home will be seen to be a vehicle for commenting on conflicts between the two sets of values and the resulting clash of ideals and realities that exists within the American Dream.

The Long, Long Trailer: Mobile Homes and the Modern American Family

But don't you see, if we had a trailer, no matter where we went I could make a home for you. And when the job was over we could just hitch up our house and go on to the next place.

Tracy, The Long, Long Trailer

The most complete treatment of a mobile home in film occurs in Vincent Minnelli's 1954 Lucille Ball-Desi Arnaz vehicle, *The Long, Long Trailer*. Ball and Arnaz play newlyweds on a tight budget who are unable to afford an acceptable house and are unable to settle down because the husband's job requires him to move around the country to work on construction projects. In an effort to have it all—the complete modern home, the convenient escape to the American vacation lands which post-war highway expansion opened up to Americans, and the chance for the wife to be with her career-mobilized husband—Tracy (Lucille Ball) convinces Nicky (Desi Arnaz) to buy the state-of-the-art home on wheels.

The mobile home becomes a symbol of Tracy and Nicky's modern marriage, as the film comments on the rootlessness of post-war careers and marriages. This point is reiterated throughout the film as problems with the mobile home reflect the problems in the marriage. From the outset, the long, long trailer represents the demands of married life upon Nicky. Eventually it comes to represent those upon Tracy, as well.

Nicky is overwhelmed by the unexpected costs of marriage and (mobile) home ownership. The home costs much more than Nicky expected it would, but, to satisfy his wife, he buys it on credit and extends his debt for countless years into the future. As hidden costs continue to surface and Nicky is forced to trade in his sporty car for one more capable of pulling the load of his new obligations, the former bachelor is pummeled by the reality that his new home and wife are major commitments which will force him into the slow lane—in both style and substance.

While *The Long, Long Trailer* is a comedy, the mobile home is used to show the difficulties that come with the modern marriage. Nicky quickly discovers that he may pay for the home and drive it, but there's almost no room inside it for him or his possessions (a point stressed by the home being in Tracy's name). On the other hand, Tracy is continually unable to be the traditional housewife she wants to be in their mobile home. She ends up battered—in both senses of the word—when she tries to cook while her husband obliviously drives down the highway. Tracy's insistence on collecting memorabilia and canned preserves to make the mobile house "a home" almost destroys everything.

The possibility of marital and mobile catastrophe are never far from Nicky's mind. Beginning with a terrifying driving lesson that stresses how close he is to destroying his home at all times, Nicky's attempts to pilot his mobile home through life puts him in conflict with everyone from the police and Tracy's relatives to Tracy herself. Their penultimate climb up a mountain almost fails because of Tracy's refusal to part with her romantic souvenirs. Nicky is continually reminded of the dangers that await his happy new home if he allows his vigilance to waver.

The mobile home also gives the young couple entry into a caricature of suburban life in the form of a trailer park. Trailer park living—a hellishly pleasant image of order and community—is not for them, however. This early version of the mobile suburban ideal is shown to be filled with noisy and nosy children and well-intentioned neighbors who intrude into every aspect of their lives. It is also the most positive image of a trailer park that will emerge in the films discussed in this essay.

Tracy and Nicky quickly decide to follow the highways and escape into the American "vacationland." While they get to see beautiful national park vistas, the couple also end up trapped in a sea of mud that generates more stress and new debts. Not leaving your home behind seems to also mean you can't leave your problems behind, either. The arguments escalate until Tracy drives off with the home to get a divorce.

The requisite happy ending is the only thing that allows the ideals of the mobile home some redemption in this cinematic excursion. Ideal versions of the mobile home rarely appear unchallenged in films after this. Instead, the mobile home comes to represent what the modern middle class American family is *not*. The original ideals of the mobile home seen in *The Long, Long Trailer*—the home of the middle class upwardly mobile family, the trailer park as rolling suburb, the promise of escape *and* community—do not disappear from American film. However, recognition of the ideals is generally a means to underscore the irony of a character's failure to attain those ideals.

Outpost of Middle America

> It's all right. You know we could put some built-in gun racks right here.
> > Shopper at the Trailer Show
> > The *Long, Long Trailer*

The use of mobile homes which is closest to the ideal that inspires Tracy in *The Long, Long Trailer* occurs as the homes become the outpost of middle America. As in Tracy and Nicky's comic adventures, such horror films as *Race With the Devil* (1975) and *The Hills Have Eyes* (1977) use the RV mobile home to get suburban American families into the middle of a hostile environment. As with the film *Tremors* (1989), the vulnerability of the mobile home underscores the fragility of the community in a hostile environment. Where *Race* and *Hills* reflect a "wagon train" tradition of good people surrounded by savages, *Tremors* focuses on the isolated middle-class people and homes of Perfection, Nevada, destroyed by giant carnivorous worms. In each case, the mobility of the home fails and the good people can't get away.

Trouble in Mind (1985) makes its point by shifting the location. The threatened family—Georgia (Lori Singer) and child—lives in a mobile home that is parked in a lot behind an urban diner. The mobile home becomes the outpost of possible salvation for husband Coop (Keith Carradine) as he sinks lower and lower into the savagery of the city. Their lives bottom out when the child is stolen and the mobile home is towed away by the city. As in so many American films, the city is no place for a family. True civilization can exist there only around the outpost of the mobile home. Likewise, in the British *Mona Lisa* (1986), the closest thing to a traditionally civilized individual in a corrupt city is Thomas (Robbie Coltrane), a mobile home dweller. In Thomas' case, the mobile home is parked inside a London warehouse where he helps ex-con George (Bob Hoskins) make the transition to the outside world.

Wim Wenders' *State of Things* (1982) presents this same convention of the mobile home as refuge in a hostile city. Wenders—who has noted that in the compounding of "mobility" and "home," the mobile home is a uniquely American concept—shows a film producer (Allen Goorwitz) hiding out from mobsters who have invested in his movie and now want to kill him for not making a marketable product. As his trusted assistant drives his mobile home through the streets of Los Angeles, the producer sits in a lounge chair with his dog, debating the issues of art and commerce with his film's German director (Patrick Bauchau). To complete the caricature of a middle class suburban den, the rear window of the vehicle functions as a video or film screen through which the "real world" enters the roving refuge, transformed into an image as unreal as the mobile home itself. The living room/mobile home may become as artificial as the movie theater, but its protection is real. When the producer and director step out of the mobile home into daylight they are immediately killed.

State of Things' producer is based on Francis Ford Coppola, Wenders' actual producer for the film *Hammett* (1983), a man who has developed an increasing interest in using a mobile home filled with video technology to create his own films. As the director of *Apocalypse Now* (1979), Coppola uses a mobile home to present a surreal touch of middle America in the midst of the Vietnam War. It is in this sterile setting that assassin Captain Willard (Martin Sheen) receives his euphemized orders to kill Colonel Kurtz (Marlon Brando).

Losing Naiveté

I tell you it's a fine thing when you come home to your home and your home is gone.

Nicky, *The Long, Long Trailer*

Coppola's use of the mobile home in *Apocalypse Now* as an outpost of suburban America in the midst of war, with an MP guarding the door from a lawn table complete with umbrella, may be seen as ironic commentary. By using this banal setting as the location in which members of the military establishment deniably order a kept assassin to kill an American officer who has become an embarrassment by doing his job too well, the film critiques the supposed innocence of suburban American homelife.

The juxtaposition of this ideal of innocence and its betrayal occurs regularly in Hollywood films using mobile homes. In *Walking Tall* (1973), *Honky Tonk Freeway* (1981), *Citizen's Band* (aka *Handle With Care*) (1977) and *One Flew Over the Cuckoo's Nest* (1975) mobile homes are used as houses of prostitution. In the case of *Citizen's Band*, the fragmentation of the modern family which Tracy and Nicky experience in *The Long, Long Trailer* becomes practically cubist. A prostitute who has received her mobile home as a gift from her married lover, so as to keep up with an increasingly mobile clientele of long-haul truckers, becomes the voice of reason in a unique domestic dispute. It is the prostitute who saves *both* of her lover's two marriages. In the breakfast nook of her mobile home, the hooker brokers a deal in which her lover's two wives and their children—each of who has been living at different stops along his run—will share the trucker. In a dazed acceptance, the two wives go off with their husband to celebrate the reconciliation of their marriage matched to mobility.

The mobile home as a false symbol of innocence repeats in many recent films. In *Born in East L.A.* (1987) the supposedly innocent mobile home is driven by a stereotypically elderly middle American married couple who just happen to be major drug smugglers. Domestically, guns are sold from a mobile home in *The Hard Way* (1991) and, internationally, Bill Murray and company drive the army's state-of-the-art attack vehicle—disguised as a mobile home— across Europe in the movie *Stripes* (1981). (Perhaps it is this RV that inspires one of *Die Hard*'s (1988) "terrorist"-thieves to react to an ineffectual attack by the police assault vehicle with the announcement, "the police have themselves an RV," along with *Tango and Cash*'s [1989] use of a similarly-equipped "RV from hell" to attack multinational villains.) The juxtaposition of guns and mobile home is also used to highlight tarnished innocence in the British film, *The Long Good Friday* (1980) when one of the felons jokes that, if questioned by the police, he will explain that he has an illegal gun "to knock pigeons off the caravan."

The critique of the innocence of the middle American home takes other forms as well. In the tradition of panel trucks and vans, it is from mobile homes that government agents spy on the heroes of *Hanky Panky* (1982) and *Tequila Sunrise* (1988). The cheating boys of Ivy College who will go to any end to win a raft race, betray honor and fidelity in a mobile home that establishes their wealth as well as their corruption in *Up the Creek* (1984).

In more exaggerated cases, horrifying forces hide behind the tin walls of the mobile home in films like *Ssssss* (1973) and *Near Dark* (1987), where people turn into snakes or, in the latter case, where modern day vampires first make their identities known when they abduct the hero in their stolen mobile home.

The Parked Trailer

You know, Nicky, We don't have to stay in these trailer parks. We can go anywhere we want to. We've got wheels. Why don't we just go along till we find a nice place and just stop there and stay as long as we like.

                                                    Tracy, *The Long, Long Trailer*

Given the previously-noted conventional uses of the mobile home, it should come as no surprise that the trailer park is not a high status location in films. Combining the immobile mobile home with the long-term reliance on the apparently temporary, the trailer park comes off as a low rent suburb with all of the negatives and few of the positives of the suburban lifestyle.

Generally, a trailer park implies lower income residents who have fallen out of the mainstream of society. As we will see later, the parked trailer on its own tends to signify a dead end. This "backwater" element to the trailer park is stressed by both the juxtaposition of the trailer's promise of independence with an image of many of them clustered together and the fact that the trailer is theoretically mobile but, like its inhabitants, the trailers seem unlikely to "escape." The parked trailer and the trailer park carry a connotation of being no longer on the move toward the American dream.

Old age is one of the ways people are seen as coming to the end of their run in a trailer park. In such films as *A Flash of Green* (1984), *Bank Shot* (1974), *Lost in America* (1985) and *Little Vegas* (1990), trailer parks reflect their function as retirement communities. *A Flash of Green*'s trailer park is also the home of rabid anti-Communism, a caricature of middle American patriotism. In *Little Vegas* the dead-end quality of trailer park life is reinforced by the trailer-dwelling hero's youthfulness in contrast to his elderly, now-dead lover and the park's elderly, dying owner.

But the retirement community aspect of *Little Vegas* is secondary to the economic desperation of the central characters. The alcoholic hero tried to escape his life as a New Jersey mobster by settling in Nevada. His failure as a gigolo/mobile home salesman is seen in his living in a trailer park in the middle of a desert. The film focuses on the desperate search for money on the part of several of the residents, as the hero tries to escape his mob past and build a new life with the daughter of his now-dead lover. This daughter is a drifting figure similar to the protagonist of the Australian film *High Tide* (1987), a fired back-up singer for an Elvis impersonator who washes up in a backwater trailer park only to discover that her abandoned daughter and estranged mother live there as well. In both films the trailer park becomes a place of self-confrontation and forced decision-making as personal growth ensues.

The lower-class convention for the trailer park continues in films like *Lucas* (1986), *Charley Varrick* (1973), *One Flew Over the Cuckoo's Nest*, *The Drowning Pool* (1976), *Whore* (1991), and *Wilder Napalm* (1993). *The Legend of Billie Jean* (1985) presents a young girl who is forced into a life of rebellion by the societal bias against her and her brother because they live in a mobile home. Being "from the trailers," she is assumed to be criminal, sexually loose and dangerous (a stereotype which is later applied to the trailer resident/victim in *The Accused* [1988]). As *Urban Cowboy*'s (1980) mobile home foreshadows the tenuous nature of the marriage between John Travolta's and Debra Winger's characters, it also communicates the lower-class core to their characters which the film's narrative later confirms. (The stereotype is so established that *Wilder Napalm*'s casting director, Louis Giaimo, needed to remind auditioners for the lead role of Vida that "Just because she lives in a trailer park doesn't mean she's white trash," only to continue "She been under house arrest for a year" (Sandomar). *The Last Starfighter* (1984) alters the convention slightly by also stressing the trailer park as an outpost of unconventionality.

White Trash on Flat Wheels

So, when did you get the tenement on wheels?
Clark, *National Lampoon's Christmas Vacation*

Going even further than the lower-class connotation of the immobile mobile home, there is the convention of the—generally rusting—mobile home as a symbol of what might be simplified as "white trash." In such circumstances, the trailer or RV is isolated outside of a community and might be found outside the city proper, as in *Melvin and Howard* (1980) or *Defenseless* (1991), or just rusting behind the house in *The Silence of the Lambs* (1991).

The victim in *The Accused* eventually states the societal bias against her—that she is a lower-class slut—but the point has already been made by the fact that the woman lives in a trailer on a vacant industrial lot on what is literally the wrong side of the tracks.

The epitome of the white trash convention is probably the rusted hulk of a mobile home which brings Chevy Chase's "black sheep" brother-in-law into *National Lampoon's Christmas Vacation* (1989). The vehicle is an extension of Eddie (Randy Quaid), physically representing the repulsive disruption of the Griswold's suburban holiday by its presence. This connection is confirmed when Eddie drains the home's septic tanks into the storm sewer creating visual, aromatic and combustible evidence of Eddie's non-suburban nature.

Which is not to say that the white trash model of the mobile home cannot be exceptionally kempt. In *Raising Arizona* (1987), the lower-class roots of the characters—a repeat convenience store robber and his law officer wife who kidnap a baby to complete their idea of what a home should be—are seen in their ideal home; a neatly kept double wide trailer. When the husband's prison buddies show up reeking of raw sewage, the insubstantial and claustrophobic qualities of the trailer are revealed. This point is made most explicitly in a fight scene in the confines of the mobile home when the home itself is more damaged than the combatants.

The Mobile Office

Hey, you know, you could get a tambourine and I could get a dancing bear and we'd clean up.
Nicky, *The Long, Long Trailer*

The insubstantiality and artificiality of the mobile home are underscored by its use as a rolling office. As in real life, construction site offices are often trailers as in *Raw Deal* (1986), *Sweet Heart's Dance* (1988), *My Blue Heaven* (1990), and *The Two Jakes* (1990). The mobile home's insubstantiality becomes the key factor in *Bank Shot* a movie about stealing a bank temporarily housed in a trailer. More interestingly, the reality of the trailer being a movie's on-site dressing room in a business based on artifice is reflected in films such as *Dead Ringers* (1988), *The Dead Pool* (1988), *Into the Night* (1985), *Postcards from the Edge* (1990) and *Grand Canyon* (1991) (1). Each of these films uses the site to underscore the failure of traditional values. Drug use, egotism, sexual perversion and the death of loyalty and honor are all revealed in movie trailer-based scenes.

While it may seem to make too much of the linkage between these mobile homes and professions, it is worth remembering that the mobile office stresses that the professions have become extensions of the mobile employee—the same function they served in *The Long, Long Trailer*. This convention reflects a reality of the mobile professional, linking work and personal life while also establishing the resident as being outside the community. (In *Sweet Heart's Dance*, the construction boss is shown at the depths of his alienation from his family when he moves into his on-site mobile home.)

The most obvious mobile careers to use the mobile home are those related to the circus and carnival careers. Films such as *The Jerk* (1979), *Carny* (1980), *Wings of Desire* (1988), *Big Top Pee-Wee* (1988), and the 1981 remake of *The Postman Always Rings Twice,* accentuate the "otherness" and the lack of tradition of the carnival or the circus employee. Each of the films contain an image which stresses the alienation of the mobile home resident, juxtaposing the claustrophobia of the tiny mobile home with the ideal of freedom and escape offered to people who run off with the circus.

The Outsider and the Immobile Mobile Home

Hey, your wife told me that you guys did that "drop out" thing. Hey, I really admire you. When I get old I might try it.

Skippy, *Lost in America*

Alienation does not stop with the circus and the carny folk. The mobile home, especially the immobile mobile home, has become a shorthand designation for the outsider cut off from his or her community. (This convention is also applied to non-genuine mobile homes in *The Great Santini* [1979]—an immobile bus outside of town—and *1969* (1988)—the hero's expulsion from home and community is made clear as he lives on the edge of town in a VW micro-bus.)

Not surprisingly, the non-moving mobile home is frequently found in a desert or on a desolate beach. The desert locations also lend *Paris, Texas* (1984), *Fool For Love* (1985), *Bagdad Cafe* (1988), *Raising Arizona* and *Little Vegas* a sense of characters having missed out on the green-lawned promise of American suburban life. *Fool For Love* carries the visual metaphor a step further by showing the old man, the father of the tragic incestuous couple, living in a rusting mobile home that sits in the middle of a junk yard. The white trash convention is made explicit as the home and its resident become one more piece of trash dumped behind an empty motel in the middle of an empty desert. At the film's end, the mobile home and the old man go up in flames. *Terminator 2: Judgment Day* (1991) offers a desert-based non-moving mobile home amongst broken vehicles as the heroes' momentary refuge and supply depot. In a more optimistic desert film, *Bagdad Cafe*, the mobile home still sets its artist owner apart from the already isolated community of the cafe.

The immobile mobile home on the beach has become one of the preferred locations for the societal outcast. In a convention which may have been established through the television series *The Rockford Files*, the mobile home dweller sits on the Pacific Ocean shore, isolated from any family or community, trapped in a home that should but cannot move, graphically signifying the failure of the American Dream. The mobile home resident has gotten to the end of the land, as far as he can go, but he has yet to achieve his dreams. In both *Lethal Weapon* (1987) and *Lethal Weapon 2* (1989) the hero, Martin Riggs (Mel Gibson), is defined as outside of society through his ocean-side mobile home residence. In both films, Riggs' increasing reintegration into society is seen in the time he spends at his partner's (Danny Glover's) suburban home and in his interest in moving into his girlfriend's apartment in the sequel. In the case of *The Accused*, the victim's failed life is represented by her trailer sitting in a vacant lot by a stagnant river that leads out to the Pacific Ocean.

Even in the absence of sea and sand, the conventions of isolation continue. In *Next of Kin* (1990) it is a maladjusted cousin who lives in a mobile home on the edge of a hillbilly homestead. The cousin rejoins the community in earnest, however, when it comes time to take revenge on evil Chicagoans who have killed his relative. Another variation, *After Dark, My Sweet* (1990) shows a psychopathic drifter given a trailer at the far end of a wealthy widow's property, as far from the house as possible in an overgrown field with palm trees that exclude him while still offering him a view of the object of his financial and sexual desire. *My Own Private Idaho* (1991) evokes memories of *Fool For Love* and *Bagdad Cafe* with its alienated mail-order portrait painter living in an unmoving mobile home in the driveway of his wife (and perhaps mother)'s abandoned house in the middle of an apparent Idaho wasteland. Perhaps the subtlest use of this convention occurs in *The Deer Hunter* (1978), where Nick (Christopher Walken) and Mike (Robert DeNiro)'s house at the edge of town has been built out around a mobile home. The result is a home which seems out of scale with its inhabitants, a boy's clubhouse used by adults, that also underscores Mike's and Nick's distance from the others.

False Escapes and Real Estates

Thirty feet long. A bedroom a bath. a kitchen. A microwave that browns, a little tv. Beautiful! Beautiful! Better than our new house, it has wheels!

David, *Lost in America*

The irony of the mobile home being seen as an escape lies at the foundation of many of the cinematic uses of the mobile home. The previously mentioned immobile mobile homes and trailer parks function in part as reminders of their owners' failure to escape. The mobile home as permanent residence is itself a symbol of a dead end.

But there is a second manner in which the ideal of escape is satirized in uses of the mobile home: the ideal of escaping from civilization to "rough it" in the wild. This ironic convention was one of the earliest uses of the mobile home. When the director-hero of *Sullivan's Travels* (1941) initially takes off as a hobo to find out what the real world is truly like, he is followed by a completely stocked "land yacht" mobile home. In *Honey, I Shrunk the Kids!* (1989) the suburban next-door neighbors are seen as comically false, in part, because they are going out camping in a mobile home which they have packed full of examples of the suburban civilization they supposedly want to escape.

This convention is taken to its extreme in Albert Brooks' *Lost In America* (1985), a film which updates many of the themes of Minnelli's *The Long, Long Trailer*. Here, the central conceit is that a yuppie couple (Albert Brooks and Julie Hagerty) decide to fulfill their dream of reliving *Easy Rider's* (1969) search for authentic America by quitting their jobs and taking off on the road with a six-figure nest egg and a mobile home equipped down to the microwave oven complete with browning element. The inability of the characters to escape their upwardly mobile existences—and their blindness to that failure—is seen from the first frames of their journey as they take to the highway to the tune of "Born to be Wild" as David (Brooks) enjoys a toasted cheese sandwich. David's imagined kinship with a motorcyclist is rejected when the biker returns his bonding thumbs-up gesture with the expected more obscene one.

After the couple's nest egg is lost to Linda (Hagerty)'s all-night gambling spree in Las Vegas, the fantasy of living an "authentic life" on the road becomes reality. The couple end up in a desert town having to work as a crossing guard and a fast food employee. The claustrophobia and insubstantiality of the mobile home exaggerate David and Linda's vulnerability as they are unable to find any privacy, whether fighting at Hoover Dam or discussing their future with the wife's teen-aged boss sitting an arm's length away in the "next room."

The final visual joke of *Lost in America* inverts the premise of incongruity of the yuppie couple trying to escape to an authentic life in the mobile home. We are shown the wonderful strangeness of a mobile home driving through Manhattan at rush hour to drop David off at the advertising agency job which he refused at the beginning of the film.

Return to the Middle-American Ideal

All I was thinking of was making a home for my husband. A little place we could call our own, where I could take care of him, cook for him, a place where I could make him comfortable. If that's a horrible offense, if that makes me a criminal then I'm sorry.
Tracy, *The Long, Long Trailer*

Still, there are a few films which present the mobile home as a genuine escape. In these films the "normal" world is presented in such an off-kilter manner that escape through the mobile home is an escape not *from* but *into* the world of middle-class America.

The first of these escapes is seen in *Real Genius* (1985). As the film ends, Laslo (Jonathan Grier), the reclusive tunnel-dwelling computer genius, exploits a loophole in a Publisher's Clearinghouse-type contest. Laslo wins over half of the prizes, including a mobile home, and he and a woman who is sexually-obsessed with intelligence drive away with his booty. In an inversion of the symbol, the recluse "escapes" *into* the middle-class dream of conspicuous consumption that *Lost in America* and *Honey I Shrunk the Kids'* mobile-homers were supposedly trying to escape.

By contrast, an immobile mobile home is the refuge of the escaped Handmaid at the end of *The Handmaid's Tale* (1990). Isolated in mountains somewhere beyond the Republic of Gilead, the pregnant former Handmaid awaits her rescuer and lover. In this film, the isolated trailer at the edge of civilization represents not the failure of the American dream, but the possibility of a new American dream, with a nuclear family of outsiders beyond the oppression of a horrific society.

It is in a third movie that we come closest to the mobile home as it was seen by the characters in *The Long, Long Trailer*. At the end of Terry Gilliam's *Brazil* (1985), Sam (Jonathan Pryce) escapes his torture by withdrawing into a fantasy of life with an ideal version of the truck-driving woman (Kim Greist) who hauls elongated prefab housing units on a flatbed truck. In Sam's fantasy, the lovers escape from their tormentors in the rolling prefab home. The couple settles their rolling home into a valley hideaway, surrounded by trees and gardens with a cow and chickens.

In reality the truck-driving woman is probably dead and Sam will be soon. As with most of the cinematic mobile home dwellers, *Brazil*'s hero achieves the elusive ideal of mobile home living only in his fantasy. But in that fantasy, alone together, at one with nature, having escaped the terrors of an oppressive bureaucracy, Sam and his lover finally achieve the world of mobile home living that Tracy imagined at the beginning of *The Long, Long Trailer*:

The whole trip would be just like a dream. We'd go where we please, when we please. If we saw a beautiful spot beside a brook or a mountain lake or a lovely wood we'd stop there and we'd be all alone and it would all be for us. The moonlight and the sunsets and the sound of the tree toads far off....

Notes

[1]The "real life" version of this conventional use of mobile homes is reflected in the apparently unintended presence of trailers in some of the 19th-century battle scenes in *The Alamo* (1960).

Works Cited

Sandomar, Richard. "Seeking Ms. Right in Throngs of Ms. Wrongs." *The New York Times* 24 Nov. 1991: H 13.

Filmography

Year	Film	Director
1941	*Sullivan's Travels*	Preston Sturges
1954	*The Long, Long Trailer*	Vincent Minnelli
1960	*The Alamo*	John Wayne
1969	*Easy Rider*	Dennis Hopper
1969	*The Rain People*	Francis Ford Coppola
1973	*Charley Varrick*	Don Siegel
1973	*Slither*	Howard Zieff
1973	*Sssssss*	Bernard L. Kowalski
1973	*Walking Tall*	Phil Karlson
1974	*Bank Shot*	Gower Champion
1975	*One Flew Over the Cuckoo's Nest*	Milos Foreman
1975	*Race With the Devil*	Jack Starrett
1976	*The Drowning Pool*	Stuart Rosenberg
1976	*Jackson County Jail*	Michael Miller
1976	*Kings of the Road*	Wim Wenders (German)
1977	*Citizen's Bank* (aka *Handle With Care*)	Jonathan Demme

1977	*The Hills Have Eyes*	Wes Craven
1977	*The Deer Hunter*	Michael Cimino
1979	*Apocalypse Now*	Francis Ford Coppola
1979	*The Great Santini*	Lewis John Carlino
1979	*The Jerk*	Carl Reiner
1980	*Carny*	Robert Kaylor
1980	*The Long Good Friday*	John MacKenzie (British)
1980	*Melvin and Howard*	Jonathan Demme
1980	*Urban Cowboy*	James Bridges
1980	*Willie and Phil*	Paul Mazursky
1981	*Honkytonk Freeway*	John Schlesinger
1981	*The Postman Always Rings Twice*	Bob Rafelson
1981	*Stripes*	Ivan Reitman
1981	*Hanky Panky*	Sidney Poitier
1982	*State of Things*	Wim Wenders
1983	*Eddie and the Cruisers*	Martin Davidson
1983	*Hammett*	Wim Wenders
1984	*A Flash of Green*	Victor Nunez
1984	*The Last Starfighter*	Nick Castle
1984	*Paris, Texas*	Wim Wenders
1984	*Up the Creek*	Robert Butler
1985	*Real Genius*	Martha Coolidge
1985	*Trouble in Mind*	Alan Rudolph
1985	*Brazil*	Terry Gilliam
1985	*Fool For Love*	Robert Altman
1985	*Into the Night*	John Landis
1985	*The Legend of Billie Jean*	Matthew Robbins
1985	*Lost in America*	Albert Brooks
1986	*Friday 13th, Part VI: Jason Lives*	Tom McLoughlin
1986	*The Hitcher*	Robert Harmon
1986	*Lucas*	David Seltzer
1986	*Mona Lisa*	Neil Jordan (British)
1986	*Raw Deal*	John Irvin
1987	*Born in East L.A.*	Cheech Marin
1987	*High Tide*	Gillian Armstrong (Australian)
1987	*Lethal Weapon*	Richard Donner
1987	*Near Dark*	Kathryn Bigelow
1987	*Raising Arizona*	Joel Coen
1987	*Space Balls*	Mel Brooks
1988	*The Accused*	Jonathan Kaplan
1988	*Bagdad Cafe*	Percy Adlon (German)
1988	*Big Top Pee-Wee*	Randal Kleiser
1988	*The Dead Pool*	Buddy Van Horn
1988	*Dead Ringers*	David Cronenberg
1988	*Die Hard*	John McTiernan
1988	*1969*	Ernest Thompson

1988	*Sweet Heart's Dance*	Robert Greenwald
1988	*Tequila Sunrise*	Robert Towne
1988	*Wings of Desire*	Wim Wenders
		(German & French)
1989	*Honey, I Shrunk the Kids!*	Joe Johnston
1989	*Lethal Weapon 2*	Richard Donner
1989	*National Lampoon's*	
	Christmas Vacation	Jeremiah Chechick
1989	*Next of Kin*	John Irvin
1989	*Tango and Cash*	Andrei Konchalovsky &
		Albert Magnoli
1989	*Tremors*	Ron Underwood
1990	*After Dark, My Sweet*	James Foley
1990	*The Handmaid's Tale*	Volker Schlondorff
1990	*I Love You to Death*	Lawrence Kasdan
1990	*Little Vegas (...a Desert Story)*	Perry Lang
1990	*My Blue Heaven*	Herbert Ross
1990	*Postcards from the Edge*	Mike Nichols
1990	*The Two Jakes*	Jack Nicholson
1991	*Defenseless*	Martin Campbell
1991	*Grand Canyon*	Lawrence Kasdan
1991	*The Hard Way*	Richard Donner
1991	*My Own Private Idaho*	Gus Van Sant
1991	*Silence of the Lambs*	Jonathan Demme
1991	*Terminator 2: Judgment Day*	John Cameron
1991	*Whore*	Ken Russell (British)
1993	*Wilder Napalm*	Glen Gordon Caron

Contributors

Brenda Berstler received a BA in history from the University of Missouri. A film buff, Ms. Berstler audited a film class taught by Phil Skerry. They decided to collaborate on a study of Western costume.

Parley Ann Boswell teaches English at Eastern Illinois University in Charleston, Illinois, She has contributed essays to *Beyond the Stars* I and II, and is presently co-authoring a book with Paul Loukides on rites of passage in American film. She doesn't cook much, but she really likes people who do.

Jay Boyer teaches courses in American film and literature at Arizona State University.

Ralph R. Donald is professor and chair of the Department of Communications at the University of Tennessee at Martin. He earned his BA and MA at California State University, Fullerton, and Ph.D. at the University of Massachusetts. Research interests include propaganda and gender-related issues in mass media, and film history. He is also editor of the *Mid-Atlantic Almanack*, the journal of the Mid-Atlantic Popular/American Culture Association.

Linda K. Fuller, who teaches in the Media Department of Worcester (MA) State College, received her Master's Degree in the field of Human Technology under the Carkhuff-Berenson model of interpersonal communication at American International College. Her study here of self-advertising combines that preparation with her doctoral studies of mass communication at the University of Massachusetts. Under the same category fall Dr. Fuller's books *Communicating Comfortably* (1990) and *Communicating Quotably* (1993), both published by HRD Press. She wants it known that the only "personals" she has ever submitted was rejected—it aimed to solicit research on the phenomenon of *Media-Mediated Relationships*, a subject she is currently exploring beyond filmic representations (Haworth Press, forthcoming).

Howard Good is associate professor of journalism at the State University of New York, the College at New Paltz—and a Mets fan. He is the author of *Acquainted with the Night: The Image of Journalists in American Fiction, 1890-1930* (1986), *Outcasts: The Image of Journalists in Contemporary Film* (1989), and the forthcoming *The Journalist as Autobiographer*.

Dennis P. Grady received his bachelor's and master's degrees in speech communication from Miami University in Oxford, Ohio. He is currently working on his doctoral degree in interpersonal communication at the University of Texas—Austin.

Norma Fay Green, who owns a trenchcoat, has been a print journalist for more than 20 years. A Mass Media Ph.D. candidate at Michigan State University, she has written for numerous academic, trade and consumer publications and taught journalism courses at MSU, Northwestern University and Columbia College—Chicago.

Gary Hoppenstand has published several books and numerous articles dealing with American literature and popular culture subjects. Currently, he is writing an extensive examination of contemporary best-selling horror fiction for the University Press of Mississippi. He is also an Assistant Professor teaching in the Department of American Thought and Language at Michigan State University.

Susanna Hornig is Assistant Professor of Journalism at Texas A&M University. She has a BA in Anthropology from the University of California at Berkeley and a Ph.D. in Communications from the University of Washington. Her current projects include a book on media representations of science and technology.

John H. Lenihan is Associate Professor of History at Texas A&M University, where he specializes in American cultural-intellectual history and film. He is the author of *Showdown: Confronting Modern America in the Western Film*, published by the University of Illinois Press.

Steve Lipkin teaches film study, film and video production, and scriptwriting at Western Michigan University. This work was helped by a grant from the WMU Faculty Research and Creative Activities Fund.

Donald G. Lloyd recently completed his doctoral dissertation on the role of science in the novels of Thomas Pynchon at TCU in Fort Worth, TX. He has taught at several area institutions and has presented papers on science fiction films at both Popular Culture and Science Fiction Research Association conventions.

Paul Loukides is a Professor of English at Albion College where he teaches courses in film, creative writing and literature. He is particularly interested in the conventions of popular film and the ways in which conventions both within and across genres reflect the patterns of American culture. He is currently co-authoring with Ann Boswell a book length study of weddings, baptisms and funerals in American popular film.

Erik S. Lunde is Professor of American Thought and Language at Michigan State University, where he has offered courses in writing and film studies. He is the author of *Horace Greeley*; with Douglas A. Noverr, he has co-edited *Film History* and *Film Studies*. He has written articles in American history, sports history and film history.

Greg Metcalf teaches film at the University of Maryland, College Park, and literature at the Smithsonian Institution. He continues to write on issues of adaptation to film, Victorian culture, and Marlovian detectives, while compiling a "post-post-modern" book of film quotations and creating art historical snow domes.

Martin F. Norden teaches film as an Associate Professor of Communication at the University of Massachusetts at Amherst. His articles and reviews have appeared in such journals as *Wide Angle, Journal of Popular Film & Television, Film & History*, and *Journal of Film & Video*. His book on movie portrayals of people with physical disabilities is scheduled to be published by Rutgers University Press.

Douglas A. Noverr is a Professor in the Department of American Thought and Language at Michigan State University and teaches in the Graduate Program in American Studies. With Lawrence E. Ziewacz he has published *The Games They Played: Sports in American History, 1865-1980* (1983) and *Sport History* (1987). With Erik S. Lunde he has published *Film History* (1989) and *Film Studies* (1989). He has published a number of articles on sports films and sports history, reviews sports books for the *Journal of American Culture* and *CHOICE,* and contributed numerous articles to the five-volume *Biographical Dictionary of American Sports.*

Brooks Robards has a Ph.D. in Communication from the University of Massachusetts, Amherst, an MA from the University of Hartford and an AB from Bryn Mawr College. She does research on Film & TV and has published articles on the TV cop genre and on innovation in TV programming. She is Professor of Mass Communication at Westfield State College in Massachusetts.

Philip Skerry is Professor of English and Film at Lakeland Community College in Mentor, OH. He has published several articles on Westerns in *The Journal of Popular Film and Television* and *The New Orleans Review.* He is also a contributing author to the book *Superman at Fifty.*

Dick Stromgren is an Associate Professor of Communication at the University of Massachusetts in Amherst where he teaches courses in film history, genre studies, and film persuasion and propaganda. He has co-authored two books on film: *Light & Shadows: A History of Motion Pictures* and *Movies: A Language in Light.* His current research involves studies in social imagery and stereotyping and the evolution of screen satire. His essay on Chinese and Chinese American stereotypes—"The Chinese Syndrome"—appears in Volume I of *Beyond the Stars.*

www.ingramcontent.com/pod-product-compliance
Lightning Source LLC
Chambersburg PA
CBHW031245090426
42742CB00007B/326